The Literature of Jazz

A Critical Guide

Second edition, revised

by Donald Kennington
and Danny L. Read

American Library Association
Chicago 1980

182173

Library of Congress Cataloging in Publication Data

Kennington, Donald.
    The literature of jazz.
    Includes index.

    1. Jazz music—Bibliography. I. Read, Danny L., 1946– joint
author.   II. Title.
ML128.J3K45 1980   016.781'57   80-19837   ISBN 0-8389-0313-4

Printed in the United States of America

There were a raft of books published about jazz history, a lot of them bad, some of them very good as to facts and dates and names; a few were readable, the rest mostly for the fanatics and so packed with names, dates and written either in professors' English or reporters' prose that you had to love the stuff a lot to wade through it. But it all helped, it all made the subject serious because people are impressed by the printed word about anything.

Stephen Longstreet, *The Real Jazz, Old and New*

Contents

Preface   vii

Introduction   ix

Chapter 1.   The General Background   1

Chapter 2.   The Blues   28

Chapter 3.   The Histories of Jazz   43

Chapter 4.   The Lives of Jazz Musicians   71

Chapter 5.   Analysis, Theory, and Criticism   108

Chapter 6.   Reference Sources   133

Chapter 7.   Jazz Education   163

Chapter 8.   Jazz in Novels, Poetry, Plays, and Films   180

Chapter 9.   Jazz Periodicals   189

Name Index   203

Title Index   217

Preface

The first edition of this guide was published in Great Britain in 1970, and in the United States the following year. It created considerable interest as it was the first real attempt to provide a critical survey of the literature of jazz to that date. Since 1970, new jazz books have appeared even more rapidly and there have been many new editions of established titles, not to mention pamphlet and periodical literature, dissertations and theses.

In light of this, the author was asked to bring the earlier work up to date in collaboration with an American colleague, resulting in this much expanded second edition. Noticeable trends in jazz publishing appearing during the past nine years have been identified and are reflected in these pages. Undoubtedly, the literary standard of published work has risen with the considerable growth in the production of scholarly books by academics. These and other volumes maintain a high physical standard, and, in general, much more attention has been paid to bibliographies, sources of information, discographies, and indexing. There has also been a notable growth in the number of books written by black Americans and, since jazz originated as part of their culture, this is a welcome development. Serious literature on the blues has grown to such an extent that it has been necessary to separate it from the general background literature and allocate a separate chapter on the blues in this edition. The growth of jazz education materials has necessitated a separate chapter. A substantial growth of books in related fields such as soul, rhythm and blues, ragtime, and so on, as well as in popular music and rock in all its varieties, has been noted; the former categories have been covered to some extent, while the latter has been excluded except in cases where a book on popular music includes a significant section on jazz itself. Jazz-influenced popular artists such as Lena Horne, Bing Crosby, and Sammy Davis, Jr., are also included, as they worked closely with jazz musicians and their biographies are therefore likely to be of interest to the user of this work. A final point of interest is the emergence of publishers who specialize in jazz books and obviously find a market for their titles.

As in any work such as this, many people were consulted, and all gave freely of their help and advice. In addition to those who contributed directly to the first edition, we have also received much assistance from Norman Day, David Will, Lionel Grigson, Myra Menville, Fred Turco, Dick Collins and the staff of the Tunbridge Wells Division of Kent County Library, Marlene Coleman and the staff of the St. Louis Public Library, Gwen Watkinson, who typed the manuscript, and, most of all, from Teresa Chilton of the Bloomsbury Book Shop, London, whose stock of books proved more valuable than any library collection.

DON KENNINGTON
Tunbridge Wells, England
DANNY L. READ
St. Louis, Missouri

Introduction

The need for a guide to the rapidly growing literature of jazz music has been apparent for some time. In the fifty or so years since the first book on the subject was written, some notable bibliographical work has been done by Alan Merriam and Robert Reisner in America and Gregor von Mecklenberg in Germany but, to the best of our knowledge, there had never been an attempt at an overall, though selective, critical appraisal.

Up to the beginning of World War II only a handful of books had seriously attempted to analyze what jazz really was and from whence it came. Since that time, the literature has proliferated mainly through pamphlets in the 1940s leading to the fully published hardback books of the 1950s and 1960s. The paperback revolution of the late 1960s and 1970s was reflected in jazz publishing, and today more discerning works of a generally high literary standard are the rule. The serious jazz aficionado tends to belong to higher socioeconomic groups, often with the benefits of further or higher education. Many jazz listeners became "addicted" to the music in societies, at schools, colleges, and universities. Public libraries therefore have a steady demand for books on all aspects of the subject, but few have made any real effort to collect all the literature. Apart from the library of the Institute of Jazz Studies at Rutgers University (New Brunswick, N.J.), the collections of the Library of Congress, the New Orleans Public Library, the New York Public Library, and some private collectors, it is doubtful whether a really comprehensive collection of the literature of jazz exists. As time passes, the earlier works will disappear and the student will be unable to refer to necessary sources. Our aim in producing this guide is to indicate the significant works to the jazz newcomer and to refresh the memory of the expert. We also hope to assist the librarian in selecting both the books and journals needed to achieve a balanced collection, and to indicate sources for the location of information on the subject.

As the title indicates, this book is selective, and some ephemeral (mainly pamphlet) literature has been omitted; however, we believe that all the significant material published in English up to the end of 1979 has been listed. Most of the items listed have been examined by one of the authors and, as far as possible, all editions known to the authors are given except where Canadian and American editions have been published simultaneously. No foreign language material is listed unless it has been translated into English. Periodical articles are also not listed, but chapter 9 provides a list of jazz periodicals.

As in the first edition, the arrangement attempts to be logical, with the first chapter devoted to general background literature on black American culture, especially its African origins, slavery, minstrels, and ragtime, as well as the sociological aspects of jazz itself. An additional chapter now covers the literature devoted to that other primary ingredient—the blues—reflecting the substantial increase in analytical writing on this subject in the past few years. Jazz history proper is discussed in chapter 3, and chapter 4 examines the substantial biographical literature. There is considerable overlap between material in these two chapters and the next section on analysis, theory, and criticism, but if a particular choice is not agreeable to the user, the work sought can be located through the extensive indexes and cross references.

Reference sources of all kinds are listed in chapter 6, including encyclopedias, bibliographies, discographies, and record guides. A major part of the discography section is based on Paul B. Sheatsley's excellent "state-of-the-art" article published in *Record Research* (58:3–6) and a special acknowledgment is made to this writer.

Chapter 7 deals with jazz education materials (with the exception of "how to" books), and chapter 8 looks at jazz and fiction literature. Chapter 9 contains a list of jazz periodicals. For a listing of jazz organizations (which appeared in a separate chapter in the first edition), the reader is referred to the list published by the National Consortium of Jazz Organizations in New York. The Jazz on Film appendix in the first edition has also been deleted; the reader is referred to David Meeker's *Jazz in the Movies*, which provides a comprehensive listing of jazz on film. Indexes to book titles and names mentioned in both the text and the annotated references complete the work.

Each chapter (except chapter 4) is completed by a bibliography arranged in broad subject groupings and then in alphabetical order by authors in which, wherever possible, information is provided showing authors, title and subtitle, edition, place of publication, name of publisher and date. A single horizontal line instead of an author's name indicates that that book was written by the previous author; a second horizontal line indicates a different edition or publication of the preceding book. In many references, brief explanatory annotations are included. In chapter 4, references are arranged alphabetically under the name of the biographee and then alphabetically by author. For example:

John Coltrane

Cole, Bill. *John Coltrane*. New York: Schirmer Books, 1976.

Simpkins, Cuthbert Ormond. *Coltrane: A Biography*. New York: Herndon House, 1975.

Thomas, J. C. *Chasin' the Trane*. Garden City, N.Y.: Doubleday, 1975.

Chapter 1

The General Background

Jazz was born at the end of the nineteenth century, although the musical forms fused to bring it into being had been in existence for many years. These musical forms included the chants and work songs of West Africa, the hymn tunes of eighteenth-century Britain (from which the spiritual ultimately developed), the popular dance and operatic music of France, and the "tinge" acquired from Spanish folk music. The southern states, and particularly the port of New Orleans, were racial melting pots where these musical cultures coalesced over the years. Negro slaves provided the African ingredient of the rhythmic drive, while the settling immigrants added the European influences. France and Spain dominated the area until the Louisiana Purchase in 1803, and much of their musical heritage and culture remained, particularly among "free-born" Creoles. Other Spanish influences came from the nearby Caribbean islands, such as Cuba, which were at that time part of the Spanish Empire.

After the Civil War ended, black Americans looked for new ways to provide outlets for their natural exuberance. Their musical instincts led to the fashioning of primitive, homemade instruments and these, together with trumpets and trombones acquired from the disbanding Confederate Army, were used to produce a primitive, homemade music. Early jazz players were musically illiterate; their techniques were acquired by trial and error, with unusual fingerings producing the peculiar noises and effects that were cultivated and became the forerunners of the many varied tone colors present in jazz today.

This folk music approach is, in many ways, similar to the early stirrings of European music and, in this context, was

1

passed on from one performer to another without being documented. So it is that, in spite of the comparatively recent origins of jazz, much of its prehistory and indeed early history is shrouded in legend. An occasional white sociologist or musicologist expressed an interest in this music of the Afro-American, but few understood it, since it grew out of the appalling living conditions endured by a race in bondage. This emotive description applied as well to the post-Civil War period, since the actual conditions endured by black Americans improved very little. Indeed, the recent developments manifested in the civil rights and black power movements provide substantial evidence that considerable discrimination of various kinds continues to survive.

The documentation of the gestation period of this explosive art form is thus negligible. The early periodical articles of the 1920s were meager, ill-informed, and usually anti-jazz in outlook. European writers were the first to express interest and admiration. They were, of course, able to view this music with appropriate detachment, but this very detachment had its dangers; the European critics often came to wrong conclusions and put into print many erroneous statements that have only recently been corrected by more painstaking research.

The greatest single influence on the dissemination of knowledge about jazz was the invention of the disc-shaped phonograph record followed by the rapid development of radio in the 1920s. Records made possible the preservation of jazz fragments from 1916 onward, and their worldwide circulation created interest beyond the restricted areas of the United States in which jazz first appeared.

In the area of the musical background of jazz, over thirty years of important sociomusical research was carried out in Haiti by Harold Courlander and documented in two books of considerable interest. These are *Haiti Singing* (1939) and *The Drum and the Hoe* (1960). Courlander also turned his attention to mainland folk music with *Negro Folk Music USA* (1963). This is a serious and important book that recognizes the strength of the African roots of jazz without disputing the impact of other cultures.

Maud Cuney Hare in *Negro Musicians and Their Music*

(1936) traces the African beginnings of jazz through religious and secular folk songs to a rather confused chapter on Negro idiom and rhythm that tries to cover the blues, ragtime, and jazz itself. The book also contains a useful appendix on African musical instruments as well as extensive material on nonjazz musicians, including some non-Americans. There are two other, more recent works of importance in this category also written by women. Eileen Southern's compilation *Readings in Black American Music* (1971) is mainly general background, although some specific extracts from Ethel Waters's *His Eye Is on the Sparrow* and Mahalia Jackson's *Movin' on Up* (see chapter 4 for both titles) are included. Hildred Roach's *Black American Music: Past and Present* (1973) covers all forms of Afro-American music including much on jazz itself. A seminar held at the Black Music Center of Indiana University covered historical materials, reports of field work in Africa, soul, gospel, jazz and tribal music, and the edited proceedings, *Reflections on Afro-American Music* by Dominique de Lerma, appeared in 1973. John Storm Roberts's *Black Music of Two Worlds* (1972) provides a general overview and includes the music of the Caribbean and Latin America within its covers.

American folk music is very well documented, and we have space to quote only some of the important titles. John and Alan Lomax, a father and son team, have done many years of research in this field and have produced collections of folk songs of all kinds. *American Ballads and Folk Songs* (1934) is a fairly typical example of their efforts, but individually and together they have made an impressive contribution to this area of the literature. *Folk Song U.S.A., Adventures of a Ballad Hunter* (1947), and *Folk Songs of North America* are all examples of their output. A very early collection of *Slave Songs of the United States* was published in 1867 by William Allen and others and was followed by other important works including Odum and Johnson's *Negro Workaday Songs* (1926, reprinted in 1969), John Greenway's *American Folk Songs of Protest* (1953), and Miles Fisher's *Negro Slave Songs in the United States* (1953). Of more recent date is Dena Epstein's *Sinful Tunes and Spirituals* (1977), subtitled "Black Folk Music to the Civil War." This book has an extensive and valuable bibliography extending to 41 of its 433 pages. Bruce Jackson's *Wake Up Dead Man* (1972) is a collection of Afro-American worksongs from Texas prisons, and G. B. Johnson's *John Henry* (1929) investigates the famous legend that has become one of the widest known of all folk songs.

The world of the black American as an entertainer is explored sociologically in Robert Toll's *Blacking Up* (1974), subtitled "The Minstrel Show in Nineteenth Century America." An earlier work in this area is Hans Nathan's *Dan Emett and the Rise of Early Negro Minstrelsy* (1962). The links between jazz and popular entertainment have always been strong, and books on this aspect are of considerable interest to the student of jazz history. Marshall Stearns, who produced one of the best histories of jazz (see chapter 3) has also (in collaboration with Jean Stearns) written *The Jazz Dance* (1968). This book has excellent chapters on road shows, vaudeville, the Theatre Owners Booking Association (TOBA), and many other aspects of Afro-American music. Jack Schiffman's *Uptown–The Story of Harlem's Apollo Theatre* (1971) is also of interest as is *Black Magic* (1967), by Langston Hughes and Milton Meltzer, which is a pictorial history of the Negro in American entertainment.

The whole story of popular music in America in its widest interpretation has produced several substantial and well-written general histories. Probably the best is Gilbert Chase's monumental work *America's Music;* the revised second edition of which appeared in 1966. In its 761 pages, there are several individual chapters of direct interest to the jazz student, including chapter 21 (on ragtime), chapter 22 (on the blues), and chapter 23 (on the growth of jazz). This material is, of course, better covered elsewhere, but the main value of this scholarly work is in its linking of jazz to the mainstream of American music. The book includes an extremely useful bibliography of 29 pages. Sigmund Spaeth covers a narrower field clearly defined in his title *A History of Popular Music in America* (1948). This too has over 700 pages, of which the last 150 are devoted to detailed and extensive indexes and a bibliography.

David Ewen has written several books in this area including *Panorama of American Popular Music* (1957), *Life and*

Death of Tin Pan Alley (1964), and *American Popular Songs from the Revolutionary War to the Present* (1966).

British authors who have made contributions of note are Gammond and Clayton with their *Guide to Popular Music* (1960), and Tony Palmer with *All You Need Is Love* (1976). The latter was based on a sixteen-part television series, and includes a substantial section on jazz itself. Edward Lee's *Music of the People* (1970) is a study of popular music in Britain and, though of only marginal interest to the jazz student, provides interesting background material. The world of popular song generated its own subculture of sheet music, and in *Memory Lane* (1973) Max Wilk reproduces, in full color, around 100 sheet music covers from the period 1899–1925.

When the first edition of this guide appeared in 1970, there was a dearth of literature on ragtime. Periodical articles, some of considerable substance, had appeared; one, by Guy Waterman, attempted a musical analysis of the style and was published in the important magazine *Record Changer* in the 1940s. This pioneering essay was preserved more permanently in *The Art of Jazz* (1960), edited by Martin T. Williams. Rudi Blesh and Harriet Janis published the first comprehensive book on ragtime in 1950. *They All Played Ragtime* is still regarded by many as the definitive work on the topic and, to quote the English writer Peter Gammond, the book is "a magnificent piece of scholarship on a specific and well-defined area of music making." Ragtime, which flourished originally from the late 1890s to approximately the first world war, was locally based in the Midwest and, because it was a written music as opposed to the improvised contemporary styles of jazz proper, was often overlooked as a precursor and ingredient of mainstream jazz music. The resurgence of interest in ragtime in recent years has spawned a good deal of additional material, but Blesh and Janis remains a vital source of information on Scott Joplin and the other major exponents of this self-contained musical style. Peter Gammond's *Scott Joplin and the Ragtime Era* (1975) modestly claims to be only a primer on the subject, but it is well written and supported by an excellent bibliography, with record and music listings. An extremely important musicological study is found in Schafer

The Art of Ragtime (1973), which explains, in its subtitle, "the form and meaning of an original American art." Other works describing the history of the genre and discussing the composers and performers involved include Jasen and Tichenor's *Rags and Ragtime: A Musical History* (1978), Terry Waldo's *This Is Ragtime* (1976), and a biography of the single most important creative influence in this musical field, *Scott Joplin: The Man Who Made Ragtime* (1978) by James Haskins and Kathleen Benson. Ann Charters's *Ragtime Songbook* (1965) is a collection of pieces with a brief introduction describing the ragtime era, while Trebor Tichenor has compiled *Ragtime Rareties* (1975), which includes the complete original music for sixty-three piano rags by unknown composers.

Another important category that receives attention in this chapter is the sociological and political writings on jazz and its background. Afro-Americans in general, and the jazz musician in particular, make excellent subjects for the sociologist. The reasons are fairly obvious—the transportation of a large number of people of a completely different racial and cultural background into the midst of a diverse mass of immigrants from a hostile Europe provides a rich field for sociological enquiry. In spite of the humane pretensions of liberal whites, only in two areas are the black Americans fully accepted as equal or even superior to their white compatriots. One is in sport, in which black athletes (and particularly boxers) have dominated their sports, and the second, the concern of this book, is in jazz music. Undoubtedly the fact that the black American "invented" and developed jazz music has been a source of pride. This is not to say that no white musician can play jazz successfully, as is sometimes argued in extremist circles, but it cannot be denied that the major innovators have all been Afro-Americans. Although Louis Armstrong, Duke Ellington, and Charlie Parker all had completely different social backgrounds and their musical styles were disparate, they were major figures in what is now recognized everywhere as a major musical stream. This preamble is designed to show that an understanding of the sociological background is vital to an understanding of jazz itself, and there are some excellent literary contributions in this area.

The New Orleans socioeconomic background is covered in Henry Kmen's *Music in New Orleans* (1967), subtitled "The Formative Years, 1791–1841." This is a revised doctoral dissertation on the social history of white New Orleans music and contains some interesting material on the "prehistoric" jazz era. It has been suggested that this work helps to prove some of Rudi Blesh's theories that imply that New Orleans jazz had a social origin in the racial discriminatory laws that forcibly integrated the Creole and free Negro communities with the poor former slaves after the Civil War. It also helps to explain why jazz developed more rapidly and better in New Orleans than in other cities, and suggests that the unique part of the new music derived from the African musical tradition and was not of European origin. It is, in total, a valuable and scholarly confirmation of theories that have been widely held but insufficiently proven.

A much earlier book by Herbert Asbury, *The French Quarter* (1936), informally describes the New Orleans underworld, while Al Rose in *Storyville, New Orleans* (1974) provides what he describes as "an authenticated, illustrated account of the notorious red-light district." Jack Buerkle and Danny Barker (the latter a well-known musician) attempt a detailed sociological analysis of New Orleans musicians in *Bourbon Street Black* (1973); the book is of considerable interest because of its unusual approach.

More general studies include Neil Leonard's *Jazz and the White Americans* (1962), which explains the social and intellectual relationships of whites in America to a music associated primarily with the Negro. Leonard includes a 13-page bibliography in his book. From the other side of the color line, Le Roi Jones, a leading black intellectual and poet, produced *Blues People: Negro Music in White America* (1963). This was a major contribution to the understanding of what jazz means to the educated black American in particular and is worthy of close study. Jones, who became increasingly involved in the militant black power movement, also produced a second book, *Black Music*, in 1967. Nat Hentoff, author or coauthor of several of the most worthwhile books on various aspects of jazz, has written *The New Equality* (1964) and *The Jazz Life*, originally published in

1961 and reissued by Da Capo Press in 1975. The latter is perhaps one of the few really indispensable jazz books, and the author's main source of material was his conversations with the musicians themselves. Hentoff managed to get them to talk freely and constructively about their music, their fellow musicians, and the social background of their work and play. He put the drug problem into perspective as well, but the book loses a little by not having an index.

Ortiz M. Walton's *Music, Black, White and Blue* (1972) is an important book that covers areas not documented elsewhere in the sociological literature. It is essentially about jazz and its various ingredients and has the expressive subtitle "A Sociological Survey of the Use and Misuse of Afro-American Music." *Music and Politics* (1971) by John Sinclair and Robert Levin is made up of extracts from the journal *Jazz and Pop* and consists of reviews, interviews, and black power manifestos.

A major British contribution to this area of the literature is a fine examination of the *Jazz Scene* (1959) by Frances Newton, a pseudonym for Eric J. Hobsbawn. The Da Capo Press of New York, who has done an excellent job in selecting and reissuing many of the earlier works of consequence now out of print, republished this in 1975. Newton writes refreshingly and, although he claims to be no expert, probes deep into such interesting issues as the business world of jazz, the jazz public, and the influence of jazz on "serious" and "popular" music. There is a detailed guide to sources at the end of the book that is valuable, and the whole work is required reading for the jazz student. Another British author, Kenneth Allsopp, in *The Bootleggers* (1961), primarily the story of Chicago's prohibition era, writes entertainingly and well on the jazz of the twenties. David Dachs's *Anything Goes* (1964) is an analysis of the effect of the commercial world on popular music; Dachs includes jazz in his review.

The place of the phonograph in spreading the influence of jazz has already been mentioned. It is appropriate, therefore, to mention two books that cover the development of this invention. Roland Gelatt's *The Fabulous Phonograph: 1877–1977* is a full-length work presenting the story of the gramophone from tin foil to high fidelity and as such is a technical, rather than an economic and social history. This book originally appeared in 1956 and has been revised twice since then. More specific is Charles Graham's "Jazz and the Phonograph," which was included in Leonard Feather's *New Yearbook of Jazz* (1959). Graham combines expert knowledge of recording techniques and sound reproduction with an understanding of jazz music, and the resulting twelve-page essay is an outstanding contribution to this relatively neglected topic. It includes a brief chronology of recording from Edison in 1877 up to the widespread availability of stereophonic equipment in 1959. A brief thirty-two-page pamphlet by Michael Wyler, *A Glimpse at the Past* (1957) is useful for information on some of the early record companies that were associated with jazz.

BIBLIOGRAPHY

Black History

Abdul, Raoul. *Blacks in Classical Music*. New York: Dodd, Mead, 1977.
    Includes little commentary on jazz.

Abrahams, R. D. *Deep Down in the Jungle: Negro Narrative Folklore from the Streets of Philadelphia*. Hatboro, Pa.: Folklore Associates, 1964.

Belton, Geneva R. "The Contribution of Negro Music and Musicians in World War II." Master's thesis, Northwestern University, 1946.
    Comments on "new" gospel hymns, the "Jungleers" (a hot jazz band in the Pacific), and individuals, including Fletcher Henderson, Louis Armstrong, and Duke Ellington.

Botkin, B. A., ed. *Sidewalks of America*. Indianapolis: Bobbs-Merrill, 1954.
    Brief comments on New Orleans funerals and the beginning of bebop.

Clarke, John, ed. *Harlem, U.S.A*. New York: Collier Books, 1971.
    Contains one chapter on Harlem music by William Dixon.

Cunard, N., comp. *Negro Anthology, 1931–33*. London: Wishard, 1934.

Davis, J. P., ed. *The American Negro Reference Book*. Englewood Cliffs, N.J.: Prentice-Hall, 1966.

Covers all aspects of Negro life and is useful for general background material.

Elkins, S. M. *Slavery: A Problem in American Institutional and Intellectual Life*. Chicago: Chicago University Press, 1959.

————— —————. London: Cambridge University Press, 1960.

————— —————. New York: Grosset and Dunlap, 1963.

Frazier, E. F. *The Negro in the United States*. New York: Macmillan, 1949.

Background reference work with full bibliography; weak on musical aspects.

————— —————. Rev. ed. New York: Macmillan, 1957.

Hollander, B. *Slavery in America: Its Legal History*. London: Bowes and Bowes, 1962.

————— —————. New York: Barnes and Noble, 1963.

Huggins, Nathan Irvin. *Harlem Renaissance*. New York: Oxford University Press, 1971.

Background study on Afro-American culture.

Hughes, Langston. *Famous Negro Musicmakers*. New York: Dodd, Mead, 1955.

For children.

————— —————. New York: Dodd, Mead, 1957.

—————, and Meltzer, Milton. *Black Magic: A Pictorial History of the Negro in American Entertainment*. Englewood Cliffs, N.J.: Prentice-Hall, 1967.

Includes photos and commentary on the birth of jazz, the blues, etc.

—————. *A Pictorial History of the Negro in America*. New York: Crown, 1956.

Includes very brief commentary on James Reese Europe, Duke Ellington, and others.

Hyman, S. E. *The Promised End: Essays and Reviews 1942–1962*. Cleveland and New York: World, 1963.

Includes one chapter on "American Negro Literature and the Folk Tradition."

Johnson, James Weldon. *Black Manhattan*. New York: Alfred A. Knopf, 1930.

Brief commentary on the birth of the jazz orchestra, Jim Europe, W. C. Handy, and the nightclubs of Harlem.

————— —————. New York: Knopf, 1940.

————— —————. New York: Arno Press, 1968.

Mannix, D. P., and Cowley, M. *Black Cargoes: A History of the*

Atlantic Slave Trade, 1518–1865. New York: Viking Press, 1962.

————— —————. London: Longmans, 1963.

————— —————. New York: Viking Press, 1965.

Meier, August, and Elliott, Rudwick. *The Making of Black America. The Origins of Black Americans,* vol. 1. New York: Atheneum, 1971.

Contains one chapter on black folk music.

Scarborough, D. *On the Trail of Negro Folklore.* Hatboro, Pa.: Folklore Associates, 1963.

Schiffman, Jack. *Uptown–The Story of Harlem's Apollo Theatre.* See p. 59.

Stampp, K. M. *The Peculiar Institution: Slavery in the Antebellum South.* New York: Knopf, 1956.

Well-documented and readable account of slavery in America.

————— —————. London: Eyre and Spottiswoode, 1964.

————— —————. New York: Vintage, 1964.

Stearns, Marshall, and Stearns, Jean. *The Jazz Dance: The Story of American Vernacular Dance.* New York: Macmillan, 1968.

Excellent chapters on road shows, vaudeville, TOBA, and other aspects of Afro-American dance and music.

Szwed, John, ed. *Black America.* New York: Basic Books, 1970.

Contains chapters by Harry Oster and Don Heckman on black music.

Toll, Robert C. *Blacking Up: The Minstrel Show in Nineteenth Century America.* New York: Oxford University Press, 1974.

Marginal but interesting sociological background book.

Black Folk Music

Allen, W. F., Ware, C. P., and Garrison, L. M. *Slave Songs of the United States.* New York: A. Simpson, 1867.

————— —————. New York: P. Smith, 1929.

—————. *Slave Songs of the United States.* New York: Oak Publications, 1965.

Ames, Russell. *The Story of American Folk Song.* New York: Grosset and Dunlap, 1960.

Contains one chapter each on Negro spirituals and the blues.

Baker, Barbara W. "Black Gospel Music Styles, 1942–1975: Analysis and Implications for Music Education." Ph.D. dissertation, University of Maryland, 1978.

Bennett, Carolyn L. "African Survivals in the Religious Music Tradition of the United States Negro." Master's thesis, Depauw University, 1969.

    An excellent study, containing a discography, musical examples, song texts, and taped illustrations from black Baptist churches.

Blesh, Rudi. *O Susanna: A Sampler of the Riches of American Folk Music*. London: Evergreen Press, 1962.

Carratello, John D. "An Eclectic Choral Methodology and Its Effect on the Understanding, Interpretation, and Performance of Black Spirituals."

    See p. 170.

Carter, Albert E. "The Louisiana Negro and His Music." Master's thesis, Northwestern University, 1947.

    Contains chapters on work songs, blues, swing, Creole songs, and spirituals. Includes a long bibliography.

Cone, James H. *The Spirituals and the Blues*.

    See p. 35.

Courlander, Harold. *Negro Folk Music USA*. New York: Columbia University Press, 1963.

    Serious work that brings together much diverse material on its subject.

    ————— —————. London: Jazz Book Club, 1966.

Dixon, Christa K. *Negro Spirituals*. Philadelphia: Fortress Press, 1976.

    An examination of the meaning and background of some of the best known Negro spirituals.

Epstein, Dena J. *Sinful Tunes and Spirituals: Black Folk Music to the Civil War*. Urbana: University of Illinois Press, 1977.

    An excellent examination of vocal and instrumental black folk music. Contains an extensive bibliography.

Finkelstein, Sidney. *Composer and Nation: The Folk Heritage of Music*. London: Lawrence and Wishart, 1960.

    ————— —————. New York: International Publishers, 1960.

Fisher, Miles M. "The Evolution of Slave Songs in the United States." Ph.D. dissertation, University of Chicago, 1948.

    A thorough and well-documented examination.

    —————. *Negro Slave Songs in the United States*. Ithaca, N.Y.: Cornell University Press, 1953.

    ————— —————. London: Oxford University Press, 1954.

    ————— —————. New York: Citadel Press, 1963.

Foster, William P. "The Influence of the Negro on Music in America." Master's thesis, Wayne State University, 1950.

Somewhat lacking in documentation and contains a few errors, but offers amusing suggestions on the origins of jazz.

Grady, Edythe Rachel. "Sacred Music of the Negro in the U.S.A." Master's thesis, Union Theological Seminary, 1950.

Hansen, Chadwik Clarke. "The Ages of Jazz: A Study of Jazz in Its Cultural Context." Ph.D. dissertation, University of Minnesota, 1956.

Advocates the perpetuation of Negro folk music, claiming its superiority to white folk music. Also examines the origin of jazz and makes unsupported claims while giving a biased presentation.

Hare, Maud Cuney. *Negro Musicians and Their Music*. Washington, D.C.: Associated Publishers, 1936.

Traces African beginnings through Afro-American folk songs, both religious and secular, to a rather confined chapter on "Negro Idiom and Rhythm" that covers the blues, ragtime, and jazz itself. Includes an appendix on African musical instruments.

————— —————. New York: Da Capo Press, 1974.

Heilbut, Tony. *The Gospel Sound, Good News and Bad Times*. New York: Simon and Schuster, 1971.

A history of black gospel music.

————— —————. Garden City, N.Y.: Doubleday, 1975.

Hoyt, Charles A. "Jazz and Its Origin." Bachelor's thesis, Wesleyan University, 1953.

Depicts the relationship between jazz and African music.

Jackson, Bruce, ed. *Wake Up Dead Man: Afro-American Work Songs from Texas Prisons*. Cambridge, Mass.: Harvard University Press, 1972.

Includes a glossary and bibliography.

Jackson, Clyde Owen. *The Songs of Our Years: A Study of Negro Folk Music*. New York: Exposition Press, 1968.

A brief history of black folk music.

Johnson, G. B. *John Henry: Tracking down A Negro Legend*. Chapel Hill: University of North Carolina Press, 1929.

Covers the story behind the Negro folk song.

————— —————. London: Oxford University Press, 1929.

Jones, Geraldine Wells. "The Negro Spiritual and Its Use as an Integral Part of Music Education."
See p. 173.

Jones, Max, ed. *Folk: Review of People's Music*. London: Jazz Music Books, 1945.

Kennedy, R. E. *Mellows: A Chronicle of Unknown Singers*. New York: Boni, 1925.

Negro work songs, street cries, and spirituals.

_____. *More Mellows*. New York: Dodd, Mead, 1931.

Krehbiel, Henry E. *Afro-American Folksongs*. New York: Schirmer, 1914.

Analyses of black folk music as to idiom, origin, and characteristic elements.

_____ _____. New York: Frederick Ungar, 1962.

Landeck, Beatrice. *Echoes of Africa*. New York: David McKay, 1961.

An examination of the roots of African music surviving in American folk songs.

_____ _____. 2nd ed. New York: David McKay, 1961.

Lefkowits, Judith W. "The Afro-American—His Literature and Music." Trenton, N.J., Ewing High School, 1968.

Livengood, Karen S. "Negro Music and Its Influence on American Music." Master's thesis, University of Louisville, 1968.

An excellent study of the elements of a variety of black folk music.

Locke, Alain. *The Negro and His Music*. Washington, D.C.: Associates in Negro Folk Education, 1936.

An examination of black folk music with interesting comments on the origin of jazz.

_____ _____. Port Washington, N.Y.: Kennikat, 1968.

_____ _____. New York: Arno, 1969.

_____, ed. *The New Negro*. New York: Albert and Charles Boni, 1925.

Contains chapters on Negro spirituals and the origin and development of jazz. Also contains a bibliography of spirituals and folk songs and a list of composers influenced by black folk idioms.

_____ _____. New York: Atheneum, 1968.

Lomax, John, and Lomax, Alan. *Adventures of a Ballad Hunter*. New York: Macmillan, 1947.

Autobiographical reminiscences.

_____. *American Ballads and Folk Songs*. New York: Macmillan, 1934.

Covers the whole range of American songs with words and

music. Particularly interesting sections are "The Chain Gang Songs," "Negro Bad Men," "The Blues," "Creole Negroes," and "Negro Spirituals."

————. *The Leadbelly Legend: A Collection of World-Famous Songs by Huddie Ledbetter*. New York: Folkways Music Publishers, 1959.

Words and music with brief introductory matter.

———— ————. 2nd rev. ed. New York: Folkways Music Publishers, 1965.

————. *Negro Songs as Sung by Leadbelly: King of the Twelve-String Guitar Players of the World, Long-Time Convict in the Penitentiaries of Texas and Louisiana*. New York: Macmillan, 1936.

Lovell, John. *Black Song: The Force and the Flame*. New York: Macmillan, 1972.

Origin, development, and influences of the Negro spiritual.

———— ————. London: Collier-Macmillan, 1972.

Lucas, John Samuel. "Rhythms of Negro Music and Negro Poetry." Master's thesis, University of Minnesota, 1945.

Martinez, Raymond Joseph. *Portraits of New Orleans Jazz: Its Peoples and Places*. New Orleans: Hope, 1971.

A very interesting account of prejazz influences with a number of photos.

Mitchell, George. *Blow My Blues Away*. Baton Rouge: Louisiana State University Press, 1971.

A firsthand account of blues, field songs, work songs, and spirituals found in Mississippi today. Contains many photos and interviews.

Nathan, Hans. *Dan Emett and the Rise of Early Negro Minstrelsy*. Norman: University of Oklahoma Press, 1962.

Nettl, Bruno. *Folk and Traditional Music of Western Continents*. Englewood Cliffs, N.J. Prentice-Hall, 1965.

————. *An Introduction to Folk Music in the United States*. Detroit: Wayne State University Press, 1960.

Very brief comments on black folk music and its relationship to Africa.

———— ————. 2nd ed. Detroit: Wayne State University Press, 1962.

———— ————. 3rd ed. Detroit: Wayne State University Press, 1976.

Revised and expanded by Helen Myers.

Odum, Howard W., and Johnson, Guy B. *The Negro and His Songs: A Story of Typical Negro Songs in the South*. Chapel Hill: University of North Carolina Press, 1925.

————— —————. Hatboro, Pa.: Folklore Associates, 1964.

—————. *Negro Workaday Songs: With Musical Notes and a Bibliography*. Chapel Hill: University of North Carolina Press, 1926.

————— —————. London: Oxford University Press, 1926.

————— —————. New York: Negro Universities Press, 1969.

Pearson, Boyce N. "A Cantometric Analysis of three Afro-American Songs Recorded in the Commerce, Texas Area." Master's thesis, East Texas State University, 1978.

Reagon, Bernice. "A History of the Afro-American through His Songs."

See p. 176.

Ricks, George R. *Some Aspects of the Religious Music of the United States Negro*. New York: Arno Press, 1977.

History, sociocultural background, and contemporary style of black religious music.

Riedel, Johannes. *Soul Music–Black and White*. Minneapolis: Augsburg, 1975.

Deals with the nature and ramifications of black music. Somewhat superficial and lacking in authenticity.

Roach, Hildred. *Black American Music—Past and Present*.

See p. 128.

Rock, John, and Wilberforce, Christopher. *Africa Sings and the Psychology of Jazz*. Colombo, Ceylon: General, 1946.

Rublowsky, John. *Black Music in America*. New York: Basic Books, 1971.

The history of black music primarily up to 1900.

Russell, Tony. *Blacks, Whites and Blues*. London: Studio Vista, 1970.

The history of both white and black folk music.

————— —————. New York: Stein and Day, 1970.

Scarborough, Dorothy, and Gulledge, O. L. *On the Trail of Negro Folk-Songs*. Cambridge, Mass.: Harvard University Press, 1925.

Lyrics and commentary on a wide variety of black folk songs.

————— —————. Hatboro, Pa: Folklore Associates, 1963.

Shaw, Arnold. *The World of Soul: Black America's Contribution to the Pop Music Scene*. New York: Cowles, 1970.

A well-constructed book covering blues singers, jazz singers, rhythm and blues, gospel music, and contemporary soul and blues music.

Shelton, R., and Raim, W. *The Josh White Song Book.*
See p. 41.

Southern, Eileen. *The Music of Black Americans: A History.*
See p. 55.

————. *Readings in Black American Music.*
See p. 55.

Taylor, John Earl. "The Sociological and Psychological Implications of the Texts of the Antebellum Negro Spirituals." Ed.D. dissertation, University of Northern Colorado, 1971.

Thurman, Howard. *Deep River: Reflections on the Religious Insight of Certain of the Negro Spirituals.* Port Washington, N.Y.: Kennikat Press, 1969.

Townsend, A. O. "The American Folk-Song and Its Influence on the Works of American Composers." Master's thesis, University of Southern California, 1938.

Walden, Jean Elizabeth. "The History, Development, and Contribution of the Negro Folk Song." Master's thesis, Northwestern University, 1945.

A history of black folk songs, spirituals, gospels, social tunes, and the blues.

White, N. L. *American Negro Folk-Songs.* Cambridge, Mass.: Harvard University Press, 1928.

Important work with extensive bibliography.

———— ————. Hatboro, Pa.: Folklore Associates, 1965.

Work, J. W., ed. *American Negro Songs and Spirituals: A Comprehensive Collection of 230 Folk Songs, Religious and Secular.* New York: Crown, 1940.

Brief chapters on the "Origins," "The Spiritual," "The Blues," "Work Songs," and "Social and Miscellaneous." Contains primarily words and music.

———— ————. New York: Howell, Soskin, 1940.

————. *Folk Song of the American Negro.* Nashville, Tenn.: Fisk University Press, 1915.

White Folk Music

Baggelaar, Kristin, and Milton, Donald. *Folk Music, More Than a Song.* New York: Crowell, 1976.

Bokelman, Marina. "The Coon Con Game: A Blues Ballad Tradition." Master's thesis, University of California at Los Angeles, 1968.

An examination of a Texas blues ballad tradition originating after the Civil War.

Greenway, John. *American Folk Songs of Protest*. Philadelphia: University of Pennsylvania Press, 1953.

―――― ――――. London: Oxford University Press, 1953.

Jackson, George Pullen. *White and Negro Spirituals*. Locust Valley, N.Y.: J. J. Augustin, 1943.

Contains stories on the origin of religious folk songs and a bibliography of books containing folk songs.

Kmen, Henry. *Music in New Orleans: The Formative Years, 1791–1841*. Baton Rouge: Louisiana State University Press, 1967.

The social history of white New Orleans music.

Lomax, Alan. *The Folk Songs of North America*. London: Cassell, 1960.

Lomax, John. *Folksong U.S.A*. New York: Duell, Sloan and Pearce, 1947.

Ragtime

Blesh, Rudi, and Janis, Harriet. *They All Played Ragtime: The True Story of an American Music*. New York: Knopf, 1950.

Considered by many to be the definitive work on ragtime. Includes a discography, a list of compositions, and sixteen complete scores.

―――― ――――. London: Sidgwick and Jackson, 1958.

―――― ――――. Rev. ed. New York: Grove Press, 1959.

―――― ――――. New York: Music Sales, 1963.

―――― ――――. New York: Oak Publications, 1971.

Charters, A., ed. *The Ragtime Songbook*. New York: Oak Publications, 1965.

Contains historical notes about the ragtime era and ragtime tunes.

Evans, Mark. *Scott Joplin and the Ragtime Years*. New York: Dodd, Mead, 1976.

A well-researched biography for younger audiences.

Gammond, Peter. *Scott Joplin and the Ragtime Era*. New York: St. Martin's Press, 1975.

A well-written book examining the composers of ragtime, its stylistic characteristics, and its influences on jazz.

—————— ——————. Rev. ed. New York: St. Martin's Press, 1976.

—————— ——————. London: Abacus, 1975.

—————— ——————. London: Angus and Robertson, 1975.

Haskins, James, and Benson, Kathleen. *Scott Joplin*. Garden City, N.Y.: Doubleday, 1978.

A well-written biography about "The Man Who Made Ragtime."

Jasen, David A., and Tichenor, Trebor. *Rags and Ragtime: A Musical History*. New York: Seabury Press, 1978.

An excellent book depicting the history of ragtime and the contributions of its composers. Contains a listing of 3,000 rags with a structural analysis of several individual compositions.

Nettl, Paul. *The Story of Dance Music*. New York: Philosophical Library, 1947.

Very brief comments on ragtime, jazz, and swing.

—————— ——————. Westport, Conn.: Greenwood Press, 1969.

Reed, Addison. "The Life and Works of Scott Joplin." Ph.D. dissertation, University of North Carolina at Chapel Hill, 1973.

Biography, analysis of style characteristics, and a list of the works of Scott Joplin. Also examines the rudiments of ragtime.

Schafer, William J., and Riedel, Johannes. *The Art of Ragtime*. Baton Rouge: Louisiana State University Press, 1973.

Examines composers, musical characteristics, and the influences of ragtime. Contains transcriptions of original rags. Well researched.

—————— ——————. New York: Da Capo, 1977.

Tichenor, Trebor, comp. *Ragtime Rareties: Complete Original Music for 63 Piano Rags*. New York: Trebor Publications, 1975.

Contains pieces by unknown or little-known composers.

—————— ——————. London: Constable, 1976.

Waldo, Terry. *This Is Ragtime*. New York: Hawthorn Books, 1976.

An examination of the roots, development, and influences of ragtime written in a very entertaining style.

Williams, Martin. *The Art of Jazz*.

See p. 131.

Popular Music

Boeckman, Charles. *And the Beat Goes On: A Survey of Pop Music in America*. Washington, D.C.: Robert B. Luce, 1972.

Contains two chapters on blues and one on the big bands.

Chase, Gilbert. *America's Music: From the Pilgrims to the Present*. New York: McGraw-Hill, 1955.
  Contains chapters on ragtime, the blues, and jazz.
_____ _____. 2nd ed. New York: McGraw-Hill, 1966.
_____ _____. London: McGraw-Hill, 1966.
Dachs, D. *Anything Goes: The World of Popular Music*. Indianapolis: Bobbs-Merrill, 1964.
  Includes a chapter on jazz.
Ewen, David. *All the Years of American Popular Music*. Englewood Cliffs, N.J.: Prentice-Hall, 1977.
  Contains four or five chapters of jazz-related material.
_____. *American Popular Songs: From the Revolutionary War to the Present*. New York: Random House, 1966.
_____. *Life and Death of Tin Pan Alley*. New York: Funk and Wagnalls, 1964.
_____. *Panorama of American Popular Music: The Story of Our National Ballads and Folk Songs, the Songs of Tin Pan Alley, Broadway and Hollywood, New Orleans Jazz, Swing and Symphonic Jazz*. Englewood Cliffs, N.J.: Prentice-Hall, 1957.
Fong-Torres, Ben, ed. *What's That Sound?* Garden City, N.Y.: Anchor Books, 1976.
  Includes one chapter on jazz and rock by Bob Palmer.
Gammond, Peter, and Clayton, Peter. *A Guide to Popular Music*.
  See p. 150.
_____. *Dictionary of Popular Music*.
  See p. 150.
Hall, S., and Whannel, P. *The Popular Arts*. London: Hutchinson Educational, 1964.
  Treats jazz intelligently in a wide-ranging survey of popular arts. Shows contrast with "pop" music and uses illustrations from jazz (as well as other arts) in suggesting new methods of communicating with young adults. Good annotated bibliography.
_____ _____. New York: Pantheon Books, 1965.
Kaufmann, Helen L. *From Jehovah to Jazz*. New York: Dodd, Mead, 1937.
  Includes two chapters on black folk music and one on jazz.
_____ _____. Freeport, N.Y.: Books for Libraries Press, 1968.
_____ _____. Port Washington, N.Y.: Kennikat, 1970.
Lee, Edward. *Music of the People: A Study of Popular Music in Great Britain*. London: Barrie and Jenkins, 1970.

Marginal interest to the jazz reader but interesting background reading.

Palmer, Tony. *All You Need Is Love: The Story of Popular Music*. New York: Grossman, 1976.

Contains brief histories of jazz, blues, swing, and rhythm and blues.

———— ————. London: Weidenfeld and Nicolson, 1976.

Pearsall, Ronald. *Popular Music of the Twenties*. Totowa, N.J.: Rowman and Littlefield, 1976.

Contains one chapter on ragtime and jazz.

———— ————. London: David and Charles, 1976.

Pleasants, Henry. *The Great American Popular Singers*. London: Victor Gollancz, 1974.

Includes commentary on Bessie Smith, Louis Armstrong, Billie Holiday, Ella Fitzgerald, and Mahalia Jackson.

Shapiro, Nat, ed. *Popular Music: An Annotated Index of American Popular Songs*. New York: Adrian Press, vol. 1, 1964; vol. 2, 1965, vol. 3, 1967; vol. 4, 1968.

Spaeth, S. G. *A History of Popular Music in America*. New York: Random House, 1948.

Fascinating background book on American popular songs up to 1948.

———— ————. London: Phoenix House, 1960.

———— ————. London: Jazz Book Club, 1962.

Wilk, Max, comp. *Memory Lane: Ragtime, Jazz, Foxtrot and Other Popular Music Covers*. London: Studio Art, 1973.

Full-color reproductions of about 100 sheet music covers from 1899 to 1925.

Sociology of Jazz

Allsopp, Kenneth. *The Bootleggers: The Story of Chicago's Prohibition Era*.

See p. 56.

Becker, Howard Saul. "The Professional Dance Musician in Chicago." Master's thesis, University of Chicago, 1949.

A sociological examination of internal and external relationships among professional musicians.

Buerkle, Jack Vincent, and Barker, Danny. *Bourbon Street Black: The New Orleans Black Jazzman*. New York: Oxford University Press, 1973.

A sociological view of the lifestyles of early New Orleans jazz musicians. Contains many quotes by the musicians themselves.

Burton, Roger V. "The Personality of the Contracted Studio Musician: An Investigation Using the Guilford-Zimmerman Temperament Survey." Master's thesis, University of Southern California, 1955.

Davis, Nathan Tate. "Charlie Parker's Kansas City Environment and Its Effect on His Later Life." Doctor of Arts dissertation, Wesleyan University, 1974.

Of more psychological and sociological interest than musical.

de Lerma, Dominique-Rene. *Reflections on Afro-American Music*. Kent, Ohio: Kent State University Press, 1973.

Transcripts of lectures and discussions including several by David Baker and Cannonball Adderley. One topic covered is the "Social Role of Jazz."

Denisoff, R. Serge, and Peterson, Richard A., eds. *The Sounds of Social Change*. Chicago: Rand McNally, 1972.

Contains chapters on the protest aspect of avant-garde jazz, the relationship of the jazz musician and his audience, and the business aspect of jazz.

Faulkner, Robert Roy. "Studio Musicians: Their Work and Career Contingencies in the Hollywood Film Industry." Ph.D. dissertation, University of California at Los Angeles, 1968.

An investigation of the careers and business relationships of studio musicians based on taped interviews with seventy-three musicians.

Gumina, Michael J. "The Problems of the Black Jazz Musician." Master's thesis, Jersey City State College, 1973.

An excellent paper depicting the social struggle of the black jazz musician.

Haralambos, Michael. *Right On: From Blues to Soul in Black America*. London: Eddison Press Ltd., 1974.

Attempts to trace the relationship between black society and culture and black music; especially seeks to explain the decline in popularity of the blues and rise in popularity of soul music.

Hentoff, Nat. *The Jazz Life*. New York: Dial Press, 1961.

Readable and lucid sociological approach based on discussions with musicians.

———— ————. London: Peter Davies, 1962.

———— ————. London: Hamilton, 1964.

———— ————. New York: Da Capo, 1975.

——. *The New Equality*. New York: Viking Press, 1964.

—— ——. Rev. ed. New York: Viking Press, 1965.

Jones, Le Roi. *Black Music*. New York: Morrow, 1967.

Collection of essays on modern jazz black musicians, 1959–1966. Has much sociological content and has, according to one critic, "enormous value quite apart from the light it throws on jazz . . . Lets you know what it has felt like at various times to be a Negro in the United States."

—— ——. London: MacGibbon and Kee, 1969.

—— ——. New York: Morrow, 1971.

——. *Blues People: Negro Music in White America*. New York: Morrow, 1963.

Important book by leading black intellectual.

—— ——. London: MacGibbon and Kee, 1965.

—— ——. New York: Apollo Editions, 1965.

—— ——. London: Jazz Book Club, 1966.

Kofsky, Frank. *Black Nationalism and the Revolution in Music*. New York: Pathfinder, 1970.

Examines social, economic, and cultural factors in contemporary black jazz. John Coltrane, Elvin Jones, McCoy Tyner, and Albert Ayler are focused on in this excellent book.

Lambert, C. *Music Ho!: A Study of Music in Decline*. London: Faber, 1934.

Refers to the work of jazz musicians without seeing the essence of jazz.

—— ——. Rev. London: Faber, 1938.

—— ——. London: Penguin Books, 1948.

—— ——. 3rd ed. London: Faber, 1948.

Leonard, Neil. "The Acceptance of Jazz by Whites in the United States, 1918–1942."

See p. 68.

——. *Jazz and the White Americans: The Acceptance of a New Art Form*.

See p. 68.

Levy, Louis H. "The Formalization of New Orleans Jazz Musicians: A Case Study of Organizational Change." Ph.D. dissertation, Virginia Polytechnic Institute and State University, 1976.

Studies of the social structures of New Orleans jazz musicians.

McCue, George, ed. *Music in American Society 1776–1976*. New Brunswick, N.J.: Transaction Books, 1977.

Contains one chapter on "Jazz as an Urban Music" by Dan Morgenstern.

MacLeod, Bruce Alan. "Music for All Occasions: The Club Date Business of Metropolitan New York City." Ph.D. dissertation, Wesleyan University, 1979.

Focuses primarily on 200 full-time club date musicians in New York City. Treats this group as a subculture and examines the specialized cultural knowledge needed by them.

Middleton, Richard. *Pop Music and the Blues: A Study of the Relationship and Its Significance*. London: Victor Gollancz, 1972.

An original and valuable cultural analysis based on the study of the blues and blues-influenced pop music. Deals with socio-psychological relationships.

Miller, W. R. *The World of Pop Music and Jazz*.

See p. 126.

Mordden, Ethan. *That Jazz*. New York: G. P. Putnam's Sons, 1978.

Sociological history of the 1920s, very little of jazz interest.

Nanry, Charles Anthony. "The Occupational Subculture of the Jazz Musician: Myth and Reality." Ph.D. dissertation, Rutgers University, 1970.

Examines attitudinal positions of both professional jazz musicians and those trying to achieve professional status.

Newton, Francis. *The Jazz Scene*.

See p. 126.

Ramsey, Frederic. *Been Here and Gone*. Brunswick, N.J.: Rutgers University Press, 1960.

Useful and authoritative book.

————— —————. London: Cassell, 1960.

————— —————. London: Jazz Book Club, 1962.

—————. *Chicago Documentary: Portrait of a Jazz Era*.

See p. 59.

Routley, E. *Is Jazz Music Christian?* London: Epworth Press, 1964.

Shaw, George Washington. "Relationships between Experiential Factors and Percepts of Selected Professional Musicians in the United States Who Are Adept at Jazz Improvisation." Ph.D. dissertation, University of Oklahoma, 1979.

Sinclair, John, and Levin, Robert. *Music and Politics*. New York: World, 1971.

An excellent discussion of social and political aspects of rock and avant-garde black jazz. Very informative.

Stebbins, Robert Alan. "The Jazz Community: The Sociology of a Musical Subculture." Ph.D. dissertation, University of Minnesota, 1964.

Contains an analysis of the inner structure of the jazz community and how this community interacts with the community as a whole. More valuable to sociologists than musicians.

———. "The Minneapolis Jazz Community: The Conflict between Musical and Commercial Values." Master's thesis, University of Minnesota, 1962.

An excellent sociological view of the jazz musician's personality and employment and audience relationships.

Walton, Ortiz M. *Music: Black, White and Blue*.
See p. 69.

Wheaton, Jack. "The Technological and Sociological Influences on Jazz as an Art Form in America."
See p. 69.

Whitten, Norman E., and Szwed, John. *Afro-American Anthology*. New York: The Free Press, 1970.

Chapters on the origin of Afro-American folk music, soul music, and blues. Mainly of sociological interest.

The Phonograph and Jazz

Barnouw, Erik. *A History of Broadcasting in the United States to 1933: A Tower in Babel*. New York: Oxford University Press, 1966.

Contains brief commentary on race records and the denunciation of jazz espoused by many broadcasters.

Dexter, Dave. *Playback*. New York: Billboard Publications, 1976.

Comments on the pop music business and Dexter's relationship with Capitol Records. Briefly mentions a few jazz musicians.

——— ———. New York: Watson-Guptil, 1976.

Feather, Leonard. *New Year Book of Jazz*. New York: Horizon Press, 1958.

Contains an article by Charles Graham entitled "Jazz and the Phonograph."

Gelatt, Roland. *The Fabulous Phonograph: From Tin Foil to High Fidelity*. Philadelphia: Lippincott, 1955.

A technical, rather than an economic and social history.

————. *The Fabulous Phonograph: The Story of the Gramophone from Tin Foil to High Fidelity*. London: Cassell, 1956.

———— ————. Rev. ed. London: Cassell, 1965.

————. *The Fabulous Phonograph: From Edison to Stereo*. New York: Appleton, 1966.

————. *The Fabulous Phonograph: 1877–1977*. London: Cassell, 1977.

    Updates the earlier editions.

Hammond, John. *John Hammond on Record*. New York: Ridge Press, Summit Books, 1977.

    Biography describing Hammond's life and experiences in the music business.

Wyler, M. *A Glimpse at the Past: An Illustrated History of Some Early Record Companies That Made Jazz History*. West Moors, England: Jazz Publications, 1957.

The History of New Orleans

Asbury, Herbert. *The French Quarter: An Informal History of the New Orleans Underworld*. New York: Knopf, 1936.

———— ————. London: Jarrolds, 1937.

Bellocq, Ernest. *Storyville Portraits*. New York: New York Museum of Modern Art, 1970.

Haskins, James. *The Creoles of Color of New Orleans*. New York: Thomas Y. Crowell, 1975.

    Brief comments on the contribution of Creoles to the development of jazz.

Huber, Leonard. *New Orleans, A Pictorial History*. New York: Crown, 1971.

    Includes photos on New Orleans jazz, past and present.

Kane, Harnett. *Queen New Orleans*. New York: Morrow, 1949.

    Contains one chapter on the history of jazz in New Orleans.

Longstreet, Stephen. *Sportin' House: A History of the New Orleans Sinners and the Birth of Jazz*. Los Angeles: Sherbourne Press, 1965.

    Social background to early jazz that is superficial and jejune.

Rose, Al. *Storyville, New Orleans: Being an Authentic, Illustrated Account of the Notorious Red-Light District*. University, Ala.: University of Alabama, 1974.

    Not intended as a history of Storyville but attempts to evoke a feeling of the place and time.

African Music

Bebey, Francis. *African Music: A People's Art*. Translated by Josephine Bennett. London: Harrap, 1975.
   Well-written and illustrated text with a selective discography. Updated by Richard Hill.

Jenkins, Mildred Leona. "The Impact of African Music upon the Western Hemisphere." Master's thesis, Boston University, 1942.

Jones, A. M. *Studies in African Music*. London: Oxford University Press, 1959.

Kaufman, Fredrich, and Guckin, John P. *The African Roots of Jazz*. Sherman Oaks, Calif.: Alfred Publishing Co., 1978.

Nketia, J. H. K. *The Music of Africa*. New York: W. W. Norton, 1974.

——— ———. London: Gollancz, 1975.

Oliver, Paul. *Savannah Syncopators: African Retentions in the Blues*.
   See p. 40.

Other Influences

Courlander, Harold. *The Drum and the Hoe: Life and Lore of the Haitian People*. Berkeley: University of California Press, 1960.
   Includes 109 pages of native music.

———. *Haiti Singing: With the Airs of Songs and with Plates*. Chapel Hill: University of North Carolina Press, 1939.

Leaf, Earl. *Isles of Rhythm*. New York: A. S. Barnes, 1948.
   Examines the various kinds of dances found in the West Indies.

Roberts, John Storm. *Black Music of Two Worlds*. New York: Praeger, 1972.
   An examination of black music other than jazz and blues found in North and South America and the Caribbean.

——— ———. London: Allen Dare, 1973.

Terry, Richard R. *Voodooism in Music*. London: Burns, Oates and Washbourne, 1934.

Chapter 2

The Blues

The literature on the blues, and to a somewhat lesser extent that on gospel, rhythm and blues, and soul, is of considerable interest to the jazz student. It also has a specialized readership of its own. As an ingredient of jazz itself, the blues is of special significance, particularly as the basic twelve-bar format provides a vehicle on which countless improvisations are possible. Many jazz bands, large and small, are firmly based on the blues, and most individual musicians will acknowledge that their playing is considerably influenced by it. There is a particularly strong sociological content to the blues literature, since it is a folk music very closely interwoven with all aspects of black American life styles, whether rural or urban. As blacks moved from the rural south into the big cities of the north, their music reflected their changing lives, and several writers have captured this successfully in print.

The leading British authority on the blues is Paul Oliver. His reputation for scholarly research is probably unequalled, and his excellent books make a tremendous contribution to understanding blues development. He has also been responsible for editing a complete series of important, if brief, monographs by specialized authors on individual styles and performers. Oliver's first major work was *Blues Fell This Morning* (1960), which was published in the United States in 1963 as *The Meaning of the Blues*. This important and pioneering study uses 350 blues citations to illustrate aspects of the life of the rural black, and has chapters on work, gambling, travel, love, crime, etc. It is illustrated with extracts from the "race" catalogs of the record companies, and is well-documented with a full discography of quoted blues, an index of quoted blues singers, and a four-page select bibliography. Oliver's second book, *Conversation with the Blues* (1965) is a sequel to the first, and consists of verbatim extracts from the conversations the author had with sixty-eight singers during an extensive field trip in 1960. Again, it is well-illustrated with eighty unusual photographs, and there is an appendix on selected recordings of the singers quoted, as well as biographical details. One critic suggested that "this book conveys more of the essence of the blues than any other." It is certainly an extremely valuable source book. *Screening the Blues* (1968) is a series of illuminating essays on several major themes, and in it Oliver attempts to interpret the blues enigma by explaining how a vocabulary of allusion, symbol, and imagery carries code implications for the black audience. This allows blues singers to get their songs on record and past the screen of white censorship. A review of this work in the leading British newspaper the *Sunday Times* described it as "a remarkable piece of scholarship, almost completely persuasive in its argument (and) meticulous in its research detail." *The Story of the Blues* (1969) is a balanced historical narrative with over 500 illustrations, and *Savannah Syncopaters* (1970) traces the West African roots of the blues, linking it to American developments. This work is one of the first in the Blues Paperbacks series that appeared in the early 1970s. It is remarkable that anyone so geographically, racially, and socially removed from his subject as is Oliver could produce such authoritative work.

American scholars have also produced some excellent studies; Samuel Charters is one who has specialized largely in this field. He is a prolific documentor of the music starting with *The Country Blues* (1959), which is both highly readable and a mine of information on the early country singers such as Blind Lemon Jefferson, Leroy Carr, Bill Broonzy, and Lightnin' Hopkins. It is still a useful source book though it is now partly superseded by later research findings. The English edition of this work appeared in 1960, and included an extra appendix. Charters followed this in 1967 with *The Bluesmen*, an excellent study of pre-World War II country blues in Mississippi, Texas, and Alabama; his *Sweet as the Showers of Rain* (1977) is the second volume of this work. Its descriptive subtitle, "The Story and the Music of the Men Who Made the Blues," including Furry Lewis, Willie McTell, Blind Blake, Blind Boy Fuller, and others, indicates its scope. Another significant study by Charters is *The Poetry of the Blues* (1963, reprinted in 1970), which looks at blues lyrics as literature and includes much interpretative and explanatory material. A monograph on *Robert Johnson* (1973) tells the story of Johnson's life and music and is based on reminiscences of other musicians who knew and played with him plus musical transcriptions of his recorded repertoire. This review of Charters's work so far is completed by reference to *The Legacy of the Blues* (1975), subtitled "A Glimpse into the Art and Lives of Twelve Great Bluesmen."

Earlier works by American authors include W. C. Handy's *Blues* (1926), an anthology that traces "the development of the most spontaneous and appealing branch of Negro folk music," according to its extended title. It includes complete words and music of sixty-seven songs by Handy with a historical and critical text by Abbe Niles, and was reissued in 1949 under the title *A Treasury of the Blues*. Handy's autobiography *Father of the Blues* (1941, reissued in 1970) is also of interest. Other autobiographical works by blues singers include "Big Bill" Broonzy's *Big Bill Blues* (1955), which was completely revised by his collaborator, Yannick Bruynoghe, after Broonzy's death, and published in the United States in 1964. This is a valuable book that provides background details to the lives of rural singers in Mississippi. There are some excellent line drawings by Paul Oliver and a comprehensive discography of Broonzy's recorded work included as well. Another book of significance is Perry Bradford's *Born with the Blues* (1965), which includes interesting details of early jazz in New York.

Huddie Ledbetter, who was known as Leadbelly, was a major figure in blues history, and his work and songs are discussed in a number of published sources. John and Alan Lomax's *Negro Songs as Sung by Leadbelly* (1936) was an early work in the blues field, and its subtitle succinctly described Ledbetter as "King of the Twelve-String Guitar Players of the World (and) Long-Time Convict in the Penitentiaries of Texas and Louisiana." Alan Lomax was also associated with Moses Asch in the briefer *Leadbelly Song-*

book, published by Oak Publications in 1963. An even briefer pamphlet by British critics Max Jones and Albert McCarthy, *Tribute to Huddie Ledbetter*, appeared in 1946, and is still of some considerable interest.

An excellent series of television programs about the blues was produced by the British Broadcasting Corporation and was solidly based on documentary sources. An edited text of these broadcasts was published as *The Devil's Music: A History of the Blues* (1976) by Giles Oakley. Another useful general overview, written in a popular and readable style, is Bruce Cook's *Listen to the Blues* (1973), while James H. Cone's *The Spirituals and the Blues: An Interpretation* (1972) is a useful introduction, though stronger on spirituals than blues.

The Blues Paperbacks series produced some important titles in 1970 and 1971. This series examines important musicians, styles, traditions, and themes, and the history and influence of the blues. It is aimed, in the words of the publisher, Studio Vista, at "enthusiasts of modern musical idioms, sociologists and folklorists, and students of the popular arts." Several titles are biographical studies of individual singers and typical of these are *Tommy Johnson* (1971) by David Evans, *Charley Patton* (1970) by John Fahey, *The Devil's Son-in-Law: The Story of Peetie Wheatstraw and His Songs* (1971) by Paul Garon, and *Deep South Piano: The Story of Little Brother Montgomery* (1970) by Karl Gert zur Heide. Others in the series deal with groups of singers from a particular area or sharing a particular style. Bengt Olsson's *Memphis Blues and Jug Bands* (1970) and William Ferris's *Blues from the Delta* (1970) are examples of the latter. Ferris's book is a study of black folklore from the Mississippi Delta, and examines the creative processes of the blues through interviews and recording sessions with singers. Derrick Stewart-Baxter's *Ma Rainey and the Classic Blues Singers* (1970) is a critical discussion of the women singers of the 1920s who first recorded the blues and established its relationship to jazz. It is appropriate to mention Bessie Smith at this juncture, and especially the excellent biography by Chris Albertson, *Bessie* (1972), which is dealt with more fully in chapter 4 along with other biographies of major figures. The work of Blind Boy Fuller and fellow singers of the blues in the Carolinas and North Georgia is documented in Bruce Baston's *Crying for the Carolinas* (1971); a final title in this excellent series is Bob Groom's *The Blues Revival* (1971). This traces the growth of blues appreciation, especially in the British context.

Charles Keil's *Urban Blues* (1966) is a scholarly work of considerable interest. Keil has produced a masterly account of a limited field, and propounds the thesis that the urban blues is part of a valid, valuable, and distinctly black culture. There are vivid chapters on B. B. King and Bobby Bland skillfully intertwined within his analysis. He is trained in the fields of musicology, anthropology, and sociology, all of which are vital to a balanced analysis of this musical culture, and has also worked as a practicing jazz musician. Keil is exceptionally well qualified in the fields he is discussing, and thus brings authority of the highest order to this important document.

Mike Leadbitter, who died at the age of 32, was a leading British enthusiast who edited the pioneering journal *Blues Unlimited* from its inception in 1963 to 1970. His book *Nothing but the Blues: An Illustrated Documentary* (1971) is a compilation of material that originally appeared in its pages. Leadbitter also produced *Delta Country Blues* (1968), which is a very readable booklet concentrating on the 1940s and early 1950s. Paul Garon, whose contribution to the Blues Paperbacks' series has been previously mentioned, published *Blues and the Poetic Spirit* (1975) in the Eddison Blues Books series edited by Tony Russell. This title includes a brief chapter on "The Literature of the Blues." Another in the Eddison series is Mike Rowe's *Chicago Breakdown* (1973), which studies the blues singers of Chicago. It is well researched, authoritative, and particularly good on the development of postwar styles. A very well-illustrated volume is *Blues* (1975), compiled by Robert Neff and Anthony Connor. This conveys the personal experiences of some fifty-five singers rather than being either a musicological treatise or a history of the blues.

Books of musical transcriptions include Eric Kriss's *Six Blues-Root Pianists* (1973), which includes pieces by Jimmy Yancey, Champion Jack Dupree, Little Brother Montgomery, Speckled Red, Roosevelt Sykes, and Otis Spann. It also has a useful, though brief, annotated bibliography. Earlier works in the same vein include Shirley's *The Book of the Blues* (1964) and Jerry Silverman's *Folk Blues* (1958). The former includes some 100 items for guitar with useful discographical notes on each title and brief biographical details of the alleged composer. A manual on *The Country Blues Guitar* (1968) by Stefan Grossman includes guitar instruction with examples and lyrics from early records, while Tony Glover's *Blues Harp* (1965) is an instruction method for playing the blues harmonica.

A remarkable and lengthy book edited by Eric Sackheim, *The Blues Line* (1969), completes this section. Sackheim is a lifelong collector of blues lyrics and a publisher of poetry. The book contains 270 carefully selected verses laid out artistically and very effectively on its pages. The authors range from Leadbelly to Muddy Waters. As one reviewer said, "the text sings with the voices of the men and women from whose lives the songs grew." It is brilliantly illustrated, a minor masterpiece.

Blues-related popular music together with gospel is worthy of brief mention here, especially as there are several superior texts among many mediocre ones. John Broven's *Walking to New Orleans* (1974) is the story of New Orleans rhythm and blues, and particularly relates this to earlier New Orleans jazz. It is an especially useful study of the period 1946–73, and has excellent coverage of artists, clubs, and recordings. A more general work, *The Sound of the City* (1970) by Charlie Gillett, is subtitled "The Rise of Rock and Roll" and is claimed to be the best history of rhythm and blues, soul, and rock, as well as rock and roll itself. Another important work is Michael Haralambos's *Right On* (1974), which attempts to trace the relationship between black society and culture and black music, and especially to explain the decline in popularity of the blues and the rise in popularity of soul. This is another excellent title from the Eddison Blues Books series. Also on soul is Phyl Garland's *The Sound of Soul* (1969) and Ian Hoare's *The Soul Book* (1975), while gospel is covered by Tony Heilbut's *The Gospel Sound! Good News and Bad Times* (1971). Finally, a book which, according to some critics, appears not to have received the attention it merits is

Richard Middleton's *Pop Music and the Blues* (1972), which offers an original and valuable cultural analysis based on the study of the blues and how it influenced popular music as a musical form. British trumpeter and writer Ian Carr regards it as "a fascinating attempt to explain the music in terms of its sociopsychological background in the fusion of western and nonwestern cultures."

BIBLIOGRAPHY

Albertson, Chris. *Bessie*.
    See p. 104.
————, and Schuller, Gunther. *Bessie Smith, Empress of the Blues*. New York: Macmillan, 1975.
    Brief biography, analysis of her singing style, and many beautiful photos. Most of the book consists of tunes she was associated with.
Asch, Moses, and Lomax, Alan. *The Leadbelly Songbook*. New York: Oak Publications, 1962.
Baker, David. "The Rhetorical Dimensions of Black Music Past and Present."
    See p. 116.
Baston, Bruce. *Crying for the Carolinas*. London: Studio Vista, 1971.
    Study of the blues of the Carolinas and North Georgia, and especially the work of Blind Boy Fuller.
The Blues Project: The Sound. New York: McGraw-Hill, 1968.
Bokelman, Marina. "The Coon Con Game: A Blues Ballad Tradition."
    See p. 18.
Bradford, Perry. *Born with the Blues: The True Story of the Pioneering Blues Singers and Musicians in the Early Days of Jazz*. New York: Oak Publications, 1965.
———— ————. New York: Oak Publications, 1966.
Broonzy, William, and Bruynoghe, Yannick. *Big Bill Blues: William Broonzy's Story as Told to Yannick Bruynoghe*.
    See p. 90.
Broven, John. *Walking to New Orleans: The Story of New Orleans Rhythm and Blues*. Bexhill-on-Sea, England: Blues Unlimited, 1974.

Covers the period from 1946 to 1973. Brief comments on individual performers, record companies, and groups.

Bruynoghe, Yannick. *Big Bill Blues*. 2nd ed. New York: Oak Publications, 1964.

Revised after Broonzy's death with a new discography.

Charters, Samuel B. *The Bluesmen: The Story and the Music of the Men Who Made the Blues*. New York: Oak Publications, 1967.

The singers and the styles from Mississippi, Alabama, and Texas up to World War II, with brief consideration of some of the traceable relationships between the blues and African song.

————— —————. New York: Music Sales, 1967.

—————. *The Country Blues*. New York: Rinehart, 1959.

Source book for the early country blues; well researched and contains some unusual illustrations.

————— —————. London: M. Joseph, 1960.

————— —————. London: Jazz Book Club, 1961.

————— —————. New York: Da Capo, 1975.

—————. *The Legacy of the Blues*.

See p. 84.

—————. *The Poetry of the Blues*. New York: Oak Publications, 1963.

Significant study of Negro folk blues based on extensive research and field recordings. Includes much interpretative and explanatory material on the words of blues songs.

————— —————. New York: Music Sales, 1963.

————— —————. New York: Avon Books, 1970.

—————. *Robert Johnson*.

See p. 98.

—————. *Sweet as the Showers of Rain*. New York: Oak Publications, 1977.

A study of regional blues styles before World War II. An excellent book.

Cone, James H. *The Spirituals and the Blues: An Interpretation*. New York: The Seabury Press, 1972.

A discussion of the meaning and depth of spirituals and blues tunes. Illustrates cultural, sociological, and theological applications of these songs.

Cook, Bruce. *Listen to the Blues*. New York: Charles Scribner's Sons, 1973.

A history of the blues and its important exponents. Very enjoyable and entertaining reading.

————— —————. New York: Charles Scribner's Sons, 1975.

————— —————. London: Robson Books, 1975.

Dixon, Robert M. W., and Godrich, John. *Recording the Blues*. New York: Stein and Day, 1970.

An examination of the content of "race records" produced between 1920 and 1945. Also examined is how record companies discovered talent, how they recorded the singers, and how they marketed the records.

————— —————. London: Studio Vista, 1970.

Ellington, Duke. *Piano Method for Blues*.

See p. 120.

Evans, David. *Tommy Johnson*.

See p. 98.

Fahey, John. *Charley Patton*.

See p. 103.

Ferris, William. *Blues from the Delta*. London: Studio Vista, 1970.

A documentary on the music and musicians of the Mississippi Delta. Well written with photos, bibliography, and discography.

————— —————. Garden City, N.Y.: Anchor Press, 1978.

Garland, Phyl. *The Sound of Soul*. Chicago: Henry Regnery, 1969.

A well-written book centering around such notable rhythm and blues musicians as B. B. King, Nina Simone, and Aretha Franklin. Also contains an important chapter on John Coltrane and on the history of soul music.

Garon, Paul. *Blues and the Poetic Spirit*. London: Eddison Press, 1975.

Includes a brief chapter on "The Literature of the Blues" and a bibliography.

————— —————. New York: Da Capo, 1978.

—————. *The Devil's Son-in-Law: The Story of Peetie Wheatstraw and His Songs*.

See p. 106.

Garwood, Donald. *Masters of Instrumental Blues Guitar*.

See p. 121.

Gert zur Heide, Karl. *Deep South Piano: The Story of Little Brother Montgomery*.

See p. 101.

Gillett, Charlie. *The Sound of the City: The Rise of Rock and Roll*. New York: Outerbridge and Dienstfrey, 1970.

Two chapters on rhythm and blues, 1945 to 1956.

Glover, Tony. *Blues Harp: An Instruction Method for Playing the Blues Harmonica*. New York: Oak Publications, 1965.

Groom, Bob. *The Blues Revival*. London: Studio Vista, 1971.

Traces the growth of blues appreciation, especially in the British context.

Grossman, Stefan. *The Country Blues Guitar*. New York: Oak Publications, 1968.

―――. *Rev. Gary Davis/Blues Guitar*. New York: Oak Publications, 1974.

Contains an interview, notes on notation, many musical examples, two brief articles on Davis, and a discography.

Guralnick, Peter. *Feel like Going Home: Portraits in Blues and Rock'n Roll*. New York: Outerbridge and Dienstfrey, 1971.

A history of the blues with chapters on Muddy Waters, Johnny Shines, Skip James, Robert Pete Williams, Howlin' Wolf, Sam Phillips, Jerry Lee Lewis, and Charlie Rich. Contains a bibliography and discography.

Handy, W. C. *Father of the Blues: An Autobiography*.
See p. 96.

Handy, W. C., and Niles, A. *Blues: An Anthology*. New York: Boni, 1926.

Traces the development of black folk blues tunes through fifty-three songs, and includes a critical text.

――― ―――. New York: Collier Books, 1972.

――― ―――. New York: Collier Books, 1975.

―――. *A Treasury of the Blues: Complete Words and Music of the Great Songs from Memphis Blues to the Present Day*. New York: Boni, 1949.

Includes a historical and critical text.

Haralambos, Michael. *Right On: From Blues to Soul in Black America*.
See p. 22.

Heilbut, Tony. *The Gospel Sound, Good News and Bad Times*.
See p. 13.

Hoare, Ian, ed. *The Soul Book*. London: Methuen, 1975.

Hodes, Art, and Hansen, Chadwick, eds. *Selections from the Gutter*. Berkeley: University of California Press, 1977.

Contains a number of autobiographical articles by prominent jazz and blues musicians between 1943 and 1947.

Holiday, Billie, and Duffty, W. *Lady Sings the Blues*. Garden City, N.Y.: Doubleday, 1956.

———— ————. London: Barrie and Rockliff, 1958.

Howe, Martin. *Blue Jazz*. Bristol, England: Perpetua Press, 1934.

———— ————. Bristol, England: White and White, 1936.

Jones, Max, and McCarthy, Albert. *Tribute to Huddie Ledbetter*. London: Jazz Music Books, 1946.

Joy of Boogie and Blues. New York: Amsco Music Service, n.d.

Keil, Charles. *Urban Blues*. Chicago: Chicago University Press, 1966.

> A scholarly work written by an author trained in musicology, anthropology, and sociology who is also a practicing jazz musician.

Kriss, Eric. *Six Blues-Roots Pianists*. New York: Oak Publications, 1973.

> Examines Jimmy Yancey, Jack Dupree, Little Brother Montgomery, Speckled Red, Roosevelt Sykes, and Otis Spann. Also examines barrelhouse and ragtime styles.

Lang, I. *Background of the Blues*. London: Workers Music Assn., 1943.

> Brief volume expanded into *Jazz in Perspective*.

————. *Jazz in Perspective: The Background of the Blues*. London: Hutchinson, 1947.

> Influential book, particularly in Britain. Good on the blues.

———— ————. London: Jazz Book Club, 1957.

———— ————. New York: Da Capo, 1976.

Leadbitter, Mike. *Delta Country Blues*. Bexhill, England: Blues Unlimited, 1968.

> Concentrates on the 1940s and early 1950s.

————. *Nothing but the Blues: An Illustrated Documentary*. London: Hanover Books, 1971.

> Articles from the periodical *Blues Unlimited* from 1963 to 1970.

———— ————. New York: Music Sales, 1972.

Lee, G. W. *Beale Street, Where the Blues Began*. New York: R. O. Ballou, 1934.

Lomax, John, and Lomax, Alan, eds. *The Leadbelly Legend: A Collection of World-Famous Songs by Huddie Ledbetter*.
> See p. 15.

————. *Negro Songs as Sung by Leadbelly: King of the Twelve-*

String Guitar Players of the World, Long-Time Convict in the Penitentiaries of Texas and Louisiana.
　　See p. 15.

Lydon, Michael. *Rock Folk: Portraits from the Rock 'n Roll Pantheon.* New York: Dial Press, 1971.
　　Contains one chapter on B. B. King.
　　————— —————. New York: Dell, 1973.

McGhee, W. G. *Guitar Styles of Brownie McGhee.*
　　See p. 100.

McIlwaine, Shields. *Memphis Down in Dixie.* New York: E. P. Dutton, 1948.
　　Contains a partial chapter on Beale Street and W. C. Handy.

Mann, Woody. *Six Black Blues Guitarists.*
　　See p. 86.

Middleton, Richard. *Pop Music and the Blues: A Study of the Relationship and Its Significance.*
　　See p. 24.

Mitchell, George. *Blow My Blues Away.*
　　See p. 15.

Moore, Thurston W., ed. *Rhythm and Blues Scrapbook.* Cincinnati: Artist Publications, 1952.

Murray, Albert. *The Omni-Americans.* New York: Outerbridge and Dienstfrey, 1970.
　　Contains one partial chapter on the blues.
　　—————. *Stomping the Blues.* New York: McGraw-Hill, 1976.
　　An interpretation of the blues as performed by a number of jazz instrumentalists and singers. Offers an insight into the blues not found in other books. Highly recommended.
　　————— —————. London: Quartet Books, 1978.

Myrus, D. *Ballads, Blues and the Big Beat.* New York: Macmillan, 1966.

Neff, Robert, and Connor, Anthony. *Blues.* Boston: David R. Godine, 1975.
　　A collection of autobiographical comments by fifty-five blues musicians.
　　————— —————. London: Latimer New Dimensions, 1976.

Oakley, Giles. *The Devil's Music: A History of the Blues.* London: British Broadcasting Corp., 1976.
　　An excellent book including photos and a detailed bibliography. Highly recommended.
　　————— —————. New York: Taplinger, 1977.

Oliver, Paul. *Aspects of the Blues Tradition*. New York: Oak Publications, 1970.

  Originally published as *Screening the Blues*.

———. *Bessie Smith*.

  See p. 105.

——— ———. New York: A. S. Barnes, 1961.

———. *Blues Fell This Morning: The Meaning of the Blues*. London: Cassell, 1960.

  Well-documented and scholarly work.

——— ———. New York: Horizon Press, 1961.

———. *Conversation with the Blues*. London: Cassell, 1965.

  Written by the leading British authority on the blues. The text is taken from conversations with sixty-eight blues musicians. It is well illustrated with eighty photos and includes a selective discography.

——— ———. New York: Horizon Press, 1965.

——— ———. London: Jazz Book Club, 1967.

———. *The Meaning of the Blues*. New York: Collier Books, 1963.

  A sociological work depicting the life of the rural American Negro. Extremely well documented with a discography, an index of blues singers, and a selective bibliography.

———. *Savannah Syncopators*. London: Studio Vista, 1970.

  A well-written book depicting the survival of the cultural content of African music in Afro-American music and particularly the blues. Well documented through field studies in Africa.

——— ———. New York: Stein and Day, 1970.

———. *Screening the Blues*. London: Cassell, 1968.

  One of a series of illuminating essays on the blues.

———. *The Story of the Blues*. London: Barrie and Rockliff, 1969.

  An excellent history of the blues. Includes musical examples, a bibliography, and a discography.

——— ———. London: Crenet Press, 1969.

——— ———. Radnor, Pa.: Chilton, 1975.

Olsson, Bengt. *Memphis Blues and Jug Bands*. London: Studio Vista, 1970.

Oster, Harry. *Living Country-Blues*. Hatboro, Pa.: Folklore Associates, 1969.

  Contains lyrics from 230 blues tunes recorded in Louisiana between 1955 and 1961. Primarily deals with analysis and interpretation of the lyrics.

——— ———. New York: Minerva Press, 1975.

Reed, Lawrence N. *Rock Is Rhythm and Blues*. Ann Arbor: Michigan State University Press, 1974.

Includes brief commentary on the birth and development of blues and rhythm and blues.

Rowe, Mike. *Chicago Breakdown*. London: Eddison Press, 1973.

An important history of blues in Chicago.

——— ———. New York: Drake Publishers, 1975.

Russell, Tony. *Blacks, Whites and Blues*. London: Studio Vista, 1970.

See p. 16.

Sackheim, Eric. *The Blues Line: A Collection of Blues Lyrics from Leadbelly to Muddy Waters*. New York: Grossman, 1969.

——— ———. New York: Schirmer Books, 1975.

——— ———. London: Collier-Macmillan, 1977.

Shaw, Arnold. *Honkers and Shouters: The Golden Years of Rhythm and Blues*. New York: Macmillan, 1977.

A thorough and well-written book containing many quotes by the musicians themselves.

——— ———. New York: Collier Books, 1978.

———. *The World of Soul: Black America's Contribution to the Pop Music Scene*.

See p. 16.

Shelton, R., and Raim, W. *The Josh White Song Book*. Chicago: Quadrangle Books, 1963.

Biography of Josh White, along with simple arrangements of tunes associated with him.

——— ———. London: Elek Books, 1964.

Shirley, K. *The Book of the Blues*. New York: Crown, 1964.

One hundred pieces for the guitar together with notes on recordings and composers.

Shockett, Bernard I. "A Stylistic Study of the Blues as Recorded by Jazz Instrumentalists, 1917–1931."

See p. 129.

Silverman, Jerry. *Folk Blues*. New York: Macmillan, 1958.

——— ———. New York: Macmillan, 1967.

——— ———. New York: Oak Publications, 1968.

Stewart-Baxter, Derrick. *Ma Rainey and the Classic Blues Singers*. New York: Stein and Day, 1970.

A discussion of the various characteristics of classic blues and the important singers. Includes a brief bibliography and discography.

——— ———. London: Studio Vista, 1970.

Surge, Frank. *Singers of the Blues*.

See p. 87.

Titon, Jeff. *Early Downhome Blues*. Urbana: University of Illinois Press, 1977.

A musical and cultural analysis of blues tunes with an accompanying recording. Examines social and cultural influences on blues tunes.

———. "Ethnomusicology of Downhome Blues Phonograph Records, 1926–30." Ph.D. dissertation, University of Minnesota, 1971.

Deals with the musical styles of the downhome blues and the viewpoints of recording artists, record industry, and record audience.

Chapter 3

The Histories of Jazz

The history of jazz proper spans about eighty years. Even within this relatively brief time, it is possible to identify ages or periods based on the evolution of styles and on the principal centers where these styles matured. In general, the literature does not divide in this way, and we therefore intend to look at the historical literature somewhat differently. Nevertheless, the early New Orleans period is of particular interest, since this city had the primary role in the coalescence of many diverse strands into something recognizable as a quite distinct musical style.

The upheaval caused by the United States Navy in 1917, through their closing of many of the brothels in the Storyville district, has been romanticized and perhaps accorded a greater historical significance than the action warranted. The coincidence of this event, with the development of the phonograph record, undoubtedly had a major impact and caused many musicians to move to other parts of the United States to seek their living. In the following few years, the growth of radio broadcasting provided another important element in improving the dissemination of this new musical sensation.

The Original Dixieland Jazz Band made the first phonograph records of jazz in 1917. This group of white imitators achieved worldwide fame because of this lucky chance and attained an importance rather out of proportion to their talents. The events surrounding this development are well documented in H. O. Brunn's *Story of the Original Dixieland Jazz Band,* published in 1960. Little jazz history was recorded in those early years and when the first authors finally recorded their thoughts, their recollections were partially factual and partially legendary. They also interlaced historical record with attempts at critical analysis; in some ways these early works could just as easily fit into chapter 5. We believe, however, that their interest today is of an almost completely historical nature.

These early books possessed many similarities. They claimed to be serious works on the history and development of jazz, and three of them included the word in their titles. They all have interest to the jazz historian since they show how difficult it was for critics of that period to understand what it was they were trying to describe. Henry Osgood's *So This Is Jazz* (1926) contains some interesting material but has many weaknesses, since it concentrates on the work of dance band musicians who proved to have had little or no influence on the development of jazz. Osgood showed no faith in the future of what he regarded as jazz and was obsessed with the necessity for it to become "respectable" in the manner of George Gershwin. The book was considerable in spite of its many faults; it apparently was the only work read by Percy Scholes leading to his completely inaccurate and worthless assessment of jazz in the 1954 edition of the *Oxford Companion to Music*, a standard and usually very reliable work. In Britain, and consequently even farther from the roots and origins of jazz, R. W. S. Mendl produced *The Appeal of Jazz* in 1927. This too is of limited value; the author's main aim was to place jazz in the mainstream of music and, since Mendl was totally lacking in information on the work of major musicians of the period like Oliver, Armstrong, etc., this was an impossible task. The result is a volume on jazz comparable to a book on "serious" music with no mention of Bach, Beethoven, and Mozart. *All about Jazz* (1934) by Stanley Nelson concentrates on the activities of English musicians of the early 1930s. It is of little value except in its revelation of the attitudes of the supposedly well-informed music critics of the period. Although it is, with hindsight, easy to criticize these pioneering works, they should not be totally dismissed, since they broke the way for other literary efforts, and they reflect how jazz was regarded at the time.

European writers such as Robert Goffin, a Belgian, and Hugues Panassie of France were the first to recognize the important differences between true jazz and other popular music of the day, which was often placed into the same general category. Goffin made numerous contributions to the literature of jazz between 1921 (*Jazz Band*) and 1944 (*Nouvelle Histoire du Jazz, du Congo au Bebop*). All of these were originally published in French and only his biography of Louis Armstrong, *Horn of Plenty*, and *Jazz from the Congo to the Metropolitan* were translated into English. This latter work, titled *Jazz from Congo to Swing* (1946) in its British edition, deals in an informed way with early jazz and, unlike some other books, had a strong confidence in the future of the music. The English edition was widely read and very influential just after World War II, when very little jazz literature in book form was available.

Panassie has also written prolifically. His books on analysis and criticism, biography, and in the reference field appear in various chapters of this work, but much of his effort has gone into recording historical data. Panassie's earlier books, like those of all the European critics writing at the time, are not always as strictly accurate as they might be owing to his difficulty in locating relevant source material. The main value of his early work was its important role in making jazz respectable and a subject worthy of being written about.

Substantial works written by Americans eventually followed, with Ramsey and Smith's *Jazzmen* (1939) probably the first really informed full-length appraisal to appear. It was particularly interesting to the historian because it contained accurate assessments based on data collected by the authors and was, therefore, in direct contrast to the well-meaning but sometimes inaccurate commentaries of the pioneer European critics just discussed. Useful chapters on record collecting (by Stephen Smith) and "Consider the Critics" (by R. P. Dodge) are included. The latter discussed the early written references to jazz in the periodical literature of the 1920s. Undoubtedly this work is a watershed in jazz literature, in that it provoked and inspired many of the subsequent books.

The work of Rudi Blesh has been previously mentioned, but perhaps his major contribution to the literature of jazz is *Shining Trumpets*, which first appeared in 1946 and subsequently in further editions and reprints up to 1976. Blesh has a fine enthusiasm for the earlier period of traditional jazz and this book exerted wide influence when it first appeared. Because Blesh stubbornly refused to acknowledge the mainstream and modern schools, his reputation suffered among many enthusiasts in the 1950s. Now that his work can be seen in perspective, and also because many of his conclusions on the African roots of jazz have tended to be confirmed by uncommitted scholarly authors, his place as a writer of importance in jazz history seems to be assured. *Shining Trumpets* is well documented and has extensive appendixes that include a discography and forty-eight musical examples. Blesh was a constant propagandist for his view of jazz and, through broadcasts and lectures, did much to present it to a wider public.

Barry Ulanov's *History of Jazz in America* (1952) is a reliable history which, unlike many others, does not concentrate on the early days at the expense of the swing and modern eras. Marshall Stearns's work *The Story of Jazz*, which appeared four years after Ulanov's, is outstanding. It is a major work of scholarship, thoroughly researched and documented. Stearns was the founder of the Institute of Jazz Studies at Rutgers University, and was connected with it until his death in 1966; his contributions to the literature of jazz and his efforts to elevate it into a subject worthy of independent study are extremely important. *The Story of Jazz* covers all aspects of the music in a broad-minded, mature fashion and ran to several editions (including one in paperback). An extensive bibliography by Robert G. Reisner and a syllabus of fifteen lectures on the history of jazz were included in the third edition.

Shapiro and Hentoff's *Hear Me Talkin' to Ya* (1955) has been referred to as the best single book on the subject. It is the story of jazz as told directly by the men who made it and does not attempt to duplicate any of the formal histories. Nevertheless, it does complement the work of Stearns and others exceedingly well. It is arranged chronologically and is recognized as a major source for historical information on jazz. Several editions of the work have appeared since 1955, including both paperback and book club editions.

Nat Hentoff was also joint editor, with Albert McCarthy,

of *Jazz* (1959), which is subtitled "New Perspectives on the History of Jazz, etc. by Twelve of the World's Foremost Jazz Critics and Scholars." These essays, of a substantial nature, are particularly interesting and include Ernest Borneman on "The Roots of Jazz," Guy Waterman on "Ragtime," and Gunther Schuller on "The Ellington Style."

Three recent works that deal with jazz history in a comprehensive manner are Joachim-Ernst Berendt's *The Story of Jazz* (1978), Frank Tirro's *Jazz: A History* (1977), and James Lincoln Collier's *The Making of Jazz* (1978). The latter is a wide-ranging and readable history of jazz from African roots to John Coltrane, while Tirro's book is perhaps the best since Stearns. It is scholarly yet extremely readable and is well organized with a good index and a comprehensive bibliography. It also includes a useful glossary of jazz terminology. Berendt has built a high reputation for his work, and *The Story of Jazz* is thorough and competent.

Rex Harris, a critic influential in Britain in the 1950s, wrote the original paperback book *Jazz* that first appeared in 1952 and ran to five editions before 1957. This book provides good information on the roots of jazz, but his work generally needs to be approached with caution, owing to his narrow view of the subject.

An excellent series of books produced under the general title of the Macmillan Jazz Masters series were edited by Martin Williams, a leading American critic. Somewhat uneven in quality, they are nevertheless a most useful summary of the various periods of jazz history. The basic approach is by brief essays on the work of the major figures of the period. Titles so far published are *Jazz Masters of the Fifties* (1965) by Joe Goldberg and *Jazz Masters of the Forties* by Ira Gitler (1966); *Jazz Masters of the Twenties* by Richard Hadlock (1965); *Jazz Masters of New Orleans* by the series editor, Williams, in 1967; *Jazz Masters in Transition* (1970), also by Williams; and *Jazz Masters of the Thirties* (1972) by Rex Stewart. Goldberg's was the first in the series and covered the work of Gerry Mulligan, Thelonius Monk, Art Blakey, Miles Davis, Sonny Rollins, Charles Mingus, John Coltrane, and others. Hadlock's volume covered Armstrong (to 1931), Hines, Beiderbecke, Waller, Teagarden, Bessie Smith, Eddie Lang, and the Chicagoans.

Gitler's book deals with Parker, Gillespie, and the other major instrumentalists of the forties and, like the other volumes, does not have a great deal of original material but puts what it does have together well. Martin Williams covers the pioneering New Orleans musicians and Rex Stewart includes particularly interesting material on Duke Ellington.

The era of the big swing bands is very well documented. Typical examples include Leo Walker's *The Wonderful Era of the Great Dance Bands* (1964), which covers the period 1925–1945 and gives details,with illustrations, of the work of Whiteman, Goldkette, Goodman, Dorsey, and others. It also includes the work of nonjazz orchestras. Gene Fernett's *A Thousand Golden Horns* (1966) is a shorter work that deals with the ten years between 1935 and 1945. All the main bands are covered, but particularly valuable is the information on the lesser known orchestras of those years that often featured famous jazz musicians of all styles. More substantial than either of these is George Simon's *The Big Bands* (1967; revised and enlarged in 1971). Simon's book is remarkable in its scope and shows clearly, though in a gossipy style, how deeply the big bands shaped a whole generation of popular and jazz musicians in the 1920s, 1930s, and 1940s. It includes profiles of 72 major bands of the era and shorter biographies of more than 300 less-important orchestras.

Albert J. McCarthy's two volumes, *The Dance Band Era* (1971) and *Big Band Jazz* (1974), are also of some interest. The former covers the period 1910–1950 and is a well-illustrated account of the major big bands of this period, relating their work to the mainstream of jazz development. *Big Band Jazz* concentrates heavily on the formative years of the big band movement and shows McCarthy to be an indefatigable cataloger of names and places rather than an acute musical analyst.

A valuable work of reference on a specialized area of jazz history is Charters's and Kunstadt's *Jazz: A History of the New York Scene* (1962). As the subtitle indicates, this detailed and scholarly book confines itself to the developments of jazz in New York from 1920 to 1962. This book is also good on the big bands of the swing era.

Another book that concentrates on historical aspects of jazz in New York City is Arnold Shaw's *52nd Street* (1977). This was originally published as *The Street That Never Slept* in 1971, and is a review of the historical associations of 52nd Street. Duncan Schiedt examines in detail the jazz scene in Indiana in *The Jazz State of Indiana* (1977), while Burt Goldblatt's *Newport Jazz Festival* (1977) is a comprehensive review of the important events in one of the major festivals of jazz.

The history of jazz in individual countries outside the United States has been recorded in a number of books of varying quality. David Boulton's *Jazz in Britain* (1958) is an attempt to cover the whole field of British jazz, and has some useful chapters on the pre-1939 period. It is, however, a disappointing book overall, with many major omissions and too much space allocated to relatively unimportant matters. Arthur Jackson's *The World of Big Bands* (1977) is especially useful for the information it contains on British big bands, and Benny Green's *Swingtime in Tottenham* (1976) describes the semiprofessional jazz musicians working in north London in the post-World War II period. Green also produced a pamphlet on Ronnie Scott's world famous jazz club entitled *Jazz Decade* (1969).

Robert Pernet's *Jazz in Little Belgium* (1967) took six years to prepare, and is obviously of importance in the documentation of European jazz, but it is spoiled by being physically of poor quality and also by the irritating manner in which it changes language from French to English and back again. The book includes 338 pages of discography (out of 518 pages) of all jazz records by or with Belgian musicians. There is also a bibliography of some ninety books (divided into "background books" and "jazz books") and twenty jazz periodicals.

In conclusion, there are several photographic collections that are relevant. Max Jones's *Jazz Photo Album: A History of Jazz in Pictures* (1947) was followed by Keepnews's and Grauer's *Pictorial History of Jazz* (1955). This photographic tour de force is spoiled somewhat as a history by the lack of definite dates for many of the captions. There was an improved second edition in 1966. Some interesting photographs of musicians associated with the various Condon bands appear in *The Eddie Condon Scrapbook of Jazz* (1973), which is a collection of pictures from the Condon family album with some linking commentary.

BIBLIOGRAPHY

Complete Histories

Bennington, Billy D. "A Brief History of Jazz." Master's thesis, East Texas State University, 1950.

Berendt, Joachim-Ernest. *The Jazz Book: From New Orleans to Rock and Free Jazz*. New York: Lawrence Hill, 1974.

A valuable book that historically examines style characteristics, the musicians, the elements of performance, the instruments, the vocalists, big bands, and combos. Provides a variety of viewpoints to a historical perspective.

————— —————. New York: Lawrence Hill, 1975.

————— —————. London: Paladin Books, 1976.

————— —————. St. Albans, England: Hart-Davis, McGibbon, 1976.

—————. *The New Jazz Book: A History and Guide*. New York: Hill and Wang, 1962.

————— —————. London: Peter Owen, 1964.

————— —————. London: Jazz Book Club, 1965.

—————, ed. *The Story of Jazz*. Englewood Cliffs, N.J.: Prentice-Hall, 1978.

A beautiful and well-organized book with many photos and an excellent bibliography and discography.

————— —————. London: Barrie and Jenkins, 1978.

Blesh, Rudi. *Shining Trumpets: A History of Jazz*. New York: Knopf, 1946.

An in-depth examination of jazz history from prejazz influences to the beginnings of jazz in New York and the development of boogie-woogie and stride piano (1930s). Excellent coverage but limited in scope owing to the author's prejudice against post-1930 jazz.

————— —————. London: Cassell, 1949.

————— —————. 2nd rev. ed. New York: Knopf, 1958.

————— —————. London: Cassell, 1958.

————— —————. New York: Da Capo, 1975.

————— —————. New York: Da Capo, 1976.

Collier, James Lincoln. *The Making of Jazz: A Comprehensive History*. Boston: Houghton Mifflin, 1978.

A reevaluation of the history of jazz based on a study of recorded jazz. Excellent text for a college-level jazz history course.

——— ———. London: Hart-Davis, McGibbon, 1978.

Dexter, Dave. *Jazz Cavalcade: The Inside Story of Jazz*. New York: Criterion Press, 1946.

——— ———. New York: Da Capo, 1977.

———. *The Jazz Story: From the 90's to the 60's*. Englewood Cliffs, N.J.: Prentice-Hall, 1964.

Superficial and written in poor journalese.

Erlich, Lillian. *What Jazz Is All About: Illustrated with a Portrait Gallery of Jazz Greats*. New York: Messner, 1962.

Designed as an introductory text to jazz.

——— ———. London: Gollancz, 1963.

——— ———. Rev. ed. New York: Messner, 1975.

Feather, Leonard. *The Book of Jazz: A Guide to the Entire Field*. New York: Horizon Press, 1957.

An authoritative work including a particularly useful section analyzing the role of the various instruments in jazz.

——— ———. London: A. Barker, 1959.

——— ———. New York: Meridian Books, 1960.

——— ———. London: Jazz Book Club, 1961.

——— ———. New York: Paperback Library, 1961.

———. *The Book of Jazz from Then till Now: A Guide to the Entire Field*. New York: Horizon Press, 1965.

Revised edition of *The Book of Jazz*.

Fox, Charles. *Jazz in Perspective*. London: British Broadcasting Corp., 1969.

Based on a series of excellent broadcasts on B.B.C. radio. Includes bibliography and discography.

Fox, Sidney. *The Origins and Development of Jazz*. Chicago: Follett Education Corp., 1968.

A brief pamphlet with accompanying records.

Francis, A. *Jazz*. Translated by Martin Williams. New York: Grove Press, 1960.

Includes discography and bibliography.

——— ———. New York: Da Capo, 1976.

Goffin, Robert. *Jazz, from the Congo to the Metropolitan*. Translated by Walter Schaap and Leonard Feather. New York: Doubleday, 1944.

182173

Deals mainly with early jazz, but is optimistic about the future. Quite influential in the 1940s.

————— —————. New York: Da Capo, 1975.

—————. *Jazz, from Congo to Swing.* (Orginally entitled *Jazz, from the Congo to the Metropolitan*). London: Musicians Press, 1946.

Gridley, Mark C. *Jazz Styles.*

See p. 122.

Harris, Rex. *Jazz.* London: Penguin Books, 1952.

Good on the roots of jazz and traditional styles. Contains a bibliography.

————— —————. 2nd ed. London: Penguin Books, 1953.

————— —————. 3rd ed. London: Penguin Books, 1954.

————— —————. 4th ed. London: Penguin Books, 1956.

————— —————. 5th ed. London: Penguin Books, 1957.

—————. *The Story of Jazz.* New York: Grosset and Dunlap, 1955. Abridged edition of *Jazz.*

————— —————. New York: Grosset and Dunlap, 1960.

Hennessey, Thomas Joseph. "From Jazz to Swing: Black Jazz Musicians and Their Music, 1917–1935."

See p. 123.

Hentoff, Nat, and McCarthy, Albert J., eds. *Jazz: New Perspectives on the History of Jazz, etc. by Twelve of the World's Foremost Jazz Critics and Scholars.* New York: Rinehart, 1959.

Substantial essays of a high standard and a very full list of recommended records covering all styles of jazz, blues, and African music. Contains articles by Ernest Borneman, "The Roots of Jazz"; Charles Edward Smith, "New Orleans and the Traditions in Jazz"; Guy Waterman, "Ragtime"; Martin Williams, "Jelly Roll Morton"; Paul Oliver, "Blues to Drive the Blues Away"; Max Harrison, "Boogie-Woogie"; John Steiner, "Chicago"; Hsio Wen Shih, "The Spread of Jazz and the Big Bands"; Frank Driggs, "Kansas City and the Southwest"; Gunther Schuller, "The Ellington Style: Its Origin and Early Development"; Max Harrison, "Charlie Parker"; Martin Williams, "Bebop and After: A Report"; Albert J. McCarthy, "The Re-emergence of Traditional Jazz"; and Nat Hentoff, "Whose Art Form? Jazz at Mid-Century."

————— —————. London: Cassell, 1960.

————— —————. New York: Grove Press, 1961.

———— ————. London: Jazz Book Club, 1962.

———— ————. New York: Da Capo, 1974.

———— ————. London: Quartet Books, 1977.

Hentoff, Nat, and Williams, Martin, eds. *Jazz Review*.
See p. 123.

Hobson, Wilder. *American Jazz Music*. New York: Norton, 1939.
Important work on pre-1939 jazz.

———— ————. London: Dent, 1941.

———— ————. London: Jazz Book Club, 1956.

———— ————. New York: Da Capo, 1976.

Hodeir, Andre. *Jazz: Its Evolution and Essence*. Translated by
David Noakes. New York: Grove Press, 1956.
Important intellectual appraisal suitable for the musically
educated, but marred by the author's misunderstanding of the
nature of the earliest kinds of jazz.

———— ————. London: Secker and Warburg, 1956.

———— ————. London: Jazz Book Club, 1958.

———— ————. New York: Da Capo, 1975.

————. *Toward Jazz*.
See p. 123.

Jensen, Robert A. "A History of American Jazz Music Illustrated
with Stone Lithography." Master's thesis, Ohio University,
1952.
Depiction of jazz history through artistic drawings having little significance.

Jones, Max. *Jazz Photo Album: A History of Jazz in Pictures*.
London: British Yearbooks, 1947.

Keepnews, Orrin, and Grauer, B. *Pictorial History of Jazz: Peo-
ple and Places from New Orleans to Modern Jazz*. New York:
Crown, 1955.
Good collection of photographs.

———— ————. London: Hale, 1956.

———— ————. Rev. ed. London: Spring Books, 1959.

———— ————. 2nd ed. New York: Crown, 1966.

———— ————. London: Spring Books, 1968.

Lee, Edward. *Jazz: An Introduction*. London: Kahn and Averill,
1972.
A complete history of jazz written for those with no previous
experience in this area. Contains musical examples, solo transcriptions, a glossary, a bibliography, and a discography. Not
very well written.

—————— ——————. New York: Crescendo, 1977.

Meller, Wilfred. *Music in a New Found Land: Themes and Development in the History of American Music*.

See p. 125.

Morgenstern, Dan. *Jazz People*. New York: Harry N. Abrams, 1976.

A beautiful book with commentary on the history of jazz and a number of photos by Ole Brask. Includes a bibliography and discography.

——————. *The Jazz Story: An Outline History of Jazz*. New York: New York Jazz Museum, 1973.

A brief but excellent history with discography and bibliography.

Niemoeller, Adolph F. *The Story of Jazz*. Girard, Kans.: Haldeman-Julius Publications, 1946.

"An Account of the Origin and Development of Hot Music."

Osgood, Henry O. *So This Is Jazz*. Boston: Little, Brown, 1926.

Early American book that totally fails to perceive the real significance of jazz.

—————— ——————. New York: Da Capo, 1978.

Polillo, A. *Jazz: A Guide to the History and Development of Jazz and Jazz Musicians*. Translated by Peter Muccini. English ed. edited by Neil Ardley. Feltham, England: Hamlyn, 1969.

Postgate, John. *A Plain Man's Guide to Jazz*.

See p. 127–28.

Quinn, James Joseph. "An Examination of the Evolution of Jazz as It Relates to the Pre-Literate, Literate, and Post-Literate Percepts of Marshall McLuhan."

See p. 128.

Ramsey, Frederic, and Smith, Charles E., eds. *Jazzmen*. New York: Harcourt, Brace, 1939.

Significant book of great importance in any study of jazz music.

—————— ——————. London: Sidgwick and Jackson, 1952.

—————— ——————. London: Jazz Book Club, 1958.

—————— ——————. New York: Harcourt, Brace, Jovanovich, 1977.

Sargeant, Winthrop. *Jazz: Hot and Hybrid*. New York: Arrow, 1938.

Valuable book that is required reading for the enthusiast.

—————— ——————. Enlarged ed. New York: Dutton, 1946.

—————— ——————. 3rd ed. New York: Da Capo, 1975.

————. *Jazz: A History*. New York: McGraw Hill, 1964.

Shapiro, Nat, and Hentoff, Nat, eds. *Hear Me Talkin' to Ya: The Story of Jazz by the Men Who Made It*. New York: Rinehart, 1955.

Vital book for all jazz students.

———— ————. London: Peter Davies, 1955.

———— ————. London: Penguin Books, 1962.

———— ————. London: Jazz Book Club, 1967.

Southern, Eileen. *The Music of Black Americans: A History*. New York: W. W. Norton, 1971.

Contains a readable but superficial history of jazz.

————, ed. *Readings in Black American Music*. New York: W. W. Norton, 1971.

Contains a history of jazz from the beginnings to the avant-garde.

Stearns, Marshall W. *The Story of Jazz*. New York: Oxford University Press, 1956.

A major jazz history text that should be required study for all jazz enthusiasts.

———— ————. London: Sidgwick and Jackson, 1957.

———— ————. With an expanded bibliography and syllabus. New York: New American Library, 1958.

———— ————. London: Muller, 1958.

———— ————. New York: Oxford University Press, 1970.

———— ————. New York: Oxford University Press, 1974.

Tallmadge, William H. *Afro-American Music*. Washington, D.C.: Music Educators National Conference, 1957.

A brief but well-written jazz history. Includes a chronology, a bibliography, and a discography.

———— ————. Rev. ed. Buffalo, N.Y.: College Bookstore—State University College, 1969.

Tanner, Paul. "A Technical Analysis of the Development of Jazz." Master's thesis, University of California at Los Angeles, 1962.

An excellent analysis.

———— and Gerow, Maruice. *A Study of Jazz*. Dubuque, Iowa: William C. Brown, 1964.

A jazz history written in a very forthright and easily understood language. An important aspect is that it presents, in outline form, the style characteristics of each period of jazz. It includes a glossary, a discography, and a bibliography.

———— ————. 2nd ed. Dubuque, Iowa: William C. Brown, 1973.

———— ————. 3rd ed. Dubuque, Iowa: William C. Brown, 1977.

Tirro, Frank. *Jazz: A History*. New York: W. W. Norton, 1977.

An excellent survey of jazz history including photographs, musical examples, solo transcriptions, a chronology, a bibliography, and a discography. Useful as a college jazz history text. The reader should be advised that there has been some critical opposition to this text.

Ulanov, Barry. *A History of Jazz in America*. New York: Viking Press, 1952.

A reliable historical text.

———— ————. London: Hutchinson, 1958.

———— ————. New York: Da Capo, 1972.

Von Haupt, Lois. "Jazz: An Historical and Analytical Study."
See p. 130.

White, Mark. *The Observer's Book of Jazz*. London: Frederick Warne, 1978.

A history of jazz and brief biographies of selected American and European jazz musicians. Includes a bibliography and a discography.

Woodward, W. *Jazz Americana: The Story of Jazz and All-Time Jazz Greats from Basin Street to Carnegie Hall*. Los Angeles: Trend Books, 1956.

Histories by Geographic Area

Allsopp, Kenneth. *The Bootleggers: The Story of Chicago's Prohibition Era*. London: Hutchinson, 1961.

Includes an excellent chapter on the jazz of the twenties.

Balliett, Whitney. *New York Notes: A Journal of Jazz in the Seventies*.
See p. 117.

Borenstein, Larry, and Russell, Bill. *Preservation Hall Portraits*.
See p. 84.

Botkin, B. A., ed. *Sidewalks of America*.
See p. 9.

Boulton, David. *Jazz in Britain*. London: W. H. Allen, 1958.

———— ————. Toronto: Smithers, 1958.

———— ————. London: Jazz Book Club, 1960.

Broven, John. *Walking to New Orleans*. Bexhill-on-Sea, England: Blues Unlimited, 1974.

A history of popular music in New Orleans from 1946 to 1973.

Brunn, H. O. *The Story of the Original Dixieland Jazz Band*. Baton Rouge: Louisiana State University Press, 1960.

Detailed study of this pioneering white band.

————— —————. London: Sidgwick and Jackson, 1961.

————— —————. London: Jazz Book Club, 1963.

Buerkle, Jack Vincent, and Barker, Danny. *Bourbon Street Black: The New Orleans Black Jazzman*.

See p. 21.

Carr, Ian. *Music Outside: Contemporary Jazz in Britain*. London: Latimer New Dimensions, 1973.

Based on lengthy interviews with leading British musicians and composers. A well-written and valuable guide with a discography and bibliography.

Charters, Samuel Barclay. *Jazz: New Orleans 1885–1957*. Belleville, N.J.: Walter C. Allen, 1958.

An index of New Orleans jazz musicians and a listing of brass bands and orchestral groups.

—————. *Jazz: New Orleans 1885–1963*. New York: Oak Publications, 1963.

—————, and Kunstadt, L. *Jazz: A History of the New York Scene*. Garden City, N.Y.: Doubleday, 1962.

Valuable work of reference on jazz in New York.

Claxton, William. *Jazz West Coast*. Hollywood: Linear Productions, 1954.

Commentary on the history and current scene (1954) of jazz on the West Coast. Contains a number of photos and a listing of musicians. A beautiful and valuable book.

Condon, Eddie, and Sugrue, Thomas. *We Called It Music: A Generation of Jazz*. New York: Holt, 1947.

A descriptive piece on the Prohibition Era and, in particular, on the white Chicago-style musicians of the time. Includes a twenty-two page discography by John Swingle.

————— —————. London: Peter Davies, 1948.

————— —————. London: Jazz Book Club, 1956.

————— —————. London: Corgi Books, 1962.

————— —————. Westport, Conn.: Greenwood Press, 1970.

Cotterrell, Roger, ed. *Jazz Now: The Jazz Centre Society Guide*. London: Quartet Books, 1976.

Attempts to give a clear and accurate view of the current jazz activity in Britain. Includes a directory of British musicians.

Godbolt, Jim. *All This and 10%.*
See p. 121.
Granholm, Ake, ed. *Finnish Jazz: History, Musicians, Discography.*
See p. 152.
Green, Benny. *Jazz Decade: Ten Years at Ronnie Scott's.* London: Kings Road Publishing Ltd., 1969.
————. *Swingtime in Tottenham.* London: Lemon Tree Press, 1976.
Grossman, William, and Farrell, Jack. *The Heart of Jazz.*
See p. 122.
Haskins, James. *The Cotton Club.* New York: Random House, 1977.
Includes photos and commentary on Lena Horne, Cab Calloway, Duke Ellington, Ella Fitzgerald, Louis Armstrong, and others significant in the Cotton Club Story.
Huber, Leonard. *New Orleans, A Pictorial History.*
See p. 26.
Kane, Harnett. *Queen New Orleans.*
See p. 26.
Martinez, Raymond Joseph. *Portraits of New Orleans Jazz: Its Peoples and Places.*
See p. 15.
Matthew, B. *Trad Mad.* London: World Distributors, 1962.
Ephemeral work on the traditional jazz boom of the early 1960s in Britain.
Nelson, S. R. *All about Jazz.* London: Heath, Cranton, 1934.
Covers the British jazz scene and dance music of the early 1930s; little to do with the mainstream of jazz itself.
Ostransky, Leroy. *Jazz City: The Impact of Our Cities on the Development of Jazz.* Englewood Cliffs, N.J.: Prentice-Hall, 1978.
Examines how jazz developed in New Orleans, Chicago, Kansas City, and New York. Also gives background data on the origin of each city. Well researched and written with wit and readability.
Ottley, Roi. *Black Odyssey: The Story of the Negro in America.* New York: Charles Scribner's Sons, 1948.
Brief comments on the importance of black jazz musicians in Harlem.
Pernet, Robert. *Jazz in Little Belgium: History (1881–1966) Discography (1894–1966).* Brussels: Editions Sigma, 1967.

Ramsey, Frederic. *Chicago Documentary: Portrait of a Jazz Era*. London: Jazz Sociological Society, 1944.

Rose, Al, and Souchon, Edmond. *New Orleans Jazz: A Family Album*.

> See p. 149.

Russell, Ross. *Jazz Style in Kansas City and the Southwest*. Berkeley: University of California Press, 1971.

> An excellent book on Kansas City jazz including chapters on Count Basie, Lester Young, Charlie Parker, and others. Highly recommended.

——— ———. Berkeley: University of California Press, 1973.

Schafer, William J., and Allen, Richard B. *Brass Bands and New Orleans Jazz*. Baton Rouge: Louisiana State University Press, 1977.

> A well-researched book covering the music of the brass bands, roster of personnel, bibliography, and discography. Also includes commentary on the different styles and performance practices.

Schiedt, Duncan. *The Jazz State of Indiana*. Pittsboro, Ind.: The Author, 1977.

> A history of jazz in Indiana covering bands from the 1920s and 1930s. Covers appearances by both local and traveling musicians.

Schiffman, Jack. *Uptown—The Story of Harlem's Apollo Theatre*. New York: Cowles, 1971.

> Includes photos and commentary on the many jazz musicians who played at the Apollo.

Shaw, Arnold. *52nd Street: The Street of Jazz*. New York: Da Capo, 1977.

> See below.

———. *The Street That Never Slept: New York's Fabled 52nd Street*. New York: Coward, McCann, and Geoghegan, 1971.

> An examination of some of the musicians who played on 52nd Street from 1934 to the 1950s; depicts sociological and economic factors affecting the scene on "Swing Street."

Williams, Martin T. *Jazz Masters of New Orleans*. New York: Macmillan, 1967.

> Brings together in readable form much data on the major figures of New Orleans pioneering days. Contains chapters on Buddy Bolden, The Original Dixieland Jazz Band, Jelly Roll Morton, King Oliver, The New Orleans Rhythm Kings, Sidney

Bechet, Louis Armstrong, Zutty Singleton, Kid Ory, and Red Allen.

Williams, Stewart. *Jazz in Chicago*. Cardiff, Wales: The Author, 1946.

————, and Rust, Brian, eds. *Jazz in New Orleans*. Cardiff, Wales: The Authors, 1946.

Histories by Decade or Period

Belton, Geneva R. "The Contributions of Negro Music and Musicians in World War II."
See p. 9.

Budds, Michael. *Jazz in the Sixties: The Expansion of Musical Resources and Techniques*.
See p. 118.

Dance, Stanley, ed. *Jazz Era: The Forties*. London: MacGibbon and Kee, 1961.
Survey of the jazz records of the period 1940–49. Covers the birth of modern jazz and the revival of traditional styles.

———— ————. London: Jazz Book Club, 1962.

Feather, Leonard. *Inside Jazz*. New York: Robbins, 1949.
Originally entitled *Inside Be-Bop*. History and technical analysis of jazz, 1940 to 1949. Also includes some biographies.

———— ————. New York: Da Capo, 1977.

Foreman, Ronald Clifford. "Jazz and Race Records, 1920–32: Their Origins and Their Significance for the Record Industry and Society."
See p. 121.

Gitler, Ira. *Jazz Masters of the Forties*. New York: Macmillan, 1966.
Covers the life and works of Charlie Parker, Dizzy Gillespie, Bud Powell, J. J. Johnson, Oscar Pettiford, Kenny Clarke, Max Roach, Dexter Gordon, Lennie Tristano, Lee Konitz, Tadd Dameron, and others. Includes a discography at the end of each chapter.

———— ————. London: Collier-Macmillan, 1967.

———— ————. London: Collier-Macmillan, 1975.

———— ————. New York: Collier Books, 1974.

Goldberg, Joe. *Jazz Masters of the Fifties*. New York: Macmillan, 1965.
Journalistic in style with no index or bibliography. Chapters on Gerry Mulligan, Thelonious Monk, Art Blakey, Miles Davis,

Sonny Rollins, the Modern Jazz Quartet, Charles Mingus, Paul Desmond, Ray Charles, John Coltrane, Cecil Taylor, and Ornette Coleman.

————— —————. London: Collier-Macmillan, 1965.

Griffin, Nard. *To Be or Not to Bop*.
See p. 122.

Hadlock, Richard. *Jazz Masters of the Twenties*. New York: Macmillan, 1965.

Contains chapters on Louis Armstrong, Earl Hines, Bix Beiderbecke, the Chicagoans, Fats Waller, James P. Johnson, Jack Teagarden, Fletcher Henderson, Don Redman, Bessie Smith, and Eddie Lang. Each chapter is completed by a list of recommended books and records.

————— —————. London: Collier-Macmillan, 1966.

————— —————. New York: Collier Books, 1974.

Jones, Le Roi. *Black Music*.
See p. 23.

Jost, Ekkehard. *Free Jazz*. Graz, Austria: Universal Editions, 1974.

One of the very few books to examine the aesthetics of free jazz and to analyze the musical technique and procedures of this music. Contains chapters on John Coltrane, Charles Mingus, Ornette Coleman, Cecil Taylor, Archie Shepp, Albert Ayler, Don Cherry, Sun Ra, and the Association for the Advancement of Creative Musicians.

Shaw, Arnold. *The Rockin' '50's*. New York: Hawthorn, 1974.

Includes brief commentary on Frank Sinatra, Nat "King" Cole, Billy Eckstine, Tony Bennett, B. B. King, Muddy Waters, Ray Charles, Sarah Vaughan, and others.

Stewart, Rex William. *Jazz Masters of the Thirties*. New York: Macmillan, 1972.

Williams, Martin T. *Jazz Masters in Transition, 1957–69*.
See p. 131.

Wilmer, Valerie. *As Serious as Your Life: The Story of the New Jazz*. London: Allison and Busby, 1977.

An important book on the work of some of the leading black innovators in jazz. Discusses the work of John Coltrane, Ornette Coleman, Eric Dolphy, Cecil Taylor, and others.

————— —————. London: Quartet Books, 1977.

Wilson, John S. *Jazz: The Transition Years, 1940–1960*.
See p. 132.

Specialized Histories

Allen, S. S. *Stars of Swing*. London: British Yearbooks, 1947.

Berendt, Joachim. *Jazz: A Photo History*. New York: Schirmer Books, 1979.

The Birdland Story. New York: 1953.

Blancq, Charles C. "Melodic Improvisation: Its Evolution in American Jazz 1943–1960."
See p. 117.

Blesh, Rudi. *This Is Jazz*. San Francisco: The Author, 1943.
A series of lectures given at the San Francisco Museum of Art.

—————— ——————. London: Jazz Music Books, 1945.

Boyd, William C. "The History of Jazz Orchestration." Master's thesis, Michigan State University, 1941.
A detailed study of the use of instruments in jazz; an excellent work.

Coin, Gregory McAfee. "Developmental Parallels in the Evolution of Musical Styles: Romanticism, Jazz, Rock 'n Roll, and American Musical Theatre."
See p. 118.

Collier, Graham. *Jazz: A Student's and Teacher's Guide*. London: Cambridge University Press, 1975.
See p. 170.

Condon, Eddie, and O'Neal, Hank. *The Eddie Condon Scrapbook of Jazz*.
See p. 92.

Cons, Carl, and Von Physter, George. *Destiny, a Study of Swing Musicians*. Chicago: Downbeat Publications, 1938.

Dankworth, Avril. *Jazz: An Introduction to Its Musical Basis*.
See p. 119.

Driggs, Frank. *Women in Jazz*. Brooklyn: Stash Records, 1977.
A rather sketchy account of women jazz musicians from around 1920 to the present.

Esquire's Jazz Book. Edited by Paul Miller. New York: Smith and Durrell, 1944.
Selections from *Esquire* magazine.

Esquire's 1945 Jazz Book. New York: Barnes, 1945.

Esquire's 1946 Jazz Book. New York: Barnes, 1946.

Esquire's 1947 Jazz Book. Edited by E. Anderson. New York: Smith and Durrell, 1947.

Esquire's World of Jazz. Edited by L. W. Gillenson. Commentary by James Poling. New York: Grosset and Dunlap, 1962.

Superb artistic publication particularly notable for the illustrations and modernistic paintings. Basically a collection of essays on jazz with a twelve-page selective discography by John Lessner.

————— —————. London: A. Barker, 1963.

————— —————. London: Jazz Book Club, 1964.

————— —————. Rev. ed. New York: Thomas Y. Crowell, 1971.

A beautiful book that focuses on the nature and history of jazz. Includes articles by the musicians themselves.

————— —————. New York: Crowell, 1973.

————— —————. New York: Crowell, 1975.

Evans, Tom, and Evans, Mary. *Guitars, from the Renaissance to Rock.* New York: Paddington Press, 1977.

Brief comments on blues and jazz guitarists.

Fox, Charles. *The Jazz Scene.* London: Hamlyn Books, 1972.

Consists largely of photographs by Valerie Wilmer.

Frankenstein, Alfred V. *Syncopating Saxophones.* New York: Baker and Taylor, 1925.

Includes one chapter each on the history of the saxophone and symphonic jazz.

————— —————. Chicago: Robert O. Ballou, 1925.

Gammond, Peter, ed. *The Decca Book of Jazz.* London: Muller, 1958.

Contributions on a wide range of topics and musicians mainly by British authors. Includes a discography.

Goldblatt, Burt. *Newport Jazz Festival: The Illustrated History.* New York: Dial Press, 1977.

Commentary and photographs of the highlights of each Newport Jazz Festival from 1954 through 1976. Includes a discography and program for each festival.

Gottlieb, William P. *The Golden Age of Jazz.* New York: Simon and Schuster, 1979.

Contains photographs and commentary on more than 200 musicians from the late 1930s through the 1940s.

————— —————. London: Quartet Books, 1979.

Grossman, William, and Farrell, Jack. *Jazz and Western Culture.* New York: New York University Press, 1956.

The Guitar Player Book. New York: Grove Press, 1978.
>A history of the guitar, including comments by a number of top professionals.

Heaton, P. *Jazz*.
>See p. 123.

Jazzways: A Yearbook of Hot Music. Edited by G. S. Rosenthal. Cincinnati: Jazzways, 1946.

————— —————. London: Musicians Press, 1947.

Longstreet, Stephen. *The Real Jazz, Old and New*. Baton Rouge: Louisana State University Press, 1956.
>Very personal account of the traditional styles of jazz. Plenty of factual errors.

————— —————. Westport, Conn.: Greenwood Press, 1956.

————— —————. Westport, Conn.: Greenwood Press, 1969.

Lyons, Jimmy, and Kamin, Ira. *Dizzy, Duke, the Count and Me: The Story of the Monterey Jazz Festival*. San Francisco: California Living Books, 1978.

Lyttelton, Humphrey. *The Best of Jazz: Basin Street to Harlem*. New York: Taplinger, 1979.

McCarthy, Albert J., ed. *Jazzbook 1947*.
>See p. 125.

—————. *Jazzbook 1955*.
>See p. 125.

—————. *The PL Yearbook of Jazz*.
>See p. 125.

—————. *The Trumpet in Jazz*.
>See p. 125.

Mendl, R. W. S. *The Appeal of Jazz*. London: P. Allan, 1927.
>First full-length book supposedly on jazz to be published in Great Britain. Author had little to say on any of the major jazz musicians; the main aim was to place the music of Whiteman, Grofe, et al. in the stream of "serious" music.

Merriam, Alan P. "Instruments and Instrumental Usages in the History of Jazz."
>See p. 126.

Miller, Paul E. *Downbeat's Yearbook of Swing*. Chicago: Downbeat, 1939.
>A history of hot jazz that deals with groups more than individuals. Contains a number of brief biographies. A valuable book.

————. *Miller's Yearbook of Popular Music*. Chicago: PEM Publications, 1943.

Published in 1939 as *Downbeat's Yearbook of Swing*.

————, and Venables, R., eds. *Jazz Book: From the Esquire Jazz Books 1944–1946*.

See p. 126.

Morgan, Alun, and Horricks, Raymond. *Modern Jazz: A Survey of Developments since 1939*.

See p. 126.

Noble, Peter. *The Illustrated Yearbook of Jazz, 1946*. Egham, England: Citizen Press, 1946.

Pease, Sharon. *Boogie-Woogie Piano Styles*. Chicago: Forster Music Publications, 1940.

Origin, history, and development of boogie-woogie. Contains brief biographies on Meade Lux Lewis, Albert Ammons, Pete Johnson, and Mary Lou Williams.

Rowe, John. *Trombone Jazz*. London: Jazz Tempo Publications, 1944.

Sablosky, Irving L. *American Music*. Chicago: University of Chicago Press, 1969.

Includes brief sections on the history of jazz.

Schaun, George. *The Story of Music in America*. Annapolis, Md.: Greenberry Publications, 1965.

Contains commentary and bibliography on jazz.

Schuller, Gunther. *Early Jazz: Its Roots and Early Development*. London and New York: Oxford University Press, 1968.

An excellent book; should be required study for all students of jazz.

Seldes, G. V. *The Seven Lively Arts*. London and New York: Harper, 1924.

Treats jazz as if it consisted of Tin Pan Alley, ragtime, and the songs of Irving Berlin.

———— ————. New York: Sagamore Press, 1957.

Sullivan, Franklin D. "Music Listening—Jazz, Music: 5635.893."

See p. 130.

Summerfield, Maurice J. *The Jazz Guitar: Its Evolution and Its Players*.

See p. 130.

Taylor, William Edward. "The History and Development of Jazz Piano: A New Perspective for Educators."

See p. 130.

Wyler, Michael. *A Glimpse at the Past*. Dorset, England: Jazz Publications, 1957.

Big Bands

Colin, S. *And the Bands Played On*. London: Hamish Hamilton, Ltd., 1977.

Dance Music Annual. London: J. Dilworth, 1951.

Dance, Stanley. *The World of Swing*. New York: Charles Scribner's Sons, 1974.

>   An examination of environmental, sociological, and economic factors that helped to shape the swing era. Much of the book is in the words of the musicians themselves.

Fernett, Gene. *Swing Out: Great Negro Dance Bands*. Midland, Mich.: Pendell, 1970.

————. *A Thousand Golden Horns: The Exciting Age of America's Greatest Dance Bands*. Midland, Mich.: Pendell, 1966.

>   Covers the work of the big swing bands as well as some non-jazz orchestras for the period 1925–1945.

Graves, Charles, ed. *100 Facts on Swing Music*. London: Naldrett Press, 1948.

Jackson, Arthur. *The World of Big Bands: The Sweet and Swinging Years*. New York: Arco, 1977.

>   A nostalgic look at both American and European big bands from the 1920s to the present. Primarily for those who remember the heyday (1930s and 1940s) of the big bands.

———— ————. London: David and Charles, 1977.

Jackson, Edgar. *Swing Music*. Middlesex, England: Gramophone Co., 1941.

>   2nd ed., 1942; 3rd ed., 1944; 4th ed., 1946; 5th ed., 1948.

————, and Hibbs, Leonard. *Encyclopedia of Swing*. London: The Decca Record Co., 1941.

Johnson, Frank, and Wills, Ron, eds. *Jam: An Annual of Swing Music*. Sydney, New South Wales: Tempo, 1938.

McCarthy, Albert. *Big Band Jazz*. New York: G. P. Putnam's Sons, 1974.

>   Coverage of a wide variety of dance, swing, and jazz bands including lesser known bands and territory bands. An important work encompassing a great deal of big band history.

———— ————. London: Barrie and Jenkins, 1974.

———— ————. New York: Berkley, 1977.

———. *The Dance Band Era: The Dancing Decades from Ragtime to Swing: 1910–1950*. Philadelphia: Chilton, 1971.

An important book including many photos, a bibliography, and a discography.

——— ———. London: Studio Vista, 1971.

——— ———. London: Spring Books, 1974.

Panassie, Hugues. *Hot Jazz: The Guide to Swing Music*.
See p. 127.

Rust, Brian. *The Dance Bands*. New Rochelle, N.Y.: Arlington House, 1974.

Examines those bands of the 1920s and 1930s that were known as dance bands rather than as jazz bands.

Simon, George T. *The Big Bands*. New York: Macmillan, 1967.

An excellent guide to the work of the swing era bands.

——— ———. London: Collier-Macmillan, 1967.

——— ———. New York: Collier Books, 1971.

——— ———. New York: Macmillan, 1971.

——— ———. New York: Macmillan, 1974.

——— ———. New York: Collier Books, 1974.

——— ———. London: Collier-Macmillan, 1974.

——— ———. Rev. ed. New York: Macmillan, 1975.

———. *The Big Bands Songbook*. New York: Thomas Y. Crowell, 1975.

Commentary on how many of the big bands became successful. Most of the book is sheet music of tunes made famous by the big bands.

———. *Simon Says: The Sights and Sounds of the Swing Era 1935–55*. New Rochelle, N.Y.: Arlington House, 1971.

Includes quite a bit of material about the dance band era. An important book of value to anyone interested in jazz.

Treadwell, Bill. *Big Book of Swing*. New York: Cambridge House, 1946.

Chapters on Harry James, Benny Goodman, the Dorseys, Glenn Miller, Gene Krupa, Artie Shaw, Woody Herman, Les Brown, Charlie Barnet, Stan Kenton, Tex Beneke, Louis Armstrong, and Count Basie. A very interesting and entertaining examination of swing musicians.

Walker, Leo. *The Big Band Almanac*.
See p. 150.

———. *The Wonderful Era of the Great Dance Bands*. Berkeley, Calif.: Howell North, 1964.

Applies a slightly different approach to the history of the dance bands; a valuable addition to the literature on big bands.

————— —————. Garden City, N.Y.: Doubleday, 1972.

—————, and Rust, Brian. *British Dance Bands*. London: Storyville, 1973.

White, Mark. *The Observer's Book of Big Bands*. London: Frederick Warne, 1978.

A history of American and European big bands and is intended for the newcomer. Also includes alphabetical lists of arrangers, bands, and bandleaders with brief biographies.

Political, Social, and Economic Histories

Backus, Rob. *Firemusic: A Political History of Jazz*. Chicago: Vanguard Books, 1977.

Backus depicts the development of black music as coinciding with the growth and development of black society in general. Includes a brief history of jazz, but most of the book has to do with black avant-garde jazz musicians. Some of the information presented cannot be found in other sources. An excellent book.

Jones, Le Roi. *Blues People: Negro Music in White America*.

See p. 23.

Kofsky, Frank. *Black Nationalism and the Revolution in Music*.

See p. 23.

Leonard, Neil. "The Acceptance of Jazz by Whites in the United States, 1918–1942." Ph.D. dissertation, Harvard University, 1960.

—————. *Jazz and the White Americans: The Acceptance of a New Art Form*. Chicago: University of Chicago Press, 1962.

Important study.

————— —————. London: Jazz Book Club, 1964.

Miller, W. R. *The World of Pop Music and Jazz*.

See p. 126.

Nanry, Charles, ed. *American Music: From Storyville to Woodstock*. New Brunswick, N.J.: Transaction Books, 1972.

A collection of writings dealing primarily with the sociological and economic aspects of jazz and rock music. A well-written and scholarly book, offering a unique approach to the history of jazz.

Ostransky, Leroy. *Understanding Jazz*.

See p. 126.

Sidran, Ben. *Black Talk: How the Music of Black America Cre-*

ated a Radical Alternative to the Values of Western Literary Tradition.
See p. 129.

Sinclair, John, and Levin, Robert. *Music and Politics.*
See p. 24.

Smith, H. L. "The Literary Manifestation of a Liberal Romanticism in American Jazz."
See p. 129.

Trone, Dolly G. "The Influence of the World War (1917) on the Art of Music in America." Master's thesis, Northwestern University, 1940.
An account of the influence of jazz on military bands. Also relates the sociological unrest after W.W. I to the development of jazz.

Walton, Ortiz. *Music: Black, White and Blue.* New York: Morrow, 1972.
An excellent examination of the African influence on jazz and a modified social and cultural history of jazz.

Wheaton, Jack. "The Technological and Sociological Influences on Jazz as an Art Form in America." Ed.D. dissertation, University of Northern Colorado, 1976.
Depicts how sociological, technological, and psychological factors affected the growth of jazz.

Jazz Histories for Young People

Blocher, Arlo. *Jazz.* Mahwah, N.J.: Troll Associates, 1975.
A brief history of jazz for young people with a number of beautiful color photos.
————— —————. Mahwah, N.J.: Troll Associates, 1976.

Boeckman, Charles. *Cool, Hot, and Blue: A History of Jazz for Young People.* Washington, D.C.: R. B. Luce, 1968.
————— —————. New York: Washington Square Press, 1970.

Collier, James Lincoln. *The Great Jazz Artists.* New York: Four Winds Press, 1977.
Includes a bibliography and discography at the end of each chapter.
—————. *Inside Jazz.* New York: Four Winds Press, 1973.
Discussion of the origin and development of jazz for young readers.

Harris, Rex. *Enjoying Jazz.*
See p. 123.

Hughes, Langston. *The First Book of Jazz*. New York: Franklin Watts, 1954.

    A history of jazz for young people.

——— ———. 2nd rev. ed. London: Mayflower Press, 1962.

——— ———. New York: Franklin Watts, 1976.

Jones, R. P. *Jazz*.

    See p. 124.

Myrus, D. *I Like Jazz*.

    See p. 126.

Chapter 4

The Lives of Jazz Musicians

Jazz is a player's art; composers, arrangers, music publishers and critics are largely secondary figures. This is in direct contrast to most other forms of music, where the composer is the key creative figure and musicians are primarily regarded as interpreters. In jazz, musicians' backgrounds and the influences on them are the most important factors. Thus biographical literature is an important element in understanding jazz, and some of the most important and informative works have appeared in this format.

Some contributors in this area have produced works of considerable substance and, in some cases, were so painstaking in their research and the documentation of their subject that it will be difficult, if not impossible, for future writers to improve on their coverage. Other biographies (and so-called autobiographies) are very much at the opposite end of the literary spectrum, and some of the least successful and satisfactory are those "ghosted" by enterprising journalists who often place undue emphasis on the sensational aspects of a musician's career, such as prison sentences, drug addiction, and the like. This gives such books an appeal to a wider readership, but leaves much to be desired in terms of accuracy. Some of the sociological studies mentioned earlier put these problems—which undoubtedly exist among jazz musicians—into a better perspective.

There are several good examples of collective biography, including Shapiro and Hentoff's *The Jazz Makers* (1957) and Robert Reisner's *The Jazz Titans* (1960), which includes thirty-three profiles of musicians. Collections of essays on modern jazz musicians include *Ten Modern Jazzmen* (1960) by Michael James, and Raymond Horricks's *These Jazzmen of Our Time* (1959). More recent collections include Whitney Balliett's *Alec Wilder and His Friends* (1974), Rudi Blesh's *Combo* (1971), Matthew Bruccoli and C. E. Clark's *Conversations with Jazz Musicians* (1977), and two works by Leonard Feather, *The Pleasures of Jazz* (1976) and *From Satchmo to Miles* (1972).

Because of the great diversity of styles and musical ability within the field, it is particularly hazardous to name the most important individual figures in jazz. As in most musical streams, innovators are the more interesting figures, and jazz music is no exception. Although a strict correlation cannot be made between, say, the number of full-length books written about an individual and that individual's place in jazz history, those who are substantially documented, such as Ellington, Armstrong, Parker, Coltrane, Beiderbecke, Waller, and Morton, did, in retrospect, make significant contributions to jazz development. All innovated within the constraints of the backgrounds and experiences they enjoyed, and all were extremely different and colorful characters. Of these six, only Beiderbecke was a white American, and only Louis Armstrong originated from the Deep South.

Armstrong recorded his own progress from early New Orleans in books published in 1936 and 1954. *Swing That Music*, the earlier of the two, was a brief record of his career to that date, and was probably the first full-length jazz biography of significance. In 1954 he produced *Satchmo: My Life in New Orleans*, which was written in the same racy style in which he spoke. This book is of interest because it clearly portrays the early life and background of a genius whose influence was worldwide and spanned several generations of musicians. *Louis Armstrong: A Self-Portrait* (1971) resulted from an interview conducted by Richard Meryman. A number of other writers have attempted to portray Armstrong in print, and several read very much like biographies. Robert Goffin's *Horn of Plenty* (1947) was translated from the original French edition; more recent and perhaps more objective works have appeared since then, including Albert McCarthy's brief biography in the Kings of Jazz series, *Louis Armstrong* (1960), and Hugues Panassie's book with the same title, which was published in English in 1971, the year Armstrong died. Also published at this time was *Louis: The Louis Armstrong Story* (1971) by Max Jones and John Chilton. This is an interesting and generally reliable account of Armstrong's career, although there are numerous irritating editing errors. There are also four books on Armstrong especially written for children, including Ruby Sanders' *Jazz Ambassador: Louis Armstrong* (1973).

The Kings of Jazz series, published by the British firm Cassell, appeared from 1959 to 1963. All were brief monographs by leading critics on important artists and covered the whole spectrum of jazz interest from Bessie Smith to Miles Davis. *Duke Ellington* (1959) by G. E. Lambert was an early contribution to the series and was well written though with little original material. Ellington is now recognized as one of the major musical figures of the twentieth century, and it is appropriate that he has attracted a number of biographers of substance—though it may be that the definitive work on him has yet to be written. The earliest was Barry Ulanov's *Duke Ellington* (1946), followed by Peter Gammond's *Duke Ellington: His Life and Music* (1958). This collection of essays by fourteen critics assesses Ellington's contribution to jazz under four main headings. The first part covers the man himself; the second deals with his music in the successive decades from the 1920s to the 1950s and with Ellington as a pianist and a composer. The third part covers the Ellington musicians, and the fourth part is a discographical guide from 1926–1957. Ellington's own autobiography, *Music Is My Mistress* (1973) has outlined his own view of an extensive career. This work has a seventy-page index, produced separately by H. E. Huon, in a three-part format—people, places, and music. Ellington's son, Mercer, whose relationship with his famous father was sometimes difficult, has (with the assistance of Stanley Dance) also written a memoir, *Duke Ellington in Person* (1978). Mercer Ellington spent many years as a trumpet player in the Ellington orchestra, and continued to tour with it after his father's death. Derek Jewell, a British journalist, has also written a sympathetic and readable biography of Ellington. Jewell's *Duke* (1977) is based largely on his friendship with Ellington in the later years of his life. Other biographies include Stanley Dance's *The World of*

Duke Ellington (1970) and Elizabeth Rider Montgomery's *Duke Ellington, King of Jazz* (1972), written for younger readers.

Charlie Parker's revolutionary impact on jazz in the early 1940s created so-called modern jazz. In association with other major innovative musicians, including trumpeter Dizzy Gillespie, Parker brought a totally new dimension into jazz, and his life and work has inspired a number of books through its mixture of inspired genius, personal tragedy, and brief span. Max Harrison's concise book in the Kings of Jazz series entitled *Charlie Parker* (1960) was the first attempt at a full-length biography; it was quickly followed in 1962 by Ross Russell's novel *The Sound*, discussed later in this book. The same year, Robert G. Reisner compiled *Bird: The Legend of Charlie Parker* (1962), a collection of articles, stories, and random memories arranged in no special order and presented with a minimum of editing and correction—even obvious errors of fact were retained. This is nevertheless a vivid and vital picture of one of the greatest jazz musicians of all time, and the society in which he lived. The most important book on Parker, however, is *Bird Lives* (1973) by Ross Russell, whose earlier novel based on Parker's life has been mentioned. Russell's biographical study is subtitled "The High Life and Hard Times of Charlie 'Yardbird' Parker," and is a first-class and reliable study.

John Coltrane's brand of innovative genius inspired three biographical studies within two years. All are well produced and contribute to an understanding of Coltrane's particular contribution to jazz. Cuthbert Simpkins's *Coltrane* and J. C. Thomas's *Chasin' the Trane* both appeared originally in 1975. The latter is an important study of a major jazz musician whose work influenced (and continues to influence) many others in the jazz field and elsewhere. The author has worked both as a jazz musician and in a symphony orchestra. This book includes an extensive discography of Coltrane's American recordings. Bill Cole's *John Coltrane* (1976) is also well documented and has a particularly useful seven-page bibliography.

Bix Beiderbecke's brief life has attracted several biographers; like Parker, his life also inspired a novel, Dorothy

Baker's *Young Man with a Horn* (1938), published some eight years after his premature death. Beiderbecke's middle class, Midwestern background made him an unlikely candidate for jazz fame, and in much of his recorded output he is surrounded by musicians of inferior quality. Nevertheless, those who heard him play attest to the quality and individuality of his musicianship, and the legends surrounding him show little sign of diminishing. Beiderbecke's influence on his contemporaries and later players has undeniably been substantial, and his life and work have now been admirably and painstakingly documented in a major tour de force, *Bix; Man and Legend* (1974), by Richard Sudhalter and Philip Evans. Their authoritative, well-researched book is unlikely to be superseded. It has detailed appendixes, including an almost day-by-day diary of Beiderbecke's life, and a detailed and comprehensive discography. The first full-length book on Beiderbecke was Wareing and Garlick's *Bugles for Beiderbecke* (1958), a sentimental and often inaccurate work. Much better was Burnett James's *Bix Beiderbecke* (1959), which was concise, easy to read, and attempted to separate fact from legend. Finally, a memoir of the cornet player by one of his friends, Ralph Berton, *Remembering Bix* (1974), contains a useful, if personalized, annotated bibliography of the major books on Beiderbecke.

Thomas "Fats" Waller, pianist, organist, composer, bandleader, and humorist, has also inspired a number of biographers including, as with Ellington, an appraisal by one of his sons. *Fats Waller* (1977) by Maurice Waller and Anthony Calabrese, details Waller's personal and musical life. It includes a substantial section on recording dates and personnel, and lists his published and unpublished songs and piano rolls. Previous works on Waller include John R. T. Davies's *The Music of Thomas "Fats" Waller* (1953), published in London, and a brief volume in the Kings of Jazz series, *Fats Waller* (1960), by Charles Fox. Ed Kirkeby, who was Waller's manager at one time, published his account *Ain't Misbehavin'* (1966), taking his title from one of the pianist's most famous compositions. Joel Vance's *Fats Waller: His Life and Times* (1977) completes this list.

Ferdinand "Jelly Roll" Morton was a fascinating character whose colorful memories and boasts are beautifully documented by Alan Lomax in his *Mister Jelly Roll*, originally published in 1950. This book has since appeared in various book club and paperback editions, and was most recently reissued by the California University Press in 1973. Lomax, of the Library of Congress Folk Music Division, was an indefatigable documentor of all types of North American folk music including jazz, and some of his works in the field are listed in an earlier chapter. This particular book stems from Morton's reminiscences, captured by Lomax on a memorable series of discs just before World War II, when Morton visited the Library of Congress for a brief period. Morton's musical career was then at its lowest ebb and he was in a bitter mood, but nevertheless these records have become of the greatest importance in filling gaps in the history of jazz. Much of what was said has to be assessed with Morton's record as a boaster in mind, and his claims to have "invented" jazz are ludicrous. In spite of this the book is a great success; Lomax allowed the colorful personality of Morton to emerge, and merely filled in the background. In the appendixes are transcripts of several of Morton's piano pieces but, unfortunately, there is no index. A forty-page discography compiled by Thomas Cusack appeared as a separate pamphlet with the original edition of the book (see the bibliography of chapter 6 for details). Another brief, and perhaps more objective work, *Jelly Roll Morton* (1962), appeared in the Kings of Jazz series, written by the American critic Martin T. Williams.

Biographies of musicians belonging to the traditional and mainstream jazz schools are plentiful and vary greatly in their literary standards. Recent years have witnessed a substantial growth in this sector, although some books originated in the early 1960s, and W. C. Handy's autobiography *Father of the Blues* was first published in 1941.

Sidney Bechet, a New Orleans-born Creole, was a major influence on the jazz clarinet and soprano saxophone. His playing career lasted over forty years, and was described in *Treat It Gentle* (1960). His last few years were spent in France, where he dominated the French traditional jazz world. The book is an edited version of tape-recorded reminiscences, and includes a complete discography by David Mylne.

Another major figure, Earl Hines, has had a playing career that covered over fifty years, starting in the 1920s when his association with Louis Armstrong at the peak of his (Armstrong's) powers launched Hines as a pianist of originality and tremendous talent. Stanley Dance's *The World of Earl Hines* (1977) is the only full-length study of Hines to appear so far.

The musicians of New Orleans are now receiving considerable critical attention, and it is appropriate that the legendary Buddy Bolden should be documented by a librarian at the New Orleans Public Library. This library has built up an impressive collection on jazz, and Donald Marquis has obviously drawn on these resources in his *In Search of Buddy Bolden* (1978). Bolden remains a shadowy figure, but has some claim to the title accorded him in Marquis's subtitle, "First Man of Jazz."

Major jazz figures whose playing careers started in the Crescent City, but who made their wider reputations in Chicago and elsewhere, include Joseph "King" Oliver, leader of a band of tremendous individual talents that collectively created early jazz history through a series of primitive but exciting recordings in the early 1920s. Martin T. Williams's *King Oliver* (1960) is a brief, factual biography. Among the musicians associated with Oliver were the Dodds brothers, and *Johnny Dodds* (1961), by G. E. Lambert, appeared in the Kings of Jazz series. *The Baby Dodds Story*, an autobiography of the drummer, was published in Los Angeles in 1959. The life of Lee Collins, a New Orleans-style trumpeter, is described fully in *Oh, Didn't He Ramble* (1974), written by Mary Collins with assistance from Frank J. Gillis and John W. Miner. Trumpet players in New Orleans enjoyed considerable status, and another colorful character, Willie "Bunk" Johnson, was "rediscovered" and recorded in the early 1940s, greatly contributing to the so-called New Orleans Revival. Johnson's career is described in *Willie Geary "Bunk" Johnson: The New Iberia Years* (1977), an eighty-nine-page work by Austin Sonnier. George Lewis, a clarinet player in these recordings, went on to become a cult figure to those who found the pure New Orleans sound authentic and totally satisfying. Two books have appeared discussing his life and influence; the earlier, *Call Him George* (1961), by Jay Allison Stuart (a pseudonym for Dorothy Tait) is less than satisfactory. Tom Bethell's *George Lewis* (1977), based on personal interviews with Lewis, is well researched and much more reliable. This book includes a substantial discography of seventy-two pages, as well as a good bibliography. George "Pops" Foster's lengthy career spanned several generations of New Orleans music, and his autobiography *Pops Foster* (1971) is, therefore, of considerable interest. The book includes a twelve-page introduction together with linking material between the chapters giving the historical context of Foster's reminiscences. Brian Rust contributes a discography of Foster's work from 1924 to 1940, and a detailed chronology of musical groups from 1899 to 1969 with whom Foster played is to also included.

Three pianists of differing but basically traditional styles are Clarence Williams, Pete Johnson, and Willie "The Lion" Smith. The latter's autobiography, *Music on My Mind* (1965, reprinted by Da Capo Press in 1975) is full of interesting facts about various musicians met during Smith's fifty years of playing experience. The book contains an excellent index that greatly adds to its value. *The Pete Johnson Story* (1965) by Hans Maurerer records the main events in the life of a pioneer of boogie-woogie, while Tom Lord's *Clarence Williams* (1976) is a largely discographical study.

White musicians in traditional and mainstream styles are also represented in this area of literature, and Mezz Mezzrow's *Really the Blues* (1946) was an early and important work that retains its interest. Mezzrow, a musician of limited technical ability, was one of the few white Americans to understand the feeling of his black colleagues. The book dwells overmuch on his association with drugs and is written in racy style, but it has much to commend it. It is infinitely better than some later works, including Smith and Guttridge's *Jack Teagarden* (1960), which one critic described as "superficial (and) unworthy of a fine musician."

"Chicago Style" and Eddie Condon are almost synonymous, and *We Called It Music* (1947) was the earliest and best of Condon's literary contributions. The book was revised in 1962 with additional discography. Although Condon was a musician of relatively moderate talent, his influ-

ence on jazz has been considerable as a publicist and organizer of excellent bands. *We Called It Music* is a valuable
descriptive piece on the prohibition era and the white
musicians of that time. Some of these musicians have written their own accounts, including Bud Freeman, whose
two collections of anecdotes are of little permanent value.
These are entitled *You Don't Look like a Musician* (1974)
and *If You Know of a Better Life, Tell Me* (1976). Max
Kaminsky, a regular Condon trumpeter, produced a rather
more interesting autobiography that throws some light on
the lifestyle of a professional jazz musician involved in touring in his *My Life in Jazz* (1963).

As jazz evolved from its small band and collective improvisation basic phase into the big band era of the 1930s,
other names appeared, and their lives and work have been
covered collectively in an earlier chapter. Some of the individual musicians and bandleaders have written their life
stories or have had them written by others, and these
belong in this section.

The period 1935–45 was the apogee of the popularity of
big swing bands, and two of the major bandleaders of this
time were Benny Goodman and Artie Shaw. Goodman's
orchestra developed from the Fletcher Henderson big
band, and used many of Henderson's arrangements. It had
tremendous influence both in its heyday and afterwards.
Goodman was the first major bandleader to front a mixed
group of black and white musicians, and this breakthrough
on the social level, plus the outstanding musicianship dis-
played by the band, have ensured Goodman an important
niche in jazz history. His autobiography *The Kingdom of
Swing* (1939) was written with journalistic help at the height
of his fame, and does not reflect his musical importance. It
was republished in paperback form in 1962, and gives some
useful data on the 1930s, but it was sharply criticized by
the English critic Benny Green in his essay on Goodman
included in *The Reluctant Art*. A lesser practitioner, both as
a performer on the clarinet and organizer of successful big
bands, was Artie Shaw. As a contributor to the literature of
jazz, however, Shaw outshines Goodman, and his book *The
Trouble with Cinderella* (1952) shows that he was an intelligent man and an able writer. This combination makes his

book worthy of some study, since few jazz musicians have had the ability to write as lucidly.

The earliest book on big band jazz, though of a totally different variety, was Paul Whiteman's *Jazz* (1926). Whiteman's chief claim to inclusion in this work was his willingness to use important jazz musicians, of whom Bix Beiderbecke was an outstanding example.

Apart from Ellington's orchestra, Count Basie has led the premier black band for most of the past forty years. Raymond Horricks's *Count Basie and His Orchestra* (1957) is really a biography of the band itself, with pen portraits of most of the musicians who played with it. Another black bandleader of considerably less significance than Basie was Cab Calloway, whose autobiography, *Of Minnie the Moocher and Me*, appeared in 1976.

The Dorsey brothers, who both ran leading big bands in the 1930s and 1940s, are the subject of Herb Sanford's *Tommy and Jimmy: The Dorsey Years* (1972), while Glenn Miller, whose life ended in a wartime air crash, is remembered in George T. Simon's *Glenn Miller and His Orchestra* (1974) and in Jonathan Green's *Glenn Miller and the Age of Swing* (1976). Stan Kenton's "progressive" orchestra is documented in Carol Easton's *Straight Ahead* (1973).

When the first edition of this guide appeared, there was a dearth of biographical studies of jazz musicians belonging to the modernist schools, with the exception of Charlie Parker, Dizzy Gillespie, and Miles Davis. This situation has changed considerably with the three books on Coltrane already discussed and others on Charles Mingus, Hampton Hawes, Eric Dolphy, and others. Charles Mingus's *Beneath the Underdog* (1971) is an unusual autobiography written in the third person. This is an important statement by an articulate musician whose work remained firmly rooted in the basic blues tradition, even though his associates have to be classified as jazz modernists. This blending of jazz styles was a prime achievement of Mingus, who died in 1978. The first biography of Miles Davis appeared in the Kings of Jazz series in 1961. This was a brief ninety-page book by Michael James entitled simply *Miles Davis*. A more extensive work was Bill Cole's *Miles Davis: A Musical Biography* (1974), which included a comprehensive discography and a seventeen-page bibliography. *Dizzy Gillespie* (1959) was also written by Michael James, a rather dull evaluation of an exceptionally colorful musician. Saxophonist Coleman Hawkins was a major innovator on his instrument, and his style of playing showed a more continuous evolution than most of his colleagues, who often tended to repeat themselves. Albert McCarthy's *Coleman Hawkins* (1963) is therefore of interest, as is Vladimir Simosko and Barry Tepperman's *Eric Dolphy* (1974). Dolphy, who died at the age of thirty-six in 1964, played alto saxophone, flute, and bass clarinet. This well-produced volume includes an excellent annotated discography by Simosko's co-author, Barry Tepperman.

Nat King Cole (1971) is a memoir by Cole's wife, assisted by Louie Robinson. Cole's early career as an exciting creative jazz pianist was overshadowed by his phenomenal success as a singer in later years. Another jazz pianist, Hampton Hawes, has written his life story *Raise Up off Me* (1973) with Don Asher, while trombonist Dicky Wells, whose work included some very formative years with the Count Basie orchestra, reminisced to jazz writer Stanley Dance to produce *The Night People* (1971).

Jazz singers, and those in the closely related field of jazz-tinged popular music, constitute an interesting group, and there are a number of important books well worth recording in this guide. Ethel Waters's connection with jazz was fleeting, but her book was the first of its kind, and is mainly of interest for its descriptions of show business in the United States in the 1920s and 1930s. This was closely linked with the contemporary jazz scene, and thus the book, *His Eye Is on the Sparrow* (1951), is of considerable interest.

Three of the more important women jazz has produced are Billie Holiday, Bessie Smith, and Mahalia Jackson. Strictly speaking, the latter two were not jazz singers; Bessie Smith sang the blues to perfection, and Mahalia Jackson was the leading figure in gospel music. Although Jackson always declared her separation from jazz itself, she undoubtedly belongs here, and at least three books have appeared describing her rise to prominence. Her own *Movin' On Up* (1966) came first, but more substantial is Laurraine Goreau's *Mahalia* (1975), which was originally published under the rather unsuitable title *Just Mahalia, Baby: A Biography for Children*. *Mahalia Jackson: Queen of Gospel Song* (1974) by Jean Cornell completes this trio.

Bessie Smith was both physically and musically a giant, and she has been lucky indeed in having a biographer of the stature of Chris Albertson. His *Bessie* (1972) is a splendid, well-researched piece of work that includes much material from family sources that has not been previously quoted and that sifts the truth from the many legends surrounding Bessie Smith, particularly at her death. Her dramatic rise to fame and her domination of the "race circuit" in the southern United States in the 1920s is also covered in Paul Oliver's contribution to the Kings of Jazz series, *Bessie Smith* (1959). A further work on Bessie Smith is *Somebody's Angel Child* (1970) by Carmen Moore.

Billie Holiday's tragic personal life dominates her ghost-written autobiography, *Lady Sings the Blues* (1956), which was later made into a very successful movie featuring Diana Ross. The book was written shortly before Billie Holiday died, and unfortunately does not thoroughly cover important musical aspects of her career. John Chilton's excellent *Billie's Blues* (1975) redresses the balance and concentrates on her career and musical importance. He includes a detailed analysis of her recordings and a substantial bibliography of books and references.

Cleo Laine has emerged as perhaps Europe's leading female jazz singer, and her career is described in *Cleo and John: A Biography of the Dankworths* (1976) by Graham Collier. Lena Horne's biography *Lena* appeared in 1965, following an earlier version, *In Person, Lena Horne* (1950).

Male entertainers such as Bing Crosby and Hoagy Carmichael have had close connections with jazz and the musicians who play it over the years, and their life stories are of considerable interest in studying the development of the music. Crosby's own book *Call Me Lucky* (1953) tells of his early days as a singer with jazz bands such as Eddie Condon's. He retained an affection for the music throughout his career. Other books on Crosby's career include *The Story of Bing Crosby* (1946) by Ted Crosby, *The Incredible Crosby* (1948) by Barry Ulanov and, more recently, *Bing: The Authorized Biography* (1976) by British journalist Charles Thompson.

Hoagy Carmichael, composer and pianist, was a close friend of Bix Beiderbecke and other Chicago-style musicians, and a number of his tunes have become standards in the jazz musician's repertoire. His autobiography *Sometimes I Wonder* was published in 1965, and supplements *The Stardust Road*, which appeared nearly twenty years earlier.

Perhaps the major European contributor to the development of jazz was the French gypsy guitarist Django Reinhardt. His work with colleagues in the Quintet of the Hot Club of France produced what has been described as a European strain of jazz, and his biography is therefore of unusual interest. Charles Delaunay's *Django Reinhardt* (1954) was originally published in French, and did not appear in English until 1961. More recently, *The Book of Django* (1973) by Max Abrams has been issued. There is a comprehensive seventy-eight-page discography included in the book. A British pioneer, Patrick "Spike" Hughes, describes his deep involvement in British jazz around 1930 in *Second Movement*. The book appeared in 1951, long after Hughes had severed all his connections with jazz, but it is a fascinating and vital work on the history of European jazz. British jazz has also been fortunate in that other highly literate musicians have contributed to the literature. Humphrey Lyttleton, whose bands have had considerable impact for the past thirty years, has written several amusing and instructive books. *I Play as I Please* (1954) is subtitled "The Memoirs of an Old Etonian Trumpeter," and describes and comments on jazz in Britain in the period 1945–54. *Second Chorus* (1958) and *Take It from the Top* (1975) complete the trilogy. The latter is particularly interesting for its descriptions of Lyttleton playing alongside leading American musicians on visits to Britain. George Melly's singing in the style of Bessie Smith created his early reputation. His description of this early phase of his life in *Owning-Up* (1965) paints an earthy pen picture of his far from glamorous life touring with an itinerant band in the 1950s. A later book by Melly, *Rum, Bum and Concertina* (1977) is of less interest to the jazz enthusiast, though it does refer to his early interest in the music.

Finally, two biographical works have been recently published that describe the jazz world from the viewpoint of nonmusician insiders. The first and more important is John

Hammond's *John Hammond on Record* (1977). Hammond is a leading jazz critic and promoter who has had considerable influence through his use of mixed bands of white and black musicians. Jim Godbolt's *All This and 10%* (1976) is in-interesting mainly because it presents a virtually undocumented viewpoint—that of the band agent. In the book, Godbolt describes his personal experience in the post-World War II British jazz scene up to 1970.

BIBLIOGRAPHY

Collective Biographies

Baker, David; Belt, Lida; and Hudson, Herman; eds. *The Black Composer Speaks.*
See p. 152.
Balliett, Whitney. *Alec Wilder and His Friends.* Boston: Houghton Mifflin, 1974.
Portraits of the daily life of Marian McPartland, Bobby Hackett, Ruby Braff, and others.
Blesh, Rudi. *Combo: U.S.A.: 8 Lives in Jazz.* Philadelphia: Chilton, 1971.
Sketches of Louis Armstrong, Sidney Bechet, Jack Teagarden, Lester Young, Billie Holiday, Gene Krupa, Charlie Christian, and Eubie Blake.
————— —————. New York: Hayden Books, 1971.
Borenstein, Larry, and Russell, Bill. *Preservation Hall Portraits.* Baton Rouge: Louisiana State University Press, 1968.
Paintings by Noel Rockmore. Portraits and brief biographies of the musicians who have played in Preservation Hall since 1961.
Bruccoli, Matthew J., and Clark, C. E., eds. *Conversations with Jazz Musicians.* Detroit: Gale Research, 1977.
Brief biographies of Louie Bellson, Leon Breeden, Dizzy Gillespie, Eric Kloss, Jimmy McPartland, Barry Miles, Sy Oliver, Charlie Spivak, Billy Taylor, Phil Woods, and Sol Yaged. An excellent book.
Charters, Samuel B. *The Legacy of the Blues.* London: Calder and Boyars, 1975.
Biographies of twelve great blues performers.
————— —————. New York: Da Capo, 1977.

Ewen, David. *Men of Popular Music*. Chicago: Ziff-Davis, 1944.
   Chapters on King Oliver, Louis Armstrong, W. C. Handy,
   Meade Lux Lewis, Duke Ellington, Paul Whiteman, and Ben-
   ny Goodman.
——— ———. New York: Prentice-Hall, 1949.
Feather, Leonard. *From Satchmo to Miles*. New York: Stein and
   Day, 1972.
   Portraits of Feather's personal relationships with Louis Arm-
   strong, Duke Ellington, Billie Holiday, Ella Fitzgerald, Count
   Basie, Lester Young, Charlie Parker, Dizzy Gillespie, Norman
   Granz, Oscar Peterson, Ray Charles, Don Ellis, and Miles
   Davis.
——— ———. New York: Stein and Day, 1974.
——— ———. London: Quartet Books, 1974.
———. *The Pleasures of Jazz*. New York: Horizon Press, 1976.
   Brief biographical pieces on a number of jazz musicians.
——— ———. New York: Dell, 1977.
Gleason, Ralph J. *Celebrating the Duke, and Louis, Bessie, Billie,
   Bird, Carmen, Miles, Dizzy, and Other Heroes*. Boston: Atlantic-
   Little, Brown and Co., 1975.
   A well-written personal commentary on these musicians.
——— ———. New York: Dell, 1976.
Graham, A. P. *Strike Up the Band: Bandleaders of Today*. New
   York: Nelson, 1949.
Green, Benny. *The Reluctant Art: Five Studies in the Growth of
   Jazz*.
   See p. 122.
Hodes, Art, and Hansen, Chadwick, eds. *Selections from the
   Gutter*. Berkeley: University of California Press, 1977.
   Autobiographical articles by a number of jazz and blues musi-
   cians.
Horricks, Raymond, et al. *These Jazzmen of Our Time*. London:
   Gollancz, 1959.
   Essays on modern jazz musicians.
Hughes, Langston. *Famous Negro Music Makers*. New York:
   Dodd, Mead, 1955.
   Brief biographical articles on Leadbelly, Jelly Roll Morton,
   Bessie Smith, Duke Ellington, Louis Armstrong, and others.
——— ———. New York: Dodd, Mead, 1957.
James, Michael. *Ten Modern Jazzmen: An Appraisal of the
   Recorded Work of Ten Modern Jazzmen*. London: Cassell,
   1960.

Collection of essays that analyze the recorded work of Charlie Parker, Dizzy Gillespie, Bud Powell, Miles Davis, Stan Getz, Thelonious Monk, Gerry Mulligan, John Lewis, Lee Konitz, and Wardell Gray.

Jones, Hettie. *Big Star Fallin' Mama*. New York: Dell, 1976.

Biographies of Ma Rainey, Bessie Smith, Mahalia Jackson, Billie Holiday, and Aretha Franklin.

Kimball, Robert, and Bolcom, William. *Reminiscing with Sissle and Blake*. New York: Viking Press, 1973.

The story of the relationship between lyricist Noble Sissle and composer/pianist Eubie Blake.

Mann, Woody. *Six Black Blues Guitarists*. New York: Oak Publications, 1973.

Bits of biographical information on Big Bill Broonzy, Memphis Minnie, Rev. Robert Wickins, Blind Willie McTell, Rev. Gary Davis, and Blind Blake.

Miller, William H. *Three Brass (O'Brien, Kaminsky, Sherock)*. Melbourne, Australia: The Author, 1945.

Neff, Robert, and Connor, Anthony. *Blues*.

See p. 39.

Reisner, Robert G. *The Jazz Titans*. Garden City, N.Y.: Doubleday, 1960.

Thirty-three biographical profiles with discographies.

——— ———. New York: Da Capo, 1977.

Rivelli, Pauline, and Levin, Robert, eds. *The Black Giants*. New York: World, 1970.

Deals with many of the new jazz musicians including John Coltrane, Pharaoh Sanders, Elvin Jones, Sunny Murray, Oliver Nelson, Ornette Coleman, Archie Shepp, Alice Coltrane, and others. An excellent book.

Roach, Hildred. *Black American Music–Past and Present*.

See p. 128.

Rollins, Charlemae. *Famous Negro Entertainers*. New York: Dodd, Mead, 1967.

Brief comments on Duke Ellington, Louis Armstrong, and Fats Waller.

Rosenkrantz, Timme. *Jazz Profiles*. Copenhagen: J. A. Hansen's Forlag, 1945.

Shapiro, Nat, and Hentoff, Nat, eds. *The Jazz Makers*. New York: Rinehart, 1957.

——— ———. New York: Grove Press, 1958.

———— ————. London: Peter Davies, 1958.

———— ————. Westport, Conn.: Greenwood Press, 1975.

Spellman, A. B. *Black Music, Four Lives*. New York: Pantheon Books, 1966.

Originally titled *Four Lives in the Bebop Business*. Deals with Cecil Taylor, Ornette Coleman, Herbie Nichols, and Jackie McLean.

———— ————. London: MacGibbon and Kee, 1967.

———— ————. New York: Schocken Books, 1970.

Surge, Frank. *Singers of the Blues*. Minneapolis: Lerner, 1969.

Brief biographies of blues singers, primarily for children.

Terkel, Studs. *Giants of Jazz*. New York: Crowell, 1957.

For younger readers.

———— ————. Rev. New York: Crowell, 1975.

Treadwell, Bill. *Big Book of Swing*.

See p. 67.

Wayne, Bennett. *3 Jazz Greats*. Champaign, Ill.: Garrard, 1973.

Biographies of W. C. Handy, Louis Armstrong, and Duke Ellington—for younger readers.

Williams, Martin. *The Jazz Tradition*. New York: Oxford University Press, 1970.

An examination of sixteen major figures in the history of jazz. Each performer's style characteristics are analyzed, with comments provided on their contribution and influences. An excellent book.

Wilmer, Valerie. *Jazz People*. New York: Bobbs-Merrill, 1970.

Brief biographical essays based on interviews with fourteen major jazz figures. Well illustrated with excellent photographs.

———— ————. 2nd ed. New York: Bobbs-Merrill, 1971.

———— ————. London: Quartet Books, 1977.

———— ————. 3rd ed. London: Allison and Busby, 1977.

Individual Biographies

Louis Armstrong (trumpeter, singer, and bandleader)

Armstrong, Louis. *Louis Armstrong: A Self-Portrait*. New York: Eakins Press, 1971.

Interview conducted by Richard Meryman. Armstrong tells of his life in New Orleans, Chicago, and New York. Charming, entertaining, and realistic. Very enjoyable.

————. *Satchmo: My Life in New Orleans*. New York: Prentice-Hall, 1954.

Portrays Armstrong's life and background up to the time he left for Chicago in 1922.

———— ————. London: Peter Davies, 1955.

———— ————. New York: Signet, 1955.

———— ————. London: Jazz Book Club, 1957.

————. *Swing That Music*. London: Longmans, 1936.

Music section edited by Horace Gerlach.

Cornell, Jean Gay. *Louis Armstrong: Ambassador Satchmo*. Champaign, Ill.: Garrard, 1972.

Written for children.

———— ————. New York: Dell, 1975.

———— ————. New York: Dell, 1977.

Eaton, J. *Trumpeter's Tale: The Story of Young Louis Armstrong*. New York: Morrow, 1955.

For children.

Goffin, Robert. *Horn of Plenty: The Story of Louis Armstrong*. Translated by James Bezou. New York: Allen, Towne and Heath, 1947.

———— ————. New York: Da Capo, 1977.

Iverson, Genie. *Louis Armstrong*. New York: Thomas Y. Crowell, 1976.

For young readers.

Jones, Max, and Chilton, John. *Louis: The Louis Armstrong Story 1900–1971*. London: Studio Vista, 1971.

Highly recommended.

———— ————. Boston: Little, Brown, 1971.

———— ————. St. Albans, England: Mayflower, 1975.

McCarthy, Albert J. *Louis Armstrong*. London: Cassell, 1960.

———— ————. New York: Barnes, 1961.

Panassie, Hugues. *Louis Armstrong*. New York: Charles Scribner's Sons, 1971.

One chapter on his biography, one on an analysis of his playing style, and one on his recordings.

Sanders, Ruby. *Jazz Ambassador; Louis Armstrong*. Chicago: Children's Press, 1973.

For children. Well written and entertaining.

Satchmo, Collector's Copy. Hollywood, Calif.: Matco, 1971.

An excellent work including many rare photos.

Pearl Bailey (singer)
Bailey, Pearl. *The Raw Pearl*. New York: Harcourt, Brace and
World, 1968.

William "Count" Basie (pianist and bandleader)
Horricks, Raymond. *Count Basie and His Orchestra*. London:
Gollancz, 1957.
A biography of Basie and of his individual musicians. In-
cludes a comprehensive discography by Alun Morgan.
——— ———. London: Jazz Book Club, 1958.
——— ———. Westport, Conn.: Negro Universities Press, 1971.

Sidney Bechet (soprano saxophonist and clarinetist)
Bechet, Sidney. *Treat It Gentle*. New York: Hill and Wang, 1960.
Complete discography by David Mylne. Autobiography of a
leading New Orleans Creole musician who was a major influ-
ence on jazz clarinet and saxophone playing. His career span-
ned over 40 years, the last few of which were spent in France.
——— ———. London: Cassell, 1960.
——— ———. London: Jazz Book Club, 1962.
——— ———. London: Transworld, 1964.
——— ———. New York: Da Capo, 1975.

Leon "Bix" Beiderbecke (cornetist)
Baker, Dorothy. *Young Man with a Horn*.
See p. 184.
Berton, Ralph. *Remembering Bix*. New York: Harper and Row,
1974.
Written in an entertaining style—more like reading a story
than a work of nonfiction.
——— ———. London: W. H. Allen, 1974.
James, Burnett. *Bix Beiderbecke*. London: Cassell, 1959.
Concise and easy-to-read with fact separated from legend.
——— ———. New York: Barnes, 1961.
Sudhalter, Richard M., and Evans, Philip R. *Bix; Man and
Legend*. New Rochelle, N.Y.: Arlington House, 1974.
A well-written biography. Includes photos, a chronology of
his life, and a discography.
——— ———. London: Quartet Books, 1974.
——— ———. New York: Schirmer Books, 1975.
Wareing, Charles H., and Garlick, George. *Bugles for Beider-
becke*. London: Sidgwick and Jackson, 1958.
A sentimental view of the Beiderbecke legend.

Bunny Berigan (trumpeter-bandleader)
Danca, Vince. *Bunny: A Biodiscography of Jazz Trumpeter Bunny Berigan*. Rockford, Ill.: The Author, 1978.

Bernard "Acker" Bilk (clarinetist and bandleader)
Leslie, P., and Gwynn-Jones, P. *Book of Bilk*. London: MacGibbon and Kee, 1961.
————— —————. London: Jazz Book Club, 1963.

Eubie Blake (pianist)
Rose, Al. *Eubie Blake*. New York: Schirmer Books, 1979.

Buddy Bolden (cornetist)
Marquis, Donald M. *In Search of Buddy Bolden*. Baton Rouge: Louisiana State University Press, 1978.
A well-researched biography with a very detailed bibliography.

Perry Bradford (blues singer)
Bradford, Perry. *Born with the Blues: The True Story of the Pioneering Blues Singers and Musicians in the Early Days of Jazz*.
See p. 34.

William "Big Bill" Broonzy (blues singer)
Broonzy, William, and Bruynoghe, Yannick. *Big Bill Blues: William Broonzy's Story as Told to Yannick Bruynoghe*. London: Cassell, 1955.
Essential reading for a real understanding of the origins of jazz and the development of the blues. Line drawings by Paul Oliver and discography by Albert McCarthy.
————— —————. London: Jazz Book Club, 1957.
————— —————. 2nd rev. ed. New York: Oak Publications, 1964.

Gary Burton (vibraphonist)
Rivelli, Pauline, and Levin, Robert, eds. *The Rock Giants*. New York: World, 1970.
Contains one chapter on Gary Burton.

Cab Calloway (singer and bandleader)
Calloway, Cab, and Rollins, Bryant. *Of Minnie the Moocher and Me*. New York: Crowell, 1976.

Also contains *The New Cab Calloway's Hipsters Dictionary*, originally published in 1938.

Hoagy Carmichael (singer, pianist, and composer)
Carmichael, Hoagy. *The Stardust Road*. New York: Rinehart, 1946.
———— ————. London: Musicians Press, 1947.
————, and Longstreet, Stephen. *Sometimes I Wonder: The Story of Hoagy Carmichael*. New York: Farrar, Straus and Giroux, 1965.
———— ————. London: Redman, 1966.
———— ————. New York: Da Capo, 1976.

Ray Charles (singer-pianist)
Charles, Ray, and Ritz, David. *Brother Ray: Ray Charles' Own Story*. New York: Dial Press, 1978.
———— ————. London: MacDonald and Janes, 1979.

Rosemary Clooney (singer)
Clooney, Rosemary, and Strait, Raymond. *This for Remembrance*. Chicago: Playboy Press, 1977.
Includes her experiences with big bands.

Nat King Cole (singer)
Cole, Maria, and Robinson, Louie. *Nat King Cole: An Intimate Biography*. New York: Morrow, 1971.

Lee Collins (trumpeter)
Collins, Mary. *Oh, Didn't He Ramble*. Edited by Frank Gillis and John W. Miner. Urbana: University of Illinois Press, 1974.
Biography of this New Orleans trumpet player of the 1920s.

John Coltrane (tenor saxophonist)
Cole, Bill. *John Coltrane*. New York: Schirmer Books, 1976.
A description of the evolution of Coltrane's music and the music of his sidemen. Contains excerpts from transcribed solos, a bibliography, and a discography.
———— ————. London: Collier-MacMillan, 1976.
————. "The Style of John Coltrane, 1955–67."
See p. 118.
Simpkins, Cuthbert Ormond. *Coltrane: A Biography*. New York: Herndon House, 1975.
Contains some very interesting commentary on Sun Ra and

Ornette Coleman concerning their association with Coltrane. Contains photos, letters, and interviews.

Thomas, J. C. *Chasin' the Trane: The Music and Mystique of John Coltrane*. Garden City, N.Y.: Doubleday, 1975.

———— ————. London: Elm Tree Books, 1976.

———— ————. New York: Da Capo, 1977.

Eddie Condon (guitarist and bandleader)

Condon, Eddie, and O'Neal, Hank. *The Eddie Condon Scrapbook of Jazz*. New York: St. Martins Press, 1973.

An entertaining depiction of Condon's life and career.

———— ————. London: Hale, 1974.

————, and Sugrue, Thomas. *We Called It Music: A Generation of Jazz*.

See p. 57.

Bing Crosby (singer)

Barnes, Ken. *The Crosby Years*. London: Elm Tree Books, 1979.

Crosby, Bing, and Martin, P. *Call Me Lucky*. New York: Simon and Schuster, 1953.

Crosby was associated with the jazz world of the late 1920s and early 1930s.

———— ————. London: Muller, 1953.

Crosby, E. J. *The Story of Bing Crosby*. Cleveland: World, 1946.

Thompson, Charles. *Bing: The Authorized Biography*. London: Star Books, 1976.

———— ————. London: W. H. Allen, 1975.

Ulanov, Barry. *The Incredible Crosby*. New York: McGraw-Hill, 1948.

John Dankworth (saxophonist, composer, and bandleader) and **Cleo Laine** (singer)

Collier, Graham. *Cleo and John: A Biography of the Dankworths*. London: Quartet Books, 1976.

Miles Davis (trumpeter)

Cole, Bill. *Miles Davis, A Musical Biography*. New York: Morrow, 1974.

One chapter is devoted to his musical style. Included are thirteen solo transcriptions, a bibliography, and a discography.

James, Michael. *Miles Davis*. London: Cassell, 1961.

Brief biography with much critical material on Davis's work.

———— ————. New York: Barnes, 1961.

Sammy Davis (singer)
Davis, Sammy; Boyar, J.; and Boyar, J. *Yes I Can: The Story of Sammy Davis Jr*. New York: Farrar, Straus, and Giroux, 1965.
————— —————. London: Cassell, 1965.

Johnny Dodds (clarinetist)
Lambert, G. E. *Johnny Dodds*. London: Cassell, 1961.
    Biography of a leading New Orleans clarinet player who played with some of Louis Armstrong's most important recorded groups.

Warren "Baby" Dodds (drummer)
Dodds, Warren, and Gara, L. *The Baby Dodds Story*. Los Angeles: Contemporary Press, 1959.
    Story of leading New Orleans jazz drummer.

Eric Dolphy (saxophonist)
Simosko, Vladimir, and Tepperman, Barry. *Eric Dolphy*. Washington, D.C.: Smithsonian, 1974.
    Career biography and discography.

Tommy and Jimmy Dorsey (trombonist, alto saxophonist, and bandleaders)
Sanford, Herb. *Tommy and Jimmy: The Dorsey Years*. New Rochelle, N.Y.: Arlington House, 1972.
    Contains an amusing collection of quotes and anecdotes about the Dorsey brothers.
————— —————. London: Ian Allan, 1972.

Duke Ellington (pianist, composer, and bandleader)
Dance, Stanley. *The World of Duke Ellington*. New York: Charles Scribner's Sons, 1970.
    Contains anecdotes, thoughts, and opinions in Ellington's own words, plus a chronology and a selective discography. Most of the book deals with some of the great players who have gone through the Ellington band.
————— —————. London: Macmillian, 1971.
————— —————. New York: Scribner's, 1972.
Darrell, R. D. *Black Beauty*. Philadelphia: (Publisher unknown), 1933.
    Probably the earliest American written comment on Ellington's work.

Ellington, Duke. *The Great Music of Duke Ellington*. Melville, N.Y.: Belwin Mills, 1974.

Includes a brief text on his career written by Leonard Feather. Most of the book is devoted to lead sheets.

————. *Music Is My Mistress*. Garden City, N.Y.: Doubleday, 1973.

A very revealing and entertaining book. Includes a discography and a list of his compositions. Highly recommended.

———— ————. London: W. H. Allen, 1974.

———— ————. New York: Da Capo, 1976.

———— ————. London: Quartet Books, 1977.

Ellington, Mercer, and Dance, Stanley. *Duke Ellington in Person: An Intimate Memoir*. Boston: Houghton Mifflin, 1978.

Adds new insight into the personal and professional life of Ellington. A very good book.

———— ————. London: Hutchinson, 1978.

Gammond, Peter, ed. *Duke Ellington: His Life and Music*. London: Phoenix House, 1958.

Essay collection.

———— ————. New York: Roy Publishers, 1958.

———— ————. London: Jazz Book Club, 1960.

———— ————. New York: Da Capo, 1977.

Gutman, Bill. *Duke: The Musical Life of Duke Ellington*. New York: Random House, 1977.

A collection of photographs and personal interviews; intended for young readers.

Jewell, Derek. *Duke: A Portrait of Duke Ellington*. New York: W. W. Norton, 1977.

Includes a chronology, a discography, and a bibliography.

———— ————. London: Elm Tree Books, 1977.

Lambert, G. E. *Duke Ellington*. London: Cassell, 1959.

Well written but with little original material.

———— ————. New York: Barnes, 1961.

Montgomery, Elizabeth Rider. *Duke Ellington, King of Jazz*. Champaign, Ill.: Garrard, 1972.

A biography especially written for young people.

———— ————. New York: Dell, 1975.

Ulanov, Barry. *Duke Ellington*. New York: Creative Age Press, 1946.

Includes discography.

———— ————. London: Musicians Press, 1947.

———— ————. New York: Da Capo, 1975.

George "Pops" Foster (bassist)

Foster, George M. *Pops Foster*. Berkeley: University of California Press, 1971.

A very interesting book with many photos. Also contains a chronology and a discography.

Pete Fountain (clarinetist)

Fountain, Pete, and Neely, Bill. *A Closer Walk: The Pete Fountain Story*. Chicago: Henry Regnery, 1972.

Roy Fox (bandleader)

Fox, Roy. *Hollywood, Mayfair and All That Jazz: The Roy Fox Story*. London: Frewin, 1975.

American bandleader who worked largely in Britain. Of marginal significance.

Bud Freeman (saxophonist)

Freeman, Bud. *If You Know of a Better Life, Please Tell Me*. See p. 121.

————. *You Don't Look like a Musician*. Detroit: Balamp, 1974.

Freeman's autobiography, including anecdotes about many of his contemporaries. Philosophical, humorous, and entertaining. Good reading.

George Gershwin (composer and pianist)

Armitage, Merle, ed. *George Gershwin*. New York: Longmans, Green, 1938.

————. *George Gershwin, Man and Legend*. Freeport, N.Y.: Books for Libraries Press, 1970.

Gershwin is of marginal significance to jazz because of his relationship with Paul Whiteman.

———— ————. New York: Duell, Sloan and Pearce, 1958.

Ewen, David. *A Journey to Greatness: The Life and Music of George Gershwin*. New York: Henry Holt, 1956.

Goldberg, Isaac. *George Gershwin, a Study in American Music*. New York: Simon and Schuster, 1931.

Jablonski, Edward, and Stewart, Lawrence D. *The Gershwin Years*. Garden City, N.Y.: Doubleday, 1958.

———— ————. Garden City, N.Y.: Doubleday, 1973.

John Birks "Dizzy" Gillespie (trumpeter)

Gillespie, Dizzy, and Fraser, Al. *To Be or Not to Bop*. Garden City, N.Y.: Doubleday, 1979.

James, Michael. *Dizzy Gillespie*. London: Cassell, 1959.

Rather dull evaluation of a colorful musician who was one of the leading influences in developing the "modern" school of jazz.

————— —————. New York: Barnes, 1961.

Jim Godbolt (band agent)

Godbolt, Jim. *All This and 10%*.

See p. 121.

Benny Goodman (clarinetist and bandleader)

Baron, Stanley. *Benny, King of Swing: A Pictorial Biography Based on Benny Goodman's Personal Archives*. London: Thames and Hudson, 1979.

Consists primarily of photographs.

Goodman, Benny, and Kolodin, Irving. *The Kingdom of Swing*. New York: Stackpole, 1939.

————— —————. New York: Ungar, 1961.

————— —————. London: Constable, 1962.

Robert Graettinger (jazz composer)

Morgan, Robert. "The Music and Life of Robert Graettinger with Cantata for Chorus and Jazz Band." D.M.A. dissertation, University of Illinois, 1974.

This includes an analysis of this composer who was affiliated with the Stan Kenton band during the 1950s. Includes a listing of existing scores and parts.

John Hammond (producer)

Hammond, John. *John Hammond on Record*. New York: Ridge Press, Summit Books, 1977.

Autobiography describing his life and experiences in the music business.

W. C. Handy (composer)

Handy, W. C. *Father of the Blues: An Autobiography*. New York: Macmillan, 1941.

————— —————. London: Sidgwick and Jackson, 1957.

————— —————. New York: Collier, 1970.

Montgomery, Elizabeth Rider. *William C. Handy, Father of the Blues*. Champaign, Ill.: Garrard, 1968.

Biography for young people.

————— —————. New York: Dell, 1972.

Hampton Hawes (pianist)

Hawes, Hampton, and Asher, Don. *Raise Up off Me*. New York: Coward, McCann and Geoghegan, 1973.

Coleman Hawkins (tenor saxophonist)

McCarthy, Albert J. *Coleman Hawkins*. London: Cassell, 1963.
  Life of influential saxophonist whose work spans several periods and styles.

Ted Heath (trombonist and bandleader)

Heath, Ted. *Listen to My Music: An Autobiography*. London: Muller, 1957.
  Life of the British orchestra leader whose band included many of the leading British jazz musicians in the 1940s and 1950s.

Fletcher Henderson (pianist and bandleader)

Allen, Walter C. *Hendersonia: The Music of Fletcher Henderson and His Musicians*. Highland Park, N.J.: The Author, 1973.
  A comprehensive account including an itinerary of engagements, a discography, and brief biographies of the musicians who played with Henderson.
  —————— ——————. Highland Park, N.J.: The Author, 1974.

Earl Hines (pianist)

Dance, Stanley. *The World of Earl Hines*. New York: Charles Scribner's Sons, 1977.
  This book contains an oral history of jazz in Chicago by many of the musicians who were involved. Most of the book is Hines's autobiography with a chronology and discography.

Billie Holiday (singer)

Chilton, John. *Billie's Blues*. New York: Stein and Day, 1975.
  Holiday's biography from the beginning of her recording career in 1933 to her death in 1959. Contains a very detailed bibliography.
  —————— ——————. London: Quartet Books, 1975.
Holiday, Billie, and Duffty, W. *Lady Sings the Blues*. Garden City, N.Y.: Doubleday, 1956.
  —————— ——————. London: Barrie and Rockliff, 1958.

Lena Horne (singer)

Horne, Lena. *In Person, Lena Horne*. New York: Greenberg, 1950.

————, and Schickel, R. *Lena*. New York: Doubleday, 1965.

————— ————. London: Deutsch, 1966.

Patrick C. "Spike" Hughes (bassist and composer)

Hughes, Patrick C. *Opening Bars, Beginning an Autobiography*. London: Pilot Press, 1946.

————. *Second Movement: Continuing the Autobiography of Spike Hughes*. London: Museum Press, 1951.

Hughes was influential on the British jazz world in the early 1930s.

Mahalia Jackson (singer)

Cornell, Jean Gay. *Mahalia Jackson: Queen of Gospel Song*. Champaign, Ill.: Garrard, 1974.

Brief biography for children.

Goreau, Laurraine. *Just Mahalia, Baby*. Waco, Tex.: Word Books, 1975.

Well-written biography.

————. *Mahalia*. Berkhamsted, England: Lean Publishing, 1976.

Jackson, Mahalia, and Wylie, Evan McLeod. *Movin' On Up*. New York: Hawthorn Books, 1966.

Milt Jackson (vibraphonist)

Wilbraham, Roy. *Milt Jackson: A Discography and Biography: Including Recordings Made with the MJQ*.

See p. 160.

Harry James (trumpeter and bandleader)

Stacy, Frank. *Harry James' Pin-Up Life Story*. New York: Arco, 1944.

Pete Johnson (pianist)

Maurerer, H. J., ed. *The Pete Johnson Story*. New York: The Author, 1965.

Life of leading boogie-woogie pianist.

Robert Johnson (singer)

Charters, Samuel. *Robert Johnson*. New York: Oak Publications, 1973.

Tommy Johnson (singer)

Evans, David. *Tommy Johnson*. London: Studio Vista, 1971.

Biography of leading Mississippi blues singer.

Willie Geary "Bunk" Johnson (trumpeter)

Sonnier, Austin M. *Willie Geary "Bunk" Johnson: The New Iberia Years*. New York: Crescendo, 1977.

Biography, photos, discography, and chronology of Bunk Johnson and other musicians in New Iberia, Louisiana, between 1900 and 1930.

Max Kaminsky (trumpeter)

Kaminsky, Max, and Hughes, W. E. *My Life in Jazz*. New York: Harper and Row, 1963.

Life and work of the Chicago-style trumpet player.

————— —————. London: Deutsch, 1964.

————— —————. London: Jazz Book Club, 1965.

Stan Kenton (pianist and bandleader)

Bauman, Dick. "A Dissection of the History and Musical Product of Stan Kenton." Master's paper, Northwest Missouri State University, 1970.

Easton, Carol. *Straight Ahead, the Story of Stan Kenton*. New York: Morrow, 1973.

A biography of Kenton's life and a description of his present work routine. Also included is commentary on some important people in his professional and personal life.

B. B. King (guitarist)

B. B. King. New York: Amsco Music Publishing Co., 1970.

Interviews and transcriptions of guitar solos.

Lydon, Michael. *Rockfolk: Portraits from the Rock 'n' Roll Pantheon*.

See p. 39.

Eartha Kitt (singer)

Kitt, Eartha. *Alone with Me: A New Autobiography*. Chicago: Henry Regnery, 1976.

George Lewis (clarinetist)

Bethell, Tom. *George Lewis, A Jazzman from New Orleans*. Berkeley: University of California Press, 1977.

The life of George Lewis. Also discusses the development of jazz in New Orleans after the closing of Storyville in 1917. Contains a number of comments by Lewis himself.

Stuart, Jay Allison. *Call Him George*. London: Peter Davies, 1961.

———— ————. New York: Crown, 1961.

———— ————. London: Jazz Book Club, 1963.

———— ————. New York: Crown, 1969.

Guy Lombardo (bandleader)

Lombardo, Guy. *Auld Acquaintance*. Garden City, N.Y.: Doubleday, 1975.

Humphrey Lyttleton (trumpeter and bandleader)

Lyttleton, Humphrey. *I Play as I Please: The Memoirs of an Old Etonian Trumpeter*. London: MacGibbon and Kee, 1954.

   Amusing and interesting comments on the British jazz scene from 1945 to 1954.

———— ————. London: Jazz Book Club, 1957.

———— ————. London: Pan Books, 1959.

————. *Second Chorus*. London: MacGibbon and Kee, 1958.

   Further comments on British jazz between 1954 and 1958.

———— ————. London: Jazz Book Club, 1960.

————. *Take It from the Top: An Autobiographical Scrapbook*. London: Robson Books, 1975.

"Wingy" Manone (trumpeter)

Manone, Wingy, and Vandervoort, P. *Trumpet on the Wing*. New York: Doubleday, 1948.

———— ————. London: Jazz Book Club, 1964.

Brownie McGhee (guitarist)

McGhee, W. B. *Guitar Styles of Brownie McGhee*. New York: Oak Publications, 1971.

   His autobiography with examples of his playing style.

George Melly (singer)

Melly, George. *Owning-Up*. London: Weidenfeld and Nicolson, 1965.

   Earthy pen picture of life with a traveling jazz band (Mick Mulligan) in Britain. Describes and removes most of the glamour from the "one-night-stand" existence of itinerant bands.

———— ————. London: Penguin Books, 1977.

————. *Rum, Bum and Concertina*. London: Weidenfeld and Nicolson, 1977.

   Personal memoirs of leading British jazz singer.

Milton "Mezz" Mezzrow (clarinetist and bandleader)

Mezzrow, Milton, and Wolfe, B. *Really the Blues*. New York: Random House, 1946.

An important work about a clarinet player who played with many leading jazz musicians and made some memorable recordings.

————— —————. London: Musicians Press, 1947.

————— —————. London: Secker and Warburg, 1957.

————— —————. London: Transworld Publishers, 1961.

————— —————. New York: Doubleday, 1972.

Glenn Miller (trombonist and bandleader)

Flower, John. *Moonlight Serenade: A Bio-Discography of the Glenn Miller Civilian Band.* New Rochelle, N.Y.: Arlington House, 1972.

An examination of the Miller Band from the mid-1930s to 1942. A well-documented and thorough book.

Green, Jonathan. *Glenn Miller and the Age of Swing.* London: Dempsey and Spurrier, 1976.

Simon, George T. *Glenn Miller and His Orchestra.* New York: Thomas Y. Crowell, 1974.

A well-written book on the career of Glenn Miller.

————— —————. London: W. H. Allen, 1974.

Charles Mingus (bassist)

Mingus, Charles. *Beneath the Underdog.* Edited by Nel King. New York: Alfred A. Knopf, 1971.

A rather esoteric glimpse into the world of Charles Mingus. Autobiographical sketches are mixed with fiction.

————— —————. London: Weidenfeld and Nicolson, 1971.

————— —————. London: Penguin Books, 1971.

————— —————. New York: St. Martins Press, 1975.

Wilbraham, Roy J. *Charles Mingus—A Biography and Discography.* London: The Author, 1967.

Little Brother Montgomery (pianist)

Gert zur Heide, Karl. *Deep South Piano: The Story of Little Brother Montgomery.* London: Studio Vista, 1970.

Ferdinand "Jelly Roll" Morton (pianist, composer, and bandleader)

Lomax, Alan. *Mister Jelly Roll: The Fortunes of Jelly Roll Morton, New Orleans Creole and "Inventor of Jazz."* New York: Duell, 1950.

Vital and important work by this indefatigable documentor of all types of American folk music.

———— ————. London: Cassell, 1952.
———— ————. New York: Grove Press, 1956.
———— ————. London: Jazz Book Club, 1956.
———— ————. London: Pan Books, 1959.
———— ————. Berkeley: University of California Press, 1973.
Smith, Charles E. *Jelly Roll Morton's New Orleans Memories*.
New York: Consolidated Records, n.d.
Williams, Martin T. *Jelly Roll Morton*. London: Cassell, 1962.

Loring "Red" Nichols (cornetist and bandleader)
Johnson, G. *The Five Pennies: The Biography of Jazz Band Leader Red Nichols*. New York: Dell, 1959.
Based on the film of the same title.

Joseph "King" Oliver (cornetist and bandleader)
Williams, Martin T. *King Oliver*. London: Cassell, 1960.
Brief life of a major jazz figure of the 1920s. Oliver led one of the most exciting and creative bands in jazz at this period.

"Hot Lips" Page (trumpeter)
Jepsen, J. G., and Mohr, Kurt. *Hot Lips Page*. (City unknown): Jazz Publications, 1961.
Brief biography and discography from 1938 to 1954.

Charlie Parker (alto saxophonist)
Davis, Nathan Tate. "Charlie Parker's Kansas City Environment and Its Effect on His Later Life." Ph.D. dissertation, Wesleyan University, 1974.
Of more psychological and sociological value than musical.
Harrison, M. *Charlie Parker*. London: Cassell, 1960.
———— ————. New York: Barnes, 1961.
Reisner, Robert George. *Bird: The Legend of Charlie Parker*.
New York: Citadel Press, 1962.
A collection of articles, stories, and random memories arranged in no particular order chronologically, and presented with the minimum of editing and correction. Obvious errors of fact are retained. A vivid and vital picture of one of the greatest jazz musicians of all time and the society in which he lived.
———— ————. London: MacGibbon and Kee, 1963.
———— ————. London: Jazz Book Club, 1965.
———— ————. New York: Da Capo Press, 1973.
———— ————. London: Quartet Books, 1974.

Russell, Ross. *Bird Lives: The High Life and Hard Times of Charlie (Yardbird) Parker*. New York: Charter House, 1973.

An excellent biography written by one of the best writers on jazz history. Also includes a bibliography and discography.

————— —————. London: McKay, 1975.

————— —————. London: Quartet Books, 1976.

Charley Patton (singer)

Fahey, John. *Charley Patton*. London: Studio Vista, 1970.

A musicological examination of the music of Charley Patton, an influential figure in the history of the blues.

Art Pepper (saxophonist)

Pepper, Art. *Straight Life: The Story of Art Pepper*. New York: Schirmer Books, 1979.

André Previn (pianist)

Greenfield, Edward. *André Previn*. New York: Drake, 1973.

An account of Previn's career and recording achievements.

Ma Rainey (singer)

Stewart-Baxter, Derrick. *Ma Rainey and the Classic Blues Singers*.

See p. 41–42.

Django Reinhardt (guitarist)

Abrams, Max. *The Book of Django*. Los Angeles: The Author, 1973.

Delaunay, Charles. *Django Reinhardt*. Translated by Michael James. London: Cassell, 1961.

Includes a seventy-eight-page discography.

————— —————. London: Jazz Book Club, 1963.

Buddy Rich (drummer)

Balliett, Whitney. *Super-Drummer: A Profile of Buddy Rich*. Indianapolis: Bobbs-Merrill, 1968.

Photos and commentary on the lifestyle of Buddy Rich, providing an interesting insight into his personality.

Bob Scobey (trumpeter)

Scobey, Jan. *Jan Scobey Presents: He Rambled 'til Cancer Cut Him Down*. Northridge, Calif.: Pal, 1976.

Biography of Dixieland trumpeter Bob Scobey.

Ronnie Scott (saxophonist)

Scott, Ronnie. *Some of My Best Friends Are Blues*. London: W. H. Allen, 1979.

Artie Shaw (clarinetist and bandleader)

Blandford, Edmund L. *Artie Shaw*. Hastings, England: The Author, 1974.

Robertson, A. *Artie Shaw '36–'55*. (City unknown): The Author, 1971.

Shaw, Artie. *The Trouble with Cinderella: An Outline of Identity*. New York: Farrar, Straus and Young, 1952.

———— ————. London: Jarrolds, 1955.

———— ————. New York: Collier, 1963.

Frank Sinatra (singer)

Barnes, Ken. *Sinatra and the Great Song Stylists*. London: Ian Allan, 1972.

Includes brief commentary on Louis Armstrong, Peggy Lee, Nat Cole, Mel Torme, Sarah Vaughan, Ethel Waters, Lena Horne, Pearl Bailey, Mildred Bailey, Jimmy Rushing, Dinah Washington, etc.

Kahn, Ely J. *The Voice*. New York: Harper, 1947.

A collection of articles about Sinatra that originally appeared in the *New Yorker*.

Ridgway, John. *The Sinatra File*. Birmingham, England: John Ridgway Books, 1977.

Shaw, Arnold. *Sinatra: Twentieth-Century Romantic*. New York: Holt, Rinehart and Winston, 1968.

Wilson, Earl. *Sinatra, An Unauthorized Biography*. New York: Macmillan, 1976.

Bessie Smith (singer)

Albertson, Chris. *Bessie*. New York: Stein and Day, 1972.

Her biography and a documentation of her live performances and recordings. A well-written book.

———— ————. London: Barrie and Jenkins, 1972.

———— ————. London: Abacus, 1975.

————, and Schuller, Gunther. *Bessie Smith, Empress of the Blues*.

See p. 34.

Moore, Carmen. *Somebody's Angel Child*. New York: Crowell, 1970.

Biography of Bessie Smith. Contains a discography, bibliography, and a list of her compositions.

——— ———. New York: Dell, 1975.

Oliver, Paul. *Bessie Smith*. London: Cassell, 1959.

Fascinating story of a great artist.

——— ———. New York: Barnes, 1961.

Willie "The Lion" Smith (pianist)

Smith, Willie, and Hoeffer, George. *Music on My Mind: The Memoirs of an American Pianist*. New York: Doubleday, 1964.

——— ———. London: MacGibbon and Kee, 1965.

——— ———. London: Jazz Book Club, 1966.

——— ———. New York: Da Capo, 1975.

Ralph Sutton (pianist)

Shacter, James D. *Piano Man, the Story of Ralph Sutton*. Chicago: Jaynar Press, 1975.

Sutton started out with Jack Teagarden and most recently played with the World's Greatest Jazz Band.

Jack Teagarden (trombonist)

Smith, J. D., and Guttridge, L. *Jack Teagarden: The Story of a Jazz Maverick*. London: Cassell, 1960.

A superficial book unworthy of the work of Teagarden, the trombonist from Texas who has played with Louis Armstrong and many other leading jazz musicians.

——— ———. London: Jazz Book Club, 1962.

Thomas "Fats" Waller (pianist, composer, and bandleader)

Davies, John R. T. *The Music of Thomas "Fats" Waller*. London: Friends of Fats, 1953.

Fox, Charles. *Fats Waller*. London: Cassell, 1960.

——— ———. New York: Barnes, 1961.

Kirkeby, W. T. E., et al. *Ain't Misbehavin': The Story of Fats Waller*. London: Peter Davies, 1966.

——— ———. New York: Dodd, Mead, 1966.

——— ———. New York: Da Capo, 1975.

Sill, Harold. *Misbehavin' with Fats*.

See p. 187.

Vance, Joel. *Fats Waller, His Life and Times*. Chicago: Contemporary Books, 1977.

A well-written biography.

Waller, Maurice, and Calabrese, Anthony. *Fats Waller*. New York: Schirmer Books, 1977.

Waller's biography, which includes a discography, a listing of his compositions, a transcription of "Ain't Misbehavin' " and a manuscript of two of his compositions.

Ethel Waters (singer)

Waters, Ethel, and Samuels, C. *His Eye Is on the Sparrow: An Autobiography*. New York: Doubleday, 1951.

———— ————. London: W. G. Allen, 1951.

———— ————. London: Jazz Book Club, 1958.

———— ————. New York: Bantam Books, 1959.

Muddy Waters (singer)

Rooney, James. *Bossmen: Bill Moore and Muddy Waters*. New York: Dial Press, 1971.

Biography of urban blues musician Muddy Waters.

Lawrence Welk (bandleader)

Welk, Lawrence. *Ah-One, Ah-Two!* Englewood Cliffs, N.J.: Prentice-Hall, 1974.

About his orchestra and how it operates.

————. *Lawrence Welk's Musical Family Album*. Englewood Cliffs, N.J.: Prentice-Hall, 1977.

Contains brief commentary on each of his musicians.

————. *My America, Your America*. Englewood Cliffs, N.J.: Prentice-Hall, 1976.

Of very marginal interest.

————. *Wunnerful, Wunnerful*. Englewood Cliffs, N.J.: Prentice-Hall, 1971.

Dicky Wells (trombonist)

Wells, Dicky. *The Night People: Reminiscences of a Jazzman*. Boston: Crescendo, 1971.

An inside look at the jazz world depicting road life with some of the great Negro jazz bands—onstage, backstage, and on the bus.

———— ————. London: Robert Hale, 1971.

Peetie Wheatstraw (singer and pianist)

Garon, Paul. *The Devil's Son-in-Law: The Story of Peetie Wheatstraw and His Songs*. London: Studio Vista, 1971.

The story of this St. Louis singer/pianist.

Paul Whiteman (bandleader)

Whiteman, Paul, and McBride, Mary Margaret. *Jazz*. New York: Sears, 1926.

Whiteman's main contribution to jazz was in providing work for some leading exponents. His band played "symphonic jazz" which had little, if any, relation to the real thing.

———— ————. New York: Arno, 1975.

Clarence Williams (pianist)

Lord, Tom. *Clarence Williams*. London: Storyville, 1976.

Chapter 5

Analysis, Theory, and Criticism

Many writers have attempted to analyze the musical structure and form of jazz. Some have found this task beyond their knowledge, either because they lacked essential experience of that elusive factor, "the feeling of jazz," or because their understanding of musical theory was faulty. This "feel of jazz" is exceedingly difficult to define; it is a pragmatic thing known instinctively to a true jazz musician. In addition, much of jazz is not written down, and even scored jazz contains nuances, impossible to notate, that vary from musician to musician. To write intelligently and critically on this subject, therefore, requires particular skill.

Hugues Panassie, the leading French critic, was one of the first writers to attempt an analysis of jazz in a manner appropriate to the type of music it was, and although much of his work is less than totally satisfactory, his pioneering efforts demand recognition. Two of his many books are of particular significance and can be considered together since they are closely connected in most ways. *Hot Jazz* (1936) and *The Real Jazz* (1940; second edition in 1960) follow a distinct pattern in their treatment of the subject. First, Panassie offers an explanation of what he believes that jazz is, followed by chapters devoted to musicians grouped by the instrument they play. The assessments of musicians at different stages in Panassie's career as a critic make interesting reading, since he wrote the first book under the severe handicap of not having heard many of the really influential players. The later book attempts to correct many of his admitted errors of judgment. Panassie has no time for modern jazz styles and contends that they do not belong to jazz itself. A great protagonist of the black American, he was most reluctant to admit that whites could play "real jazz." All his books contain a real enthusiasm for his subject; it is perhaps wiser to read his books for the spirit, rather than the letter.

Two American writers who made early and lasting contributions to this area of the literature are Winthrop Sargeant and Wilder Hobson. Sargeant's *Jazz: Hot and Hybrid* (1938) was a major essay in comparative musicology with a somewhat unusual approach. It contains many musical examples within its pages and analyzes jazz as a distinct musical idiom. It also traces its origins, dissects its anatomy, and describes in detail those features that distinguish it from other varieties of music. There is a useful bibliography of some 150 items, all published before 1940. The book is required reading for any serious jazz student. A third edition of the book was published by Da Capo Press in 1975. Another almost classic work is Hobson's *American Jazz Music* (1939). This was written at the height of the swing era in jazz history and before the birth of modern jazz. It is an intelligent and perceptive assessment of jazz up to 1940.

Sidney Finkelstein's *Jazz: A People's Music* (1948, reissued in 1975) is also a good analysis that attempts to fit jazz into its place in musical history. The book discusses improvisation and form and quotes examples of the work of major musicians. It also includes some useful record listings. An important British writer, Wilfred Mellers, writes authoritatively on all aspects of American music in his *Music in a New Found Land* (1964). A large part of the book is devoted to an excellent analysis of jazz, and Mellers's work is essential reading for anyone wanting to understand its relationship to the mainstream of music. There is a valuable seventy-page discography and a useful reading list. Another good analysis by a primarily classical composer is *The Anatomy of Jazz* (1960) by Leroy Ostransky. In the words of the preface,

> This book is an attempt, first, to present jazz in its proper perspective to those whose primary interest is in "serious" or classical music and to relate jazz theory to music theory in general. Second, to introduce to those whose primary interest is in jazz to the problems of non-jazz composers and performers by relating jazz to the history of music in general. Finally, (to try) to indicate to jazzmen what I believe to be their present position in music as well as their musical responsibility to the future.

Ostransky's book is well documented and includes a comprehensive bibliography of books and periodicals on jazz. The first part of the book is perhaps the most valuable, since the information given in the later chapters on jazz styles and periods can be found elsewhere. A later work by Ostransky, *Understanding Jazz*, was published in 1977.

Andre Hodeir's work is in complete contrast to the work of his countryman, Hugues Panassie. Many critics believe he is the leading writer on jazz in the French language and his major contributions to the literature include the influential *Jazz: Its Evolution and Essence* (1956), originally published in 1954 under the title *Hommes et Problemes du Jazz*. The book is a complex, intellectual appraisal with a bias toward the modern schools of jazz. There is a good chapter on the influence of jazz on European music and a discography of records cited in the text. In spite of some confusion over the relative importance of taste and technical skill in connection with early jazz, this is a first-class study and one of the select few major works of jazz criticism. *Toward Jazz* (1962) and *The Worlds of Jazz* (1972) by the same author are both scholarly collections of essays on aspects of jazz criticism, some of which originally appeared in various periodicals and anthologies.

Gunther Schuller writes in the manner of Hodeir. His book *Early Jazz* (1968) takes a broad view and has been described by one critic as being "among the two or three finest contributions to jazz literature." In it, the author describes and analyzes the music of the early jazz musicians up to 1930. Schuller, who is an academically trained musician and composer, offers perhaps the best interpretation yet of the African elements in jazz. He has been best known in the jazz world for his attempts to blend jazz and classical forms into third stream music. This book was intended to be the first of two volumes, but the second work has not as yet materialized.

Ross Russell's *Jazz Style in Kansas City and the South West* (1971) is a well-documented account of the musicians and styles associated with Kansas City and includes some analysis of the work of Count Basie, Bennie Moten, Charlie Parker, and Jack Teagarden. The book has both a useful discography and bibliography.

Collections of essays are a favorite format for many jazz writers, and several of Martin T. Williams's books take this form. These include *The Art of Jazz* (1959) and *Jazz Panorama* (1962), in which the thirty-nine items were selected from the important but short-lived periodical *Jazz Review*. The arrangement of the book is chronological and ranges from essays on Jelly Roll Morton and King Oliver to Ornette Coleman and Ray Charles. The earlier book by Williams is subtitled "Essays on the Nature and Development of Jazz" and these essays include a particularly interesting contribution by Ernst Ansermet on Will Marion Cook's orchestra, which toured Europe in 1918 and included Sidney Bechet in its ranks. Each essay is introduced by the editor, giving the source and date of the original publication. Williams has also contributed to the *Encyclopaedia Britannica* entries on jazz, in addition to writing several more books, including *Jazz Masters in Transition, 1957–1969* and *The Jazz Tradition*, both published in 1970. Williams is currently the jazz curator at the Smithsonian Institution. An earlier essay collection, *Frontiers of Jazz*, by Ralph de Toledano, was originally published in 1947. This collection is divided into two sections; section one, entitled "The Anatomy of Jazz," consists of five contributions including a brief one by Jean Paul Sartre; section two, "The Men Who Made Jazz," covers a wide range of earlier jazz musicians from King Oliver through the New Orleans Rhythm Kings to Benny Goodman and Duke Ellington.

Other collections of some significance include the various publications issued by *Esquire* magazine beginning in the 1940s, edited first by Paul Edward Miller and in 1947 by Ernest Anderson. All consist of brief essays that appeared originally in the magazine. After a gap of some years, *Esquire's World of Jazz* (1962) was published. This was a superb artistic production particularly notable for its use of modernistic paintings and other excellent illustrations. The most recent edition, published in 1975, is both a beautiful and informative work that would make a most impressive addition to any library. *The PL Yearbook of Jazz* (1946), edited by A. J. McCarthy, was a publication similar to the early *Esquire* yearbooks and also appeared several times rather irregularly. The *Just Jazz* series, edited by Sinclair

Traill and Gerald Lascelles, started in 1957 and ended with volume 4 in 1960, although one of the key features of each volume—a complete jazz discography for the year—was continued in Cherrington and Knight's *Jazz Catalogue* (1960–   ), which is mentioned in the chapter on reference sources.

Leonard Feather's most widely acclaimed works are his major reference volumes, previously described in some detail. Nevertheless, his critical works are also of great importance, starting with *Inside Jazz* (which appeared in 1949 as *Inside Be-Bop*) and was a combination of technical analysis and history covering the period 1940–49. *The Book of Jazz* (second edition published in 1965) is also authoritative and presents its information in a rather unusual (but very useful) way. There are four main sections: (1) the sources; (2) the instruments, sounds, and performers; (3) the nature of jazz; and (4) the future of jazz. *From Satchmo to Miles* (1972) consists of essays on important jazz musicians including Armstrong, Ellington, Billie Holiday, Basie, Lester Young, Parker, and several others, while *The Pleasures of Jazz* (1976) is a similar work covering leading performers and their lives, music, and contemporaries. Feather is currently the jazz critic of the *Los Angeles Times* and writes for a number of magazines, including *Downbeat*.

Shapiro and Hentoff's *Jazzmakers* (1957) is another exceptional work and, as with all the other publications of these authors, worthy of study. Other American writers such as Barry Ulanov and John S. Wilson have also made significant contributions to this area of the literature. Ulanov's *Handbook of Jazz* appeared in 1957, while John Wilson's *Jazz: The Transition Years, 1940–1960* (1966) is a well-produced book that includes in the final two chapters a survey of the impact of jazz outside the United States and on mass audiences everywhere.

Two other excellent books in this area are *A Study of Jazz* (originally published in 1964, with a third edition in 1977) by Paul Tanner and Maurice Gerow, and *Jazz Styles* (1978) by Mark Gridley. Both books are written to be accessible to the jazz newcomer and are particularly appropriate for college and high school students. The former is noted for its concise manner of depicting the style characteristics of various styles of jazz, while the latter attempts to explain how jazz is produced and may serve as a jazz appreciation text.

The German author Joachim Berendt produced what is regarded as one of jazz literature's best sellers in *New Jazz Book*. It sold over 200,000 copies in the German language edition before appearing in English in 1964. *The Jazz Book* (1975) is effectively the fourth edition of this excellent text, which has been recognized as a standard work for some time. This edition includes much new material and many of the sections have been rewritten. The book is an orthodox and all-embracing view of the jazz field, and its author seems to be free of the prejudices of some other leading jazz critics. The pattern followed by the book is to look at the various styles (arranged chronologically by decade), the major musicians, and the various instruments used in playing jazz. Berendt also attempts that most difficult of tasks— to define exactly what jazz is. The book is painstaking, methodical, and is so presented as to be of value to the beginner in jazz or the expert.

British critics have also made useful contributions in the analytical literature, and Benny Green's *The Reluctant Art* (1962) is a perceptive and intelligent book that takes the form of five critical essays on the work of Goodman, Holiday, Beiderbecke, Young, and Parker, all of whom are regarded by the author as major influences in jazz history. Green writes in an entertaining manner and successfully sorts out legend from fact in several cases. Another collection of essays by Green, *Drums in My Ears* (1973), includes criticism, book reviews, and obituary notices. Max Harrison's *A Jazz Retrospect* (1976) is also of British origin and represents the best type of intellectual approach to jazz. Most of the essays in this book originally appeared in the pages of *Jazz Monthly*. Another prolific essayist well worth mentioning for his eclectic tastes is Whitney Balliett, whose regular columns in the *New Yorker* have spawned some intensely readable works. Balliett's books include (in chronological order) *The Sound of Surprise* (1959), *Dinosaurs in the Morning* (1962), *Such Sweet Thunder* (1966), *Ecstasy at the Onion* (1972), *Alex Wilder and His Friends* (1974), *New York Notes* (1976) and *Improvising* (1977). The last is typical of Balliett and includes essays covering all aspects of jazz history. There is an introductory chapter on New Orleans today, pieces on trumpeters Red Allen and "King" Oliver, pianists Earl Hines, Mary Lou Williams and Jess Stacy, and other musicians playing in more modern styles such as the Modern Jazz Quartet and guitarist Jim Hall.

Some critics have specialized in assessing the work of the modern schools of jazz, among them Raymond Horricks, Alun Morgan, Barry McRae, A. B. Spellman, Ian Carr, Valerie Wilmer, and Michael James. "Modern" jazz originated with Charlie Parker and Dizzy Gillespie in the 1940s and although it now encompasses many styles of playing, it is still useful as a shorthand label for many jazz enthusiasts to identify and categorize what they hear. Barry McRae's *Jazz Cataclysm* (1967) provides a concise and readable account of developments by such jazz musicians as John Coltrane, Sonny Rollins, and, particularly, Ornette Coleman and "free form" jazz. The book has a useful selected discography to complete each of the twelve chapters. Spellman's *Black Music: Four Lives* (1966), originally published under the title *Four Lives in the Be-Bop Business*, is a critical assessment of Coleman, Cecil Taylor, Herbie Nichols, and Jackie McLean. British authors Horricks, Morgan, and others produced two books of interest, *Modern Jazz* (1956) and *These Jazzmen of Our Time* (1959). Valerie Wilmer's *Jazz People* (third edition published in 1977) is based on interviews with fourteen major figures and is very well illustrated with original photographs taken by the author. *As Serious as Your Life* (1977), by the same writer, is also an important book that discusses the work of black innovators such as Coltrane, Coleman, Eric Dolphy, Cecil Taylor, and others within the changing social and racial context of the 1960s and 1970s. The book includes brief but useful biographical information on these musicians. Ekkehard Jost's *Free Jazz* (1975) covers much of the same ground, while Frank Kofsky describes the revolution in jazz, its dynamics and the innovations of the individual revolutionists in his *Black Nationalism and the Revolution in Music* (1970). Kofsky deals in some detail with the work of John Coltrane in particular. Ian Carr's *Music Outside* (1973) covers contemporary jazz in Britain and is based on lengthy interviews with leading British musicians, and is a literate and valuable guide to this area of jazz. Another British musician and writer is Graham Collier; his *Inside Jazz* (1973) is mainly analytical but also includes a section on the jazz business and environment.

Humorous works on jazz are rare indeed, but two examples can be mentioned. Leonard Feather and Jack Tracy produced *Laughter from the Hip* (1963); in Britain *Fourteen Miles on a Clear Night* (1966), by Peter Gammond and Peter Clayton, was subtitled "An Irreverent, Skeptical and Affectionate Book about Jazz Records." This collection of brief anecdotes is not outstandingly good, but then jazz is evidently a serious subject.

A number of books on jazz have appeared in recent years for children and young adults. Some of these titles very successfully explain the basics of jazz appreciation and play an important part in catching the interest of future generations of jazz connoisseurs. (Some of these books are also listed in chapters 3 and 7.) Lillian Erlich's *What Jazz Is All About* (1962) is also a useful introductory text for adults, since she writes succinctly and accurately, and includes some good photographs, essential in this type of book; there is also a short selected bibliography of further reading. Another book, more analytical than historical, is Martin Williams's *Where's the Melody* (1966). R. P. Jones's *Jazz*, which appeared in the useful Methuen Outlines series in 1963, is compact and informative, while *Enjoying Jazz* (1960), by Rex Harris, is a young person's guide to traditional jazz; a useful seven-page guide to further reading greatly adds to the value of this book.

Other books that could be categorized as jazz primers include Gammond and Clayton's *Know about Jazz* (1963), an excellent, if brief, British contribution that gets down to basic essentials. The book is beautifully designed, well set, and contains a mixture of good photographs, line drawings, and colorful paintings. The final fifteen pages are devoted to brief biographies (listing selected records) of leading jazz artists, and the endpapers of the book contain a brief glossary of jazz terminology. Altogether the book is an excellent value, very suitable for the market it is aimed at.

Other British titles deserve mention in this context. The

first is Avril Dankworth's *Jazz: An Introduction to Its Musical Basis* (1968, reissued in paperback in 1968), which deals (as its subtitle indicates) with the musical content. The second is John Postgate's *A Plain Man's Guide to Jazz* (1973), written in a slightly patronizing but provocative style. Although Postgate attempts a review of the whole field, he is at his most perceptive in dealing with the classic pioneers, the white innovators, and the mainstream musicians. Finally, Mark White's two useful titles in the Observers' series appeared in late 1978, *The Observer's Book of Jazz* and *The Observer's Book of Big Bands*.

BIBLIOGRAPHY

Allen, Walter C., ed. *Studies in Jazz Discography*. New Brunswick, N.J.: Institute of Jazz, 1971.

    A collection of lectures and discussions about discographical research and the preservation of jazz-related materials.

Arundel, P. *This Swing Business*. London: A. Unwin, 1948.

Asman, J., and Kinnell, Bill, eds. *American Jazz*. Nottingham, England: Jazz Appreciation Society, 1940.

————. *Jazz*. Nottingham, England: Jazz Appreciation Society, 1944.

————. *Jazz Today*. Nottingham, England: Jazz Appreciation Society, 1945.

Baker, David. "The Rhetorical Dimensions of Black Music Past and Present." New York: Speech Communication Assn., 1972.

    An examination of blues lyrics and jazz forms regarding their importance in communication.

Balliett, Whitney. *Alec Wilder and His Friends*.

    See p. 84.

————. *American Singers*. New York: Oxford University Press, 1979.

————. *Dinosaurs in the Morning: 41 Pieces on Jazz*. Philadelphia: Lippincott, 1962.

    Collection of essays originally written for the *New Yorker* magazine.

———— ————. London: Phoenix House, 1964.

———— ————. London: Jazz Book Club, 1965.

————. *Ecstasy at the Onion: 31 Pieces on Jazz*. Indianapolis: Bobbs-Merrill, 1971.

Part one covers the Newport and Monterey jazz festivals, part two is devoted to Duke Ellington, and parts three and four are devoted to critical writing on important people in jazz.

————. *Improvising: Sixteen Jazz Musicians and Their Art*. New York: Oxford University Press, 1977.

A variety of jazz musicians speak about improvisation.

————. *New York Notes: A Journal of Jazz in the Seventies*. Boston: Houghton Mifflin, 1976.

A chronology of events originally appearing in the *New Yorker*.

———— ————. New York: Da Capo, 1977.

————. *The Sound of Surprise: 46 Pieces of Jazz*. New York: Dutton, 1959.

A collection of jazz articles appearing in various periodicals.

———— ————. London: Kimber, 1960.

———— ————. London: Jazz Book Club, 1962.

———— ————. London: Penguin Books, 1963.

———— ————. New York: Da Capo, 1978.

————. *Such Sweet Thunder*. New York: Bobbs-Merrill, 1966.

A collection of essays appearing in the *New Yorker*.

———— ————. London: MacDonald, 1968.

Baskerville, David Ross. "Jazz Influence on Art Music to Mid-Century." Ph.D. dissertation, University of California at Los Angeles, 1965.

Seeks to determine how jazz influenced composers of art music from 1900 to 1950. List various composers and their works that show a jazz influence.

Bauman, Dick. "The Third Stream." Master's paper, Northwest Missouri State University, 1970.

Examines Stan Kenton's Innovations Orchestra, Bill Russo, Gunther Schuller, Orchestra U.S.A., and Kenton's Neophonic Orchestra.

Berendt, Joachim. *The New Jazz Book*.
See p. 50.

Blancq, Charles C. "Melodic Improvisation: Its Evolution in American Jazz 1943–1960." Ph.D. dissertation, Tulane University, 1972.

Borneman, Ernest. *A Critic Looks at Jazz*. London: Jazz Music Books, 1946.

Brown, Robert Loran. "A Study of Influences from Euro-American Art Music on Certain Types of Jazz with Analyses and Recital of Selected Demonstrative Compositions." Ed.D. dissertation, Columbia University Teachers College, 1974.

Tries to determine what characteristics of Western European art music have been assimilated by jazz.

Brown, Sandy. *The McJazz Manuscripts*. London: Faber and Faber, 1979.

Brown, Theodore Dennis. "A History and Analysis of Jazz Drumming to 1942." Ph.D. dissertation, University of Michigan, 1976.

Examines the African influence of jazz drumming, military and dance drumming before 1900, and the styles and drummers of twentieth-century jazz.

Budds, Michael J. *Jazz in the Sixties: The Expansion of Musical Resources and Techniques*. Iowa City: University of Iowa Press, 1978.

Contains facts and an evaluation of the experimentation in the 1960s.

Carr, Ian. *Music Outside: Contemporary Jazz in Britain*.
See p. 57.

Cerulli, D., et al. *The Jazz Word*. New York: Ballantine Books, 1960.

Literary excerpts.

————— —————. London: Dobson, 1962.

————— —————. London: Jazz Book Club, 1963.

Coin, Gregory McAfee. "Developmental Parallels in the Evolution of Musical Styles: Romanticism, Jazz, Rock 'n Roll and American Musical Theatre." Master's thesis, University of Louisville, 1974.

Coker, Jerry. *Listening to Jazz*. Englewood Cliffs, N.J.: Prentice-Hall, 1978.

An excellent examination of the contents of an improvised solo. Required reading for the student improviser and for those wanting to learn to appreciate a jazz solo.

Cole, William Shadrack. "The Style of John Coltrane, 1955–67." Ph.D. dissertation, Wesleyan University, 1975.

An excellent analytical approach to Coltrane's music. Contains some solo transcriptions.

Collier, Graham. *Compositional Devices, Based on Songs for My Father*. Boston: Berklee, 1974.

An analysis of tunes recorded on "Songs for My Father."

—————. *Inside Jazz*. London: Quartet Books, 1973.

Includes a section on the jazz business and the environment of the jazz musician.

————. *Jazz: A Student's and Teacher's Guide.*
See p. 170.

Condon, Eddie, and Gehman, R., eds. *Eddie Condon's Treasury of Jazz.* New York: Dial Press, 1956.

———— ————. London: Peter Davies, 1957.

———— ————. Westport, Conn.: Greenwood Press, 1975.

Crane, Genevieve. "Jazz Elements and Formal Compositional Techniques in 'Third Stream' Music." Master's thesis, Indiana University, 1970.

An excellent analysis of three pieces by Gunther Schuller, "All about Rosie" by George Russell, and "All Set" by Milton Babbitt. Attempts to provide an understanding of third stream music.

Dance, Stanley, ed. *Jazz Era: The Forties.*
See p. 60.

Dankworth, Avril. *Jazz: An Introduction to Its Musical Basis.* London: Oxford University Press, 1968.

Brief ninety-page book that deals sketchily with the musical "guts" of jazz. Part one covers chords, forms, scales, rhythm, and tonal effects, while part two deals with the development of jazz styles and instrumentation.

———— ————. London: Oxford University Press, 1975.

de Toledano, Ralph, ed. *Frontiers of Jazz.* New York: Durrell, 1947.

A collection of essays written between 1926 and 1947, each with an introduction by the editor, selected from both jazz and nonjazz periodicals.

———— ————. 2nd ed. New York: Ungar, 1962.

———— ————. London: Jazz Book Club, 1966.

Downbeat's Yearbook of Swing. Edited by Paul E. Miller. Chicago: Downbeat, 1939.

A history of hot jazz, dealing with groups rather than individuals. A valuable book.

Downey, John. "An Analysis of the Jazz Influence in Each of the Following Contemporary Works: 'Sextet for Clarinet, Piano, and Strings,' by Aaron Copland; 'Le Creation du Monde,' by Darius Milhaud; 'L'histoire du Soldat,' by Igor Stravinsky." Master's thesis, Ithaca College, 1959.

Not very well written.

Ellington, Duke. *Piano Method for Blues*. New York: Robbins Music Corp., 1943.

A history and analysis of the blues form.

Ellison, R. *Shadow and Act*. New York: Random House, 1964.

Essay contributions to leading American literary magazines. About one-third of the collection is devoted to jazz.

————— —————. London: Secker and Warburg, 1967.

Erlich, Lillian. *What Jazz Is All About*.

See p. 51.

Esquire's Jazz Book. Edited by Paul Edward Miller. New York: Smith and Durrell, 1944.

Esquire's 1945 Jazz Book. New York: Barnes, 1945.

Esquire's 1946 Jazz Book. New York: Barnes, 1946.

Esquire's 1947 Jazz Book. Edited by Ernest Anderson. New York: Smith and Durrell, 1947.

Esquire's World of Jazz. Edited by L. W. Gillenson. Commentary by James Poling. New York: Grosset and Dunlap, 1962.

Superb artistic publication, particularly notable for the illustraditions and modernistic paintings. Basically a collection of essays on jazz with a twelve-page selective discography by John Lessner.

————— —————. London: A. Barker, 1963.

————— —————. London: Jazz Book Club, 1964.

————— —————. New York: Crowell, 1975.

Feather, Leonard. *The Book of Jazz: A Guide to the Entire Field*.

See p. 51.

—————. *The Book of Jazz from Then till Now: A Guide to the Entire Field*.

See p. 51.

—————. *From Satchmo to Miles*.

See p. 85.

—————. *Inside Jazz*.

See p. 60.

—————. *The Pleasures of Jazz*.

See p. 85.

—————, and Tracy, Jack. *Laughter from the Hip*. New York: Horizon Press, 1963.

Jazz humor.

Finkelstein, S. W. *Jazz, A People's Music*. New York: Citadel Press, 1948.

Good analytical text that attempts to fit jazz into its place in musical history.

———— ————. London: Jazz Book Club, 1964.

———— ————. New York: Da Capo, 1975.

Foreman, Ronald Clifford. "Jazz and Race Records, 1920–32: Their Origins and Their Significance for the Record Industry and Society." Ph.D. dissertation, University of Illinois, 1968.
   A historical analysis, 1920–32, of records for sale to the Negro audience. Examines the sociological conditions that produced these recordings.

Freeman, Bud. *If You Know of a Better Life, Please Tell Me*. Dublin, Ireland: Bashall Eaves, 1976.
   Collection of anecdotal memoirs on various aspects of jazz music and musicians by a leading tenor saxophonist.

Gammond, Peter, and Clayton, Peter. *Fourteen Miles on a Clear Night: An Irreverent, Skeptical and Affectionate Book about Jazz Records*. London: Peter Owen, 1966.
   Collection of humorous anecdotes about jazz.

———— ————. London: Jazz Book Club, 1967.

———— ————. *Know about Jazz*. London: Blackie, 1963.
   Introductory primer.

———— ————. Toronto: Ryerson Press, 1964.

Garwood, Donald. *Masters of Instrumental Blues Guitar*. New York: Oak Publications, 1967.
   Includes a brief analytical examination of the blues.

Gleason, Ralph Joseph, ed. *Jam Session: An Anthology of Jazz*. New York: Putnams, 1958.
   Essay collection with bibliography. Includes an important early essay on Bix Beiderbecke.

———— ————. London: Peter Davies, 1958.

———— ————. London: Jazz Book Club, 1961.

Godbolt, Jim. *All This and 10%*. London: Hale, 1976.
   Interesting mainly because it presents a virtually undocumented angle—that of the band agent—providing Godbolt's experiences in the postwar British jazz scene up to 1970.

Goddard, Chris. *Jazz Away from Home*. London: Paddington Press, 1979.

Goldberg, Isaac. *Jazz Music, What It Is and How to Understand It*. Girard, Kans.: Haldeman-Julius, 1927.

Gonzales, Babs. *I Paid My Dues: Good Times–No Bread*. New York: Lancer Books, 1967.

————, and Weston, Paul. *Boptionary: What Is Bop?* Hollywood: Capitol Records, 1941.

Gray, James M. "An Analysis of Melodic Devices in Selected Improvisations of Charlie Parker." Master's thesis, Ohio University, 1966.

Each improvisation is analyzed in terms of phrases, cadences, conjunct and disjunct motion, and sequential patterns. Includes transcriptions of four solos.

Green, Benny. *Drums in My Ears: Jazz in Our Time*. New York: Horizon Press, 1973.

A collection of articles on a variety of musicians and topics. Includes a chapter on saxophonists and one on the avant-garde. Well written.

—— ——. London: Davis-Paynter, 1973.

——. *The Reluctant Art: Five Studies in the Growth of Jazz*. London: MacGibbon and Kee, 1962.

Essays on the work of Benny Goodman, Billie Holiday, Bix Beiderbecke, Lester Young, and Charlie Parker.

—— ——. New York: Horizon Press, 1963.

—— ——. London: Jazz Book Club, 1964.

—— ——. Plainview, N.Y.: Books for Libraries Press, 1975.

Gridley, Mark C. *Jazz Styles*. Englewood Cliffs, N.J.: Prentice-Hall, 1978.

An examination of jazz styles; attempts to explain how jazz is produced. A music appreciation book dealing with jazz.

Griffin, Nard. *To Be or Not to Bop*. New York: Leo B. Workman, 1948.

An excellent examination of bebop and the musicians who played it.

Grime, Kitty (compiler). *Jazz at Ronnie Scott's*. London: Robert Hale, 1979.

Also contains photographs by Valerie Wilmer.

Grossman, William, and Farrell, Jack. *The Heart of Jazz*. New York: New York University Press, 1956.

Scholarly approach to the work of West Coast "revivalist" jazz musicians.

—— ——. London: Vision Press, 1958.

—— ——. New York: Da Capo, 1976.

——. *Jazz and Western Culture*. New York: New York University Press, 1956.

Handy, D. Antoinette. *Black Music*. Ettrick, Va.: B. M. and M., 1974.

A brief volume containing personal comments on a wide number of topics, including a few jazz concerts.

Harris, Rex. *Enjoying Jazz*. London: Phoenix House, 1960.
Young person's guide to traditional jazz, with bibliography.
——— ———. New York: Roy, 1960.
——— ———. London: Jazz Book Club, 1961.
——— ———. London: Phoenix House, 1963.
Harrison, Max. *A Jazz Retrospect*. Newton Abbot, England: David and Charles, 1976.
A collection of periodical articles that reveal different attitudes on the part of well-established performers toward aspects of their performances.
——— ———. Boston: Crescendo, 1976.
———, et al. *Modern Jazz, the Essential Records*. London: Aquarius Books, 1975.
An analysis of jazz recordings between 1945 and 1970. An excellent book.
Heaton, P. *Jazz*. London: Burke, 1964.
A primer of jazz suitable for the newcomer.
——— ———. Toronto: Ambassador Press, 1964.
Hennessey, Thomas Joseph. "From Jazz to Swing: Black Jazz Musicians and Their Music, 1917–1935." Ph.D. dissertation, Northwestern University, 1973.
A discussion of the change in jazz from a black folk music to a national popular music, 1917–1935.

Hentoff, Nat. *Jazz Is*. New York: Random House, 1976.
A selective guide and tribute to the jazz life, the players, and the music. A well-written book that tries to depict both the personal and professional personality of some of the greatest jazz musicians.
——— ———. London: W. H. Allen, 1978.
——— ———. New York: Avon Books, 1978.
———, and Williams, Martin, eds. *Jazz Review*. Millwood, N.Y.: Kraus Reprint Co., 1973.
A reprinting of the first four volumes of the periodical *Jazz Review*.

Hobson, Wilder. *American Jazz Music*.
See p. 53.

Hodeir, Andre. *Jazz: Its Evolution and Essence*.
See p. 53.

———. *Toward Jazz*. Translated by Noel Burch. New York: Grove Press, 1962.
Essay collection.

———— ————. London: Jazz Book Club, 1965.

———— ————. New York: Da Capo, 1976.

————. *The Worlds of Jazz*. New York: Grove Press, 1972.

    A critique and analysis of jazz music and musicians. Because of its allegorical devices and the fact that it reads more like a novel than a documentary, this well-written book is more for those knowledgeable about jazz.

Horricks, Raymond. *These Jazzmen of Our Time*.

    See p. 85.

James, B. *Essays on Jazz*. London: Sidgwick and Jackson, 1961.

———— ————. London: Jazz Book Club, 1960s.

————. *Living Forwards*. London: Cassell, 1961.

    Biography of a leading British music critic who frequently writes about jazz.

Jazz Guitarists; Collected Interviews from "Guitar Player" Magazine. Saratoga, Calif.: Guitar Player Productions, 1975.

    Includes a brief article on the evolution of jazz guitar by Leonard Feather.

Jazz Ways: A Yearbook of Hot Music. Edited by G. S. Rosenthal. Cincinnati: Jazz Ways, 1946.

———— ————. London: Musicians Press, 1947.

Jones, Le Roi, and Neal, Larry. *Black Fire: An Anthology of Afro-American Writing*. New York: Morrow, 1968.

    Contains one chapter on the avant-garde by A. B. Spellman.

Jones, Max, and McCarthy, Albert J., eds. *Jazz Review: A Miscellany*. London: Jazz Music Books, 1945.

    A selection of notes and essays on live and recorded jazz, most of which were written in the United States before the end of World War II.

Jones, R. P. *Jazz*. London: Methuen, 1963.

    For children.

———— ————. New York: Roy Publications, 1963.

Jost, Ekkehard. *Free Jazz*.

    See p. 61.

King, Jeffrey Michael. "Developing a Guide to the Techniques of Imitating Select Commercial Music Styles."

    See p. 174.

Kofsky, Frank. *Black Nationalism and the Revolution in Music*.

    See p. 23.

Krehbiel, Henry E. *Afro-American Folksongs*.

    See p. 14.

Kriss, Eric. *Barrelhouse and Boogie Piano*. New York: Oak Publications, 1974.

Includes a number of transcriptions and a bibliography.

—————. *Six Blues-Roots Pianists*.

See p. 38.

Larkin, P. *All What Jazz: A Record Diary, 1961–68*. London: Faber, 1970.

Collection of articles from the *Daily Telegraph*.

————— —————. New York: St. Martins, 1970.

Leonard, Neil. "The Acceptance of Jazz by Whites in the United States, 1918–1942."

See p. 68.

Lindsay, Martin. *Teach Yourself Jazz*.

See p. 174.

Longstreet, Stephen. *The Real Jazz, Old and New*.

See p. 64.

McCarthy, Albert J. *Jazzbook 1947*. London: Editions Poetry, 1947.

—————. *Jazzbook 1955*. London: Cassell, 1955.

—————. *The PL Yearbook of Jazz*. London: Editions Poetry, 1946. Essay collections

—————. *The Trumpet in Jazz*. London: Citizen Press, 1945.

—————, and Jones, M., eds. *Piano Jazz*. London: Jazz Music Books, 1945.

Biographical sketches of jazz pianists.

McRae, B. *The Jazz Cataclysm*. London: Dent, 1967.

Covers modern jazz and is particularly good on Ornette Coleman and his "free-form" style. There is a selective discography with each of the twelve chapters.

————— —————. New York: Barnes, 1967.

Marquis, Donald, *Finding Buddy Bolden*. Goshen, Ind.: Pinchpenny Press, 1978.

The story behind the search for information in writing *In Search of Buddy Bolden*. Answers how, where, and when.

Matthew, B. *Trad Mad*.

See p. 58.

Mellers, Wilfred. *Music in a New Found Land: Themes and Development in the History of American Music*. London: Barrie and Rockliff, 1964.

Required reading for all jazz students.

————— —————. New York: Knopf, 1965.

Merriam, Alan P. "Instruments and Instrumental Usages in the History of Jazz." Master's thesis, Northwestern University, 1948.

Part two of this paper provides a historical coverage of each individual instrument.

Miller, Paul E., and Venables, R., eds. *Jazz Book: From the Esquire Jazz Books 1944–1946*. London: Peter Davies, 1947.

Miller, W. R. *The World of Pop Music and Jazz*. St. Louis: Concordia, 1965.

Morgan, Alun, and Horricks, Raymond. *Modern Jazz: A Survey of Developments since 1939*. London: Gollancz, 1956.

———— ————. Westport, Conn.: Greenwood Press, 1977.

Morgan, Robert. "The Music and Life of Robert Graettinger." See p. 96.

Music Makers: A "Yale" Album of —— Your Favorite Band Leaders. London: Yale Music Corp., n.d.

Myrus, D. *Ballads, Blues and the Big Beat*. New York: Macmillan. 1966.

————. *I Like Jazz*. New York: Collier-Macmillan, 1964.

Ephemeral, anecdotal, and of no permanent value. Useful as an introductory text for children.

Newton, Francis. *The Jazz Scene*. London: MacGibbon and Kee, 1959.

Includes an examination of the business setup, the jazz public, and the influence of jazz on serious and popular music. There is a detailed guide to sources at the end of the book and a guide to further reading that is brief but very useful. Required reading for the student of jazz.

———— ————. New York: Da Capo, 1975.

Ostransky, Leroy. *The Anatomy of Jazz*. Seattle: University of Washington Press, 1960.

Well-documented analytical text that includes a comprehensive and international bibliography of books and periodicals on jazz.

———— ————. Westport, Conn.: Greenwood Press, 1974.

————. *Understanding Jazz*. Englewood Cliffs, N.J.: Prentice-Hall, 1977.

A nontechnical book aimed at creating appreciation for jazz.

Owens, Thomas. "Charlie Parker: Techniques of Improvisation. Volumes I and II." Ph.D. dissertation, University of California at Los Angeles, 1974.

The author has used about 250 of Parker's solos for this study. Much of the paper is devoted to Parker's use of principal motives, about 100 of which appear throughout his work. The author also applies Schenkerian analysis to his work.

————. "Improvisation Techniques of the Modern Jazz Quartet." Master's thesis, University of California at Los Angeles, 1965.

An examination of the Modern Jazz Quartet both individually and as a group. Contains musical examples, a long bibliography, a discography, and a glossary.

Panassie, Hugues. *Hot Jazz: The Guide to Swing Music*. Translated by Lyle and Eleanor Dowling. London: Cassell, 1936.

———— ————. New York: Witmark, 1936.

———— ————. Westport, Conn.: Negro Universities Press, 1970.

————. *The Real Jazz*. New York: Smith and Durrell, 1942.

Much more accurate assessment than *Hot Jazz*.

———— ————. 2nd rev. ed. Translated by Anne S. Williams. New York: Barnes, 1960.

———— ————. London: Yoseloff, 1960.

———— ————. London: Jazz Book Club, 1967.

———— ————. Westport, Conn.: Greenwood Press, 1973.

Paul, E. *That Crazy American Music*. Indianapolis: Bobbs-Merrill, 1957.

Ephemeral and somewhat misleading account of jazz.

———— ————. Port Washington, N.Y.: Kennikat, 1970.

————. *That Crazy Music: The Story of North American Jazz*. London: Muller, 1957.

Pease, Sharon. *Boogie Woogie Fundamentals*. Chicago: Forster Music Publications, 1945.

Pepin, M. Natalie. "Dance and Jazz Elements in the Piano Music of Maurice Ravel." D.M.A. dissertation, Boston University, 1972.

Pleasants, H. *Death of a Music? The Decline of the European Tradition and the Rise of Jazz*. London: Gollancz, 1961.

Penetrating analysis of modern classical music and jazz.

———— ————. London: Jazz Book Club, 1962.

————. *Serious Music—and All That Jazz: An Adventure in Musical Criticism*. London: Gollancz, 1969.

———— ————. New York: Simon and Schuster, 1971.

Postgate, John. *A Plain Man's Guide to Jazz*. London: Hanover Books, 1973.

Written in a slightly patronizing but provocative style, this book attempts a review of the whole field with only partial success. It is most perceptive in dealing with the early pioneers, the white innovators, and the mainstreamers; not as good on the avant-garde.

Pyke, Launcelot Allen. "Jazz, 1920 to 1927: An Analytical Study." Ph.D. dissertation, University of Iowa, 1962.

A very good work based on analysis of ten transcribed jazz tunes.

Quin, Ann. *Tripticks*. London: Calder and Boyer, 1972.

Fuses jazz improvisation and the techniques of the comic strip.

Quinn, James Joseph. "An Examination of the Evolution of Jazz as It Relates to the Pre-Literate, Literate, and Post-Literate Percepts of Marshall McLuhan." Ph.D. dissertation, George Peabody College for Teachers, 1972.

An examination of the various styles of jazz regarding performance practices, musical textures, and structural organization.

Ramsay, Jean Pamela. "Jazz Influences in the Music of Maurice Ravel." Master's thesis, California State University at Long Beach, 1975.

An examination of selected works written between 1920 and 1931. Also points out how Ravel acquired his knowledge of jazz.

Roach, Hildred. *Black American Music—Past and Present*. Boston: Crescendo, 1973.

Depicts the mutual influence of black Afro-American and European music. Focuses on black composers with a brief biography and some analyses of their compositional techniques.

————— —————. Boston: Crescendo, 1976.

Rober, Robert W. "A Stylistic Analysis of Ten Selected Dance Band Stock Orchestrations." Master's thesis, North Texas State University, 1960.

An excellent study that analyzes principles and techniques used in arranging popular ballads for dance bands.

Russell, Ross. *Jazz Style in Kansas City and the Southwest*.

See p. 59.

Sargeant, W. *Jazz: A History*.

See p. 55.

—————. *Jazz: Hot and Hybrid*.

See p. 54.

Schuller, Gunther. *Early Jazz*.
See p. 65.

Secrets of Dance Band Success. New York: Mills Music, 1949.

Shapiro, Nat, and Hentoff, Nat, *The Jazz Makers*.
See p. 86.

Shaw, Kirby H. "Inflections for the Jazz Choir: A Practical Guide." D.M.A. dissertation, University of Washington, 1976.
Deals with the style characteristics of jazz in a vocal setting. Provides an analysis of jazz singing styles.

Shockett, Bernard I. "A Stylistic Study of the Blues as Recorded by Jazz Instrumentalists, 1917–1931." Ph.D. dissertation, New York University, 1964.
Traces stylistic characteristics of the blues in jazz instrumentalists.

Sidran, Ben. *Black Talk: How the Music of Black America Created a Radical Alternative to the Values of Western Literary Tradition*. New York: Holt, Rinehart and Winston, 1971.
An excellent examination of Afro-American art music from bebop to the new jazz.

Simon, George T. *The Feeling of Jazz*. New York: Simon and Schuster, 1961.

Sinclair, John, and Levin, Robert. *Music and Politics*.
See p. 24.

Smith, Hugh L. "The Literary Manifestation of a Liberal Romanticism in American Jazz." Ph.D. dissertation, University of New Mexico, 1955.

Specht, Paul L. *How They Became Name Bands*. New York: Fine Arts Publications, 1941.
Gives advice on what some successful bandleaders have done to gain success.

Spellman, A. B. *Black Music, Four Lives*.
See p. 87.

Stewart, Milton Lee. "Structural Development in the Jazz Improvisational Technique of Clifford Brown." Ph.D. dissertation, University of Michigan, 1973.
A structural analysis applying the Schenkerian method to all four choruses of "I Can Dream, Can't I?"

Sudnow, David. *Ways of the Hand: The Organization of Improvised Conduct*. Cambridge, Mass.: Harvard University Press, 1978.
An account of how the hands learn keyboard improvisation.

Sullivan, Franklin D. "Music Listening—Jazz, Music: 5635.893" Miami, Dade County Public Schools, 1972.

A survey of jazz music and musicians, primarily since 1950.

Summerfield, Maurice J. *The Jazz Guitar: Its Evolution and Its Players*. (No location): Ashley Mark, 1978.

Tanner, Paul. "A Technical Analysis of the Development of Jazz." See p. 55.

————, and Gerow, Maurice. *A Study of Jazz*. See p. 55.

Taylor, William Edward. "The History and Development of Jazz Piano: A New Perspective for Educators." Ed.D. dissertation, University of Massachusetts, 1975.

A history of the piano in jazz, with musical examples, bibliography, and discography. Well written.

Traill, Sinclair, ed. *Concerning Jazz*. London: Faber, 1957.

Collection of essays on various topics, most by British critics.

———— ————. London: Jazz Book Club, 1958.

————. *Play That Music: A Guide to Playing Jazz*. See p. 178.

————, and Lascelles, Gerald, eds. *Just Jazz*. Vol. I—London: Peter Davies, 1957; vol. II—London: Peter Davies, 1958; vol. III—London: Landsborough Publications, 1959; vol. IV—London: Souvenir Press, 1960.

Essay collections and comprehensive discographies of each year.

———— ————. Volume IV. London: Jazz Book Club, 1961.

Trone, Dolly G. "The Influence of the World War (1917) on the Art of Music in America." See p. 69.

Tuozzolo, James Michael. "Trumpet Techniques in Selected Works of Four Contemporary American Composers: Gunther Schuller, Mayer Kupferman, William Sydeman and William Frabizio." D.M.A. dissertation, University of Miami, 1972.

Includes some jazz techniques.

Ulanov, Barry. *A Handbook of Jazz*. New York: Viking, 1957.

———— ————. London: Hutchinson, 1958.

Ullman, Michael. *Jazz Lives*. Washington, D.C.: New Republic, 1979.

Von Haupt, Lois. "Jazz: An Historical and Analytical Study." Master's thesis, New York University, 1945.

Wheaton, Jack. "The Technological and Sociological Influences on Jazz as an Art Form in America."
See p. 69.

White, Mark. *The Observer's Book of Big Bands*.
See p. 68.

———. *The Observer's Book of Jazz*.
See p. 56.

Williams, Martin T., ed. *The Art of Jazz: Essays on the Nature and Development of Jazz*. New York: Oxford University Press, 1959.

Essays on all aspects of jazz. Originally published as journal articles or as sleeve notes to record albums. Each item is introduced by the editor; source and date of the original publication is provided; brief discographies are attached to each essay.

——— ———. New York: Grove Press, 1960.

——— ———. London: Cassell, 1960.

——— ———. London: Jazz Book Club, 1962.

———. *Jazz Masters in Transition, 1957–69*. New York: Macmillan, 1970.

Observations on the important jazz musicians of this decade.

———. *Jazz Panorama: From the Pages of "Jazz Review."* New York: Crowell-Collier, 1962.

Carefully selected pieces that add up to a necessary book for anyone with more than a routine interest in jazz. Spoiled by the lack of an index.

——— ———. New York: Crowell, 1964.

——— ———. London: Jazz Book Club, 1965.

———. *The Jazz Tradition*. New York: Oxford University Press, 1970.

An examination of sixteen major figures in the history of jazz. Individual style characteristics are analyzed, along with the value of their contributions and their influence.

———. *Where's the Melody?: A Listener's Introduction to Jazz*. New York: Pantheon Books, 1966.

Analytical primer on jazz.

——— ———. New York: Minerva Books, 1967.

——— ———. New York: Pantheon Books, 1969.

Williams, Peter. *Bluff Your Way in Folk and Jazz*. London: Wolfe, 1969.

Williamson, K., ed. *This Is Jazz*. London: Newnes, 1960.

Essay collection including contributions on Count Basie, Jack

Teagarden, Miles Davis, Bill Broonzy, Duke Ellington, Ella Fitzgerald, Billie Holiday, Sarah Vaughan, and Jelly Roll Morton.

———— ————. London: Jazz Book Club, 1961.

Wilmer, Valerie. *As Serious as Your Life: The Story of the New Jazz*.

See p. 61.

————. *Jazz People*.

See p. 87.

Wilson, C. *Brandy of the Damned: Discourses of a Musical Eclectic*. London: John Baker, 1964.

————. *Chords and Discords: Purely Personal Opinions on Music*. New York: Crown, 1966.

American edition of *Brandy of the Damned*.

Wilson, John S. *Jazz: The Transition Years: 1940–1960*. New York: Appleton-Century-Crofts, 1966.

Well-produced and useful book. The last two chapters are particularly valuable, as they survey the impact of jazz in the world outside the United States and on mass audiences. Glossary, discography, and reading list are included.

Zeiger, Albert Louis. "A Study of Certain Similarities between Classical Music (1700–1961) and Jazz (1900–1961) Found in Instrumental Compositions." Ed.D. dissertation, Columbia University Teachers College, 1961.

Compares the aspects of melody, rhythm, harmony, tone color, and form between Western European art music and jazz. Musical excerpts from classical works are compared with those of jazz works.

Chapter 6

Reference Sources

Jazz was not, until relatively recent times, well covered by general reference works, and some of the major encyclopedias selected contributors who seemed to have little understanding of the complexities and subtleties of the music. Specialized music dictionaries, such as the *Oxford Companion to Music* and Grove's *Dictionary of Music and Musicians*, have also been generally inadequate, although Hugues Panassie contributed to the fifth edition of the latter in 1954. His contribution was a reasonably good survey of traditional styles of jazz, but completely ignored the more modern idioms.

By the 1960s, the two leading general encyclopedias, *Encyclopaedia Britannica* and *Chambers Encyclopedia*, had improved their coverage and their 1966 editions had useful, if brief, articles on jazz by informed critics.

The doyen of the specialized jazz reference work is undoubtedly Leonard Feather. His work is widely acclaimed, and rightly so, since his catholic and wide-ranging approach has provided the jazz student with access to a great deal of basic information. Feather produced a series of books at regular intervals, beginning in 1955, in which the basic formula remains fairly constant. Each contains a main section with biographical details of musicians, arrangers, critics, and composers, including data on instruments played, date and places of birth, career details, main recordings, and addresses. Supplementary sections include articles on aspects of jazz, discographies, a bibliography, and lists of organizations and record companies. *The Encyclopedia of Jazz* (1955) was supplemented initially by the *Encyclopedia Yearbook of Jazz* the following year, and then by the *New Yearbook of Jazz* (1958) before a second edition of the main work appeared in 1960. In 1967, *The Encyclopedia of Jazz in the Sixties* appeared. This followed the same pattern but was particularly strong on details concerning the younger musicians. *The New Edition of the Encyclopedia of Jazz* (1970) was a completely revised and enlarged edition of the previous work and, in 1976, with the assistance of Ira Gitler, Feather produced his *Encyclopedia of Jazz in the Seventies*. This is another autonomous volume that examines the ten-year period since *Encyclopedia of Jazz in the Sixties* appeared. The seventies volume includes, as well as the usual features, a useful section on jazz education by Charles Suber, a guide to jazz films by Leonard Mattin, and a bibliography of books published between 1966 and 1975.

John Chilton, the British writer and musician, has made substantial contributions to the literature, and his work is mentioned elsewhere in this guide. His *Who's Who of Jazz* (1970) is a tour de force that includes biographical details of over 1,000 American jazz musicians. This work is constantly referred to by broadcasters on jazz and by authors in search of good factual detail, since Chilton uses reliable facts, although he does not permit himself critical comments. Roger D. Kinkle's massive four-volume work *The Complete Encyclopedia of Popular Music and Jazz, 1900–1950* (1974) contains over 6,000 pages. At the other end of the scale and very specialized is Samuel Charters's *Jazz: New Orleans, 1885–1963* (1963), which is an index to the Negro musicians of New Orleans. This originally appeared in 1958, and was issued in the revised edition by a different publisher. The book is divided by periods with sections on 1885–99; 1899–1919; 1919–31 and 1931 to date. Each of these sections is further divided into biographies of musicians (in the case of section one this is further divided into the Downtown and the Uptown musicians) and details of the major brass bands and orchestras. The second edition adds some supplementary material in addenda at the end of each section. Appendixes on discographical and source material are also included, and there are indexes to names of musicians, names of bands, names of halls, cabarets, theaters, etc., in New Orleans; tune titles; and cities and towns in the Delta region of Louisiana. A more encyclopedic coverage is found in *New Orleans Jazz: A Family Album* (1967), a valuable guide to the jazz musicians of New Orleans written by Al Rose and Edmond Souchon. It includes over 1,000 biographical sketches, as well as comprehensive lists of jazz and brass bands belonging to the city. There is a unique collection of over 500 photographs, many of which were previously unpublished. Another work of interest is *Guide to Jazz* (1956) by Hugues Panassie and Madeleine Gautier. This was originally published in French in 1954, two years before the English translation appeared. The title of the British edition is *Dictionary of Jazz*. It contains the usual Panassie prejudices, and one critic described it as "a collection of opinions, peppered with facts." Nevertheless, within its limitations, it is of good value and is useful.

The Encyclopedia of Australian Jazz (1976) by Hayes, Scribner, and Magee is useful for assessing the impact of jazz in Australia, while *Jazz Now* (1976), edited by Robert Cotterrell, is an attempt to give a reasonably clear and accurate view of jazz activity in Britain. This book was published in association with the Jazz Centre Society, which has an important influence on jazz in Britain and has achieved some recognition from the Arts Council and other official bodies. Cotterrell's book includes a substantial reference section, including a directory of British musicians. A similar, but much slimmer volume on *Finnish Jazz* (1974) is edited by Ake Granholm and devotes most of its space to biographical details of jazz musicians in Finland.

More sociological than musical is Robert Gold's *Jazz Talk* (1975) which is subtitled "A Dictionary of the Colorful Language That Has Emerged from America's Own Music." It is a comprehensive and readable listing of jazz slang and terminology. Each word is defined and traced back to its earliest recorded use. Its semantic development is given, and a note of its currency or degree of obsolescence is included. The book is the product of scholarly research that updates the earlier 1964 edition. This appeared as *Jazz Lexicon: An A-Z Dictionary of Jazz Terms in the Vivid Idiom of America's Most Successful Non-Conformist Minority*.

Jazz discography is an esoteric subculture with experts of its own, and our first edition quoted extensively from Paul Sheatsley's paper in a 1964 issue of *Record Research*. This brilliantly covers the field to that date and it is still appropriate to quote in some detail:

The first important work of discography is Schleman's *Rhythm on Record*. This book is subtitled "A Who's Who and Register of Recorded Dance Music, 1906–1936" and it was published in England by the periodical *Melody Maker* early in 1936. A few months later in the same year came the first edition of the French critic Delaunay's work *Hot Discography*. It is interesting to compare these two pioneer compilations in the light of later developments in the discographical field. Schleman is largely forgotten now, and his work has become a collector's item, but his approach had much to recommend it. The listings were arranged alphabetically by artist, from Aaronson's Commanders to Zutty (Singleton)'s Band. Although Schleman did not exclude blues artists, such as Lizzie Miles, Bobby Leecan, Sylvester Weaver and Victoria Spivey (all of whom were listed later only partially or not at all by Delauney), the sub-title of his work accurately describes his interest in detailing recorded dance music. Thus, he includes along with various "hot" artists, whom we are now accustomed to find in jazz discographies, the full output of such as Jack Hylton, George Olsen and other "popular" dance band leaders of the day, including many British and American popular artists whom most jazz collectors would now find of absolutely no interest, but who, it should be noted, are still of some historical value. Additionally, Schleman planned and described his volume as "A Who's Who as Well as a Register." Before the discographical listings of each artist, Schleman gives a short biography and thus foreshadowed Leonard Feather's *Encyclopedia of Jazz* and the Panassie-Gautier *Dictionary of Jazz*. In terms of discographical detail, Schleman is sadly wanting by later standards. His personnel listings and recording dates are for the most part collective ones and the tune titles are listed, not chronologically but alphabetically by record label, with a catalogue number following each . . . Schleman was also uncritical of factual information reaching him and his book contains numerous major errors. He was outside the mainstream of "hot" record research, and his work never inspired later researchers as Delaunay's did, but it is interesting to speculate on the progress of discography if his principles of all-inclusiveness and biographical data had prevailed. Beyond its nostalgic interest *Rhythm on Record* even today provides one of the best sources of information about the personnel, recordings and bookings of the popular dance groups of the 1920s.

In view of Sheatsley's final comment, it is pleasing that Robert Hagelstein of the Greenwood Press has produced an excellent facsimile reprint of Schleman. This publisher has also made available on microfiche many early jazz periodicals, including some of specific interest to the discographer.

The French critic Charles Delaunay, who has edited jazz journals and written an excellent life of Django Reinhardt, is regarded by many as the "father of jazz discography" and, as Sheatsley stated, he inspired the field. The various and improving editions of *Hot Discography* have proved to be vital in the beginnings of a scholarly approach to jazz music. Discography is especially important in jazz because it provides historical data, particularly in those fields where little is formally documented. Delaunay is owed a great debt by all researchers in this subject. Sheatsley continues:

> Delaunay's approach was entirely different. As his title indicates . . .
> he was interested in "le jazz hot" and drew a sharp distinction between this and commercial or dance music. Furthermore, he followed Panassie's classic view of the development of jazz, from the New Orleans pioneers up the River to Chicago, thence to New York, culminating in the large and small hot Negro bands of the 1930s with their white imitators, and his discography was deliberately ordered to show this development. Instead of listing the artists alphabetically, Delaunay adopted a historical approach—starting his book with King Oliver, the Original Dixieland Jazz Band, and the New Orleans Rhythm Kings; then proceeding to discographies of the great soloists—Armstrong, Dodds, Ladnier, etc.; the great blues singers—Bessie Smith and Ma Rainey and pioneer large orchestras—Henderson, McKinney, Ellington, thence to Beiderbecke, the Chicagoans, the Nichols, Mole, Lang and Venuti combinations; Goodman, Teagarden and the Dorseys, and finally a miscellaneous selection of studio groups, ordered alphabetically by artist. As we shall see, this selective and doctrinaire approach was to have serious disadvantages, but despite Schleman's precedence chronologically and despite the weaknesses in his own approach, Charles Delaunay is the undoubted father of discography as we know it today. It was he who first saw and utilized the importance of master numbers and who from the beginning aimed at the ideal of listing each artist's work in matrix number order, with full personnels and recording date for each session.
>
> The 1936 edition was severely limited in this respect, but successive revisions in 1938, 1943, and especially in 1948, came closer to the ultimate goal, as new knowledge became available. Though the post-war edition was greatly expanded and the claim made that "this work lists nearly all discovered recordings," Delaunay's approach still remained quite selective. In this 1948 edition, post 1930 artists are grouped alphabetically without regard to style, but the first half of the book still follows the historical chronological approach. As Delaunay says in his foreword, "Some readers might prefer for their own convenience a strictly alphabetical order, but that would destroy the historical aim of this work, which turns a simple enumeration of recordings into a fascinating account of the evolution of an art form." It is true that Delaunay's selective emphasis on the major figures of early jazz history and his groupings of records into Chicago, New York and other such sections added glamour to the listings and did give a coherent if somewhat oversimplified picture of jazz development, but it is also true that

this approach produced some notable omissions and distortions, e.g. all of the records on which each major artist appeared are listed under his name, even when he was merely a side-man or accompanist to others. . . For a decade or more, Delaunay was the basic jazz discographer, and his influence was pervasive.

Orin Blackstone, the American discographer, also played a significant part in documenting much of the elusive detail associated with the early days of jazz recording. His *Index to Jazz* is another standard work of discography that was out of print for some years before being made available by University Microfilms in a paperbound photocopied facsimile edition. Paul Sheatsley says:

It was Orin Blackstone in New Orleans in the years 1945–1948 who almost single-handed managed to complete the first attempt at a definitive listing of all records of jazz or blues interest. Blackstone's four-part *Index to Jazz* was ordered from A to Z, and as explained in his foreword "because it was conceived as an index, this list follows a rigid alphabetical arrangement, according to the artists' names under which the records were originally issued." . . . Blackstone set another important standard when he stated explicitly, "It is not the purpose of this index to evaluate in any way the records listed, except that they be of interest to the jazz collector." One deficiency in Blackstone's work was his ordering of each artist's product by catalogue number rather than matrix number. This does not matter too much in most cases because the importance of the original index lies in the bare listings rather than in the richness of his discographical detail. Dates, personnels, master numbers and even instrumentation were often lacking, since Blackstone often had to rely solely on old catalogues, and no other information was available at the time, but where fuller details were known and sides from two different sessions were coupled, the ordering by release number resulted in awkward parenthetical notes to see some other date for the personnel on one of the sides. The first edition of the index was clearly announced as a trial run and the second edition was promised at an early date. Sure enough, only a year after the original part four appeared, part one of a new loose-leaf edition was mailed to subscribers. It was an impressive job. The original part one had been published in 1945, the new edition of A to E included all records issued during the intervening four years.

If Blackstone had been permitted but three more years of productive effort on the revised *Index to Jazz*, it is probable that his work would have become the standard reference for jazz discography up to the year 1950 . . . personal affairs forced his retirement from the field at this point and never again was it to be possible for one man to capture and publish the entire jazz catalog.

The major early British contribution to discography was the *Directory of Recorded Jazz and Swing Music*, which is a basic, scholarly, and useful work of reference that remained incomplete after six volumes and seven years of effort. It is often known as the "Jazz Directory" and it is under this abbreviated title that Sheatsley discusses it in the following terms:

But England, the home of Schleman, had again picked up the discographical torch. Soon after Delaunay's 1948 edition was published and almost concurrently with the revision of Blackstone's part 1, appeared volume 1 of *Jazz Directory* compiled by Dave Carey, Albert McCarthy, and Ralph Venables, a trio whose qualifications for the task were impeccable. Like Blackstone, the Directory disclaimed a selective approach: "We have admitted on the one hand Negro spiritual, gospel and 'race' recordings (of obvious historical and sociological importance) and, on the other, an extremely liberal presentation of swing and be-bop in order to reflect adequately the complete picture. . . .The non-inclusion of authentic calypso and hill-billy artists is regrettable . . . but insufficient research into their respective spheres had made it impossible to assess values at this time. . . . Commercial renderings have been included only where the prestige of the artist merits so doing or because soloists of value are featured. It seems certain that none would wish us to put in countless quasi-hot recordings by sundry aggregations, having no bearing on the subject."

A comparison between the first volume of the Directory (covering letters A and B) and the first volume of Blackstone's revised Index leaves little to choose between them. Each has a few artists, issues, dates or master numbers which the other lacks, but they are remarkably similar. . . . The Directory is far better produced, neatly printed with lots of white space. The index was photo off-set, mostly in double column format and presents a cluttered appearance. The loose-leaf idea so often recommended for discographies proved impractical (at least in my experience) since the pages gradually fell off like leaves as the volume received more and more handling. As "C-D" and subsequent volumes of the Directory appeared, this discography soon became indispensable to collectors. There was considerable delay in publishing the later volumes, and the work was eventually abandoned with volume 6, K to L. The exceedingly high cost of production in such an attractive format and perhaps even more formidably the rising flood of new jazz labels and the bewildering output of jazz and blues material on long playing and 45 r.p.m. at that time caused this sad event. It might have been better to limit the Directory's objectives, say to 1948, aiming for comprehensiveness up to that date. There would then have been available perhaps by 1952 or even earlier, a complete general discography covering all artists from A to Z for the first thirty years of jazz recording.

Brian Rust's *Jazz Records, 1897–1942* (fourth edition, published in 1978) first appeared as a private publication in 1961, and is now recognized as the basic jazz discography for those years. Rust has an unrivaled knowledge of recordings before 1940, and has shown a dogged determination to get it all into print. Rust's study of the discography of jazz of this period has resulted in a two volume work of great substance. Rust has also compiled a number of other works in more specialized areas, including *The Zonophone Studio House Bands* and *The HMV Studio House Bands*, both published in 1976. He is also joint author of *British Dance Bands* (1973).

Blues and Gospel Recordings, 1902–1942 (1964) by Robert Dixon and John Godrich complements Rust's work, and is widely regarded as the standard work in this section of the literature. *Blues Records, January 1943 to December 1966* (1968) was compiled by Mike Leadbitter and Neil Slaven as a companion volume to Dixon and Goodrich, but excluded gospel recordings. Of the comprehensive discographies, the set of volumes *Jazz Records: A Discography* by Jorgen Jepsen is quite outstanding. The Danish discographer has extended Rust's work by attempting to list all details of all jazz records from 1942 to 1962. He has also supplemented Carey and McCarthy's *Jazz Directory* and, for this reason, started his work with volume M–N. Volumes 6, 7, and 8 followed before Jepsen returned to complete volumes 1 to 4. His calculations went astray somewhat, and the total set consists of substantially more than planned. In the later volumes, Jepsen has widened his set limits, as can be seen from the bibliographical details given at the end of the chapter. This major discographical effort is already accepted as the standard work in the field.

A few further works deserve mention—the sixth edition of Delaunay, with the collaboration of Kurt Mohr, was published in France in 1951–52 under the title of *Hot Discographie Encyclopedique*. This was noteworthy because it marked a radical change in Delaunay's approach. He announced in his foreword that "this new discography, in contrast to preceding editions, will be issued in several volumes. This splitting into parts has obliged us to abandon the procedure followed in previous discographies of arrangement in sections according to affinities in style and to adopt a strictly alphabetical classification," and he adds that "the object of discography is to try to cover the entire output of recordings by the musicians and orchestras without regard to the value of the recordings. A work such as this must therefore include a considerable number of discs which do not merit acquisition by a collector but which must appear in the listing." Three volumes of *Hot Discographie Encyclopedique* appeared, bringing it alphabetically as far as Neal Hefti, but at that point publication ceased. The work was lagging behind, was less complete than *Jazz Directory*, and undoubtedly failed to sell for that reason. In 1960, Albert J. McCarthy, who had been concerned with *Jazz Directory*, made another notable contribution to discographical literature by the publication of *Jazz Discography 1958*. The purpose of this beautifully printed 271-page work was clearly stated by McCarthy in his introduction: "For some time, it has been obvious to all engaged in discographical research in the jazz field that the sheer volume of new issues is making the task of compiling a complete work and jazz directory almost impossible. It is essential to document the new issues as they appear, or within a reasonable time of their release, or else one will forever be bogged down in the task of filing comparatively new editions to the list." McCarthy attempted to list all items issued including reissues during the calendar year 1958, and he explicitly stated his intentions to compile future volumes on an annual basis. His journal *Jazz Monthly* issued a supplement listing newly released records between October 1962 and February 1966 and was a useful contribution toward continuing jazz discography.

The annual *Jazz Catalogue*, which commenced publication in 1960, provides a valuable listing of all jazz and blues issued on Bristish labels during the year under review. It has had a number of compilers in its time. It is also valuable to the bibliographer, since about one quarter of each volume is devoted to a comprehensive listing of books and articles. Coverage of this section extends beyond the purely jazz journals, adding substantially to its value as a reference work.

In more recent years, the emphasis in the discographical literature has switched to more specific topics, such as the recorded work of a single artist, an orchestra, or within a specific style of jazz. In addition, biodiscography has emerged as a favored way of examining in detail the recordings of major figures. This genre was developed very successfully by Walter C. Allen and Brian Rust in their *King Joe Oliver* (1955), which set new standards for this art. The book was a work of scholarship divided into three main sections, a bibliography, and five appendixes. The forty-three pages of section one are straight biography, while the brief section two assesses Oliver's work and influence. The discographical section consists of almost one hundred pages, and is exceptionally fine in its attention to detail. The bibliography includes references from thirty-three different publications and the appendixes include lists of orchestra itineraries, an index of recorded titles, and an index of musicians who worked with Oliver.

Another work of a similar excellent standard is Howard Waters's *Jack Teagarden's Music: His Career and Recordings* (1960). This is a later volume in the Jazz Monographs series published by Walter Allen that includes the Allen-Rust book on Oliver. There is a useful bibliography, and various indexes are a feature of a superb book. The work of Duke Ellington is documented fully in Luigi Sanfillipo's *General Catalogue of Duke Ellington's Recorded Music* (1964). This book contains all Ellington's output up to 1965, including radio and television transcriptions, v-discs, and films. This work is a continuation of Aaslund's *The "Wax Works" of Duke Ellington* (1954). From 1966 to date, *Duke Ellington's Story on Record* is continued by Luciano Massagli and some Italian colleagues.

Walter C. Allen's *Hendersonia* (1973) is number four of the Jazz Monograph series, and exhaustively covers the work of the Fletcher Henderson Orchestra in its 651 pages. Substantial and authoritative discographies on individual artists and bands include John Chilton on McKinney's Cotton Pickers (1978); Donald Connor on Benny Goodman (1958); John Flower on Glenn Miller; and Koster and Bakker on Charlie Parker (4 volumes, 1974–76). There are many more, and a selection of those available is listed in the bibliography to this chapter.

David Jasen's *Recorded Ragtime, 1897–1958* (1973) is a comprehensive discography of this specific area of jazz-related music. According to its author, it is *not* to be confused with a jazz discography, since it stresses the composition and the composer rather than the performer. A discography on *English Ragtime: A Discography 1898–1920* (1971) by Edward and Steven Walker covers a more restricted time period and geographic location.

The annotated record guides are aimed more at the general listener to jazz music. The earliest, and still one of the best, is Ramsey and Smith's *Jazz Record Book* (1942). Frederic Ramsey also produced a useful *Guide to Long Play Jazz Records* (1954), and two other important critical guides by John S. Wilson were published in the late 1950s under the titles of *Collectors Jazz: Modern* and *Collectors Jazz: Traditional and Swing.*

In the United Kingdom, *Recorded Jazz: A Critical Guide* (1958) by Rex Harris and Brian Rust provided useful critical notes on records up to 1957, but in the traditional field only. A more wide-ranging guide is *Jazz on Record* (1960) by Charles Fox and others, which is a useful guide to collecting the basic records. A revised and expanded edition of this volume by four of the leading British jazz critics appeared in 1968. This is a major tool for selecting a basic collection, and differs from the first edition in that it is not restricted to issues on British labels.

Max Harrison and some associates provided their choice of the "essential records" for the modern jazz collector in 1975. *Modern Jazz, the Essential Records* (1975) covers the period 1945–70 and, in the words of the preface, identifies all the musicians, great and small, whose contribution had real significance during 1945–70, analyzing their most representative LP's and showing how their work is related.

Other guides that need to be mentioned, since they might well be overlooked, are the catalogs of the gramophone record companies. Complete issues usually appear annually and regular supplements are published to keep them up to date. Many companies issue special catalogs for jazz with supplementary articles by jazz critics and sleeve-note writers.

Aids to jazz record collectors have included a directory listing collectors' names, addresses, and special interests, as well as works that assist in organizing a collection. An example of the former is *Who's Who in Jazz Collection* (1949) by William Love and Bill Rich, which is now very out of date.

The second category includes Derek Langridge's *Your Jazz Collection* (1970), which includes detailed guidance for the collector not only on the collecting of jazz records, books, and other materials, but also practical advice on their classification, cataloging, and arrangement. This same author's outline of a classification system for the literature of jazz was published in the British musical periodical *Brio* in 1967.

Compared to the discographical literature, the bibliographical side of jazz literature has been relatively neglected until fairly recent years. The first, and still one of the major published works in this field is Merriam and Benford's *A Bibliography of Jazz* (1954), which was published in Philadelphia by the American Folklore Society. This bibliography includes over 3,300 entries for books and periodical articles appearing before the end of 1950. The authors state that the work is not selective and entries are included that are both pro- and anti-jazz, well-written and ephemeral. Articles have been culled from both jazz and nonjazz magazines, but the bibliography makes no claim to completeness. Rather it is to be regarded as a "beginning toward the orderly gathering of the tremendous literature which has grown up around jazz music." It is divided into three parts —the first and major section consists of entries arranged alphabetically by author, and at the end of each a coding system indicates broadly what subject is discussed in the reference. Thirty-two categories range from "A and A" (analysis and appreciation) through "Tech" (technical equipment used in jazz).

The second section of the bibliography consists of a listing of magazines devoted wholly or in considerable part to jazz music. There are 113 entries in this section from all over the world. Many of the titles listed are now defunct. The third section consists of indexes to both subject and periodicals cited. This is a work of scholarship indispensable to any student of jazz literature.

The Literature of Jazz (1954), by Robert G. Reisner, formerly curator at the Institute of Jazz Studies, is also an important source book. The second revised and enlarged edition was published by the New York Public Library in

1959, and is a checklist of some 500 titles of books on jazz (including fiction) listed by author. There is also a separate list of background books and a selective list of some 850 periodical references. Reisner also included a listing of periodicals devoted wholly or principally to jazz published throughout the world at that time.

Carl Gregor Herzog zu Mecklenburg has emerged as an indefatigable jazz bibliographer based on some work originally issued in the German magazine *Jazz Podium* and subsequently published separately.

David Horn's *The Literature of American Music in Books and Folk Music Collections* (1977) is a major work. Its 556 pages contain well-organized and fully annotated entries. Another substantial bibliography is Steven Winick's *Rhythm* (1974), which covers the period 1900–1970.

Finally, mention must be made of *The International Bibliography of Discographers, Classical Music and Jazz and Blues, 1962–1972,* by David Edwin Cooper. This work, which appears in a series entitled "Keys to Music Bibliography," is subtitled "A Reference Book for Record Collectors, Dealers and Libraries." Part 2 (pp. 145–200) of the work covers jazz and blues, and is divided as follows:

A. Blues—General guides, buyer guides, and subjects
B. Blues—Recordings treated chronologically and by label
C. Jazz—General guides, buyers guides, and subjects
D. Jazz—Recordings treated chronologically and by label
E. Jazz and blues performer discography.

Part 3 covers all music, and is entitled "Summary of National Discographies, Catalogs and Major Review Sources." An excellent and unusual work of reference.

BIBLIOGRAPHY

Bibliographies

Asman, James, and Kinnell, Bill. *Jazz Writings*. Nottingham, England: Jazz Appreciation Society, 1945.
Davies, J. H. *Musicalia: Sources of Information in Music*. London: Pergamon Press and J. Curwen, 1966.
  Rather weak on jazz.

Ferris, William R. *Mississippi Black Folklore*. Hattiesburg: University and College Press of Mississippi, 1971.

A bibliography of books and articles on black folk music.

Ganfield J. *Books and Periodical Articles on Jazz in America from 1926 to 1934*. New York: Columbia University School of Library Service, 1934.

Possibly the first separately issued bibliography on the subject.

Gaskin, L. J. P. *A Select Bibliography of Music in Africa: Compiled at the International African Institute*. London: International African Institute, 1965.

Gillis, F., and Merriam, A. P. *Ethnomusicology and Folk Music: An International Bibliography of Dissertations and Theses*. Middletown, Conn.: Society for Ethnomusicology and Wesleyan University Press, 1966.

Greenway, John. *American Folk Songs of Protest*. Philadelphia: University of Pennsylvania Press, 1953.

————— —————. London: Oxford University Press, 1953.

Haselgrove, J. R., and Kennington, Donald. *Readers' Guide to Books on Jazz*. London: Library Association County Libraries Section, 1960.

Brief selective list.

————— —————. 2nd ed. London: Library Association County Libraries Group, 1965.

Herzog zu Mecklenburg, Carl Gregor. *International Jazz Bibliography: Jazz Books from 1919 to 1968*. Strasbourg, France: P. H. Heitz, 1969.

An excellent bibliography.

—————. *1970 Supplement to International Jazz Bibliography*. Graz, Austria: Universal Edition, 1971.

—————. *1971/72/73 Supplement to International Jazz Bibliography*. Graz, Austria: Universal Edition, 1975.

Horn, David. *The Literature of American Music in Books and Folk Music Collections: A fully Annotated Bibliography*. Metuchen, N.J.: Scarecrow Press, 1977.

An important, well-organized bibliography with well-annotated entries.

Kennington, Donald. *The Literature of Jazz*. London: Library Assn., 1970.

————— —————. Chicago: American Library Assn., 1971.

Markewich, Reese. *Bibliography of Jazz and Pop Tunes Sharing the Chord Progressions of Other Compositions*. New York: The Author, 1970.

⸻. *Jazz Publicity*. New York: The Author, 1967.

⸻. *Jazz Publicity Two*. New York: The Author, 1974.

"Newly revised and expanded bibliography of names and addresses of hundreds of international jazz critics and magazines."

⸻. *The New Expanded Bibliography of Jazz Compositions Based on the Chord Progressions of Standard Tunes*. New York: The Author, 1974.

Merriam, Alan P., and Benford, R. J. *A Bibliography of Jazz*. Philadelphia: American Folklore Society, 1954.

Basic work including over 3,300 entries published before 1951.

⸻ ⸻. New York: Da Capo, 1970.

Miller, E. W. *The Negro in America: A Bibliography*. Cambridge: Harvard University Press, 1966.

Oathout, Melvin C. *Bibliography of Jazz*. An unpublished manuscript housed in the Library of Congress, Washington, D.C.

Read, Danny L. "A Selective Bibliography of Periodical Literature in Jazz Education." Master's thesis, Ball State University, 1975.

An annotated listing of articles pertaining to jazz education found in both music and general interest periodicals.

Reisner, Robert George. *The Literature of Jazz*. New York: New York Public Library, 1954.

⸻. *A Selective Bibliography*. 2nd enlarged and rev. ed. of *The Literature of Jazz*. New York: New York Public Library, 1959.

This edition includes approximately 500 book titles on jazz, 850 journal references, and a select list of background books. Also lists some 125 jazz magazines.

Staffordshire County Library. *Jazz: A Selection of Books*. Stafford, England: Staffordshire County Library, 1963.

Sixty entries.

Standifer, James A., and Reeder, Barbara. *Source Book of African and Afro-American Materials for Music Educators*. Washington, D.C.: Music Educators National Conference, 1972.

Includes a bibliography of books, periodical articles, dissertations, films, tapes, and filmstrips. Also includes a discography of jazz records.

Winick, Steven. *Rhythm: An Annotated Bibliography, 1900–70.* Metuchen, N.J.: Scarecrow Press, 1974.

Encyclopedias

Case, Brian, and Britt, Stan. *The Illustrated Encyclopedia of Jazz.* London: Salamander Books, 1978.

A beautifully illustrated listing of some 400 jazz musicians including career biographies and a selective listing of their recordings.

————— —————. New York: Crown, 1978.

Charters, Samuel B. *Jazz: New Orleans 1885–1957: An Index to the Negro Musicians of New Orleans.* Belleville, N.J.: W. C. Allen, 1958.

A listing of New Orleans jazz musicians, brass bands, and orchestral groups.

—————. *Jazz: New Orleans 1885–1963.* New York: Oak Publications, 1963.

Chilton, J. *Who's Who of Jazz.* London: Bloomsbury Book Shop, 1970.

Brief biographies of over 1,000 jazz musicians and vocalists born before 1920 and born or raised in the United States.

————— —————. Philadelphia: Chilton, 1972.

Coryell, Julie, and Friedman, Laura. *Jazz-Rock Fusion.* New York: Dell, 1978.

A listing of fusion musicians categorized according to instrument. Each entry contains a brief biography and an interview. Book contains a lengthy discography.

Davis, J. P., ed. *The American Negro Reference Book.*

See p. 9.

Feather, Leonard. *The Encyclopedia of Jazz.* New York: Horizon Press, 1955.

Major reference book on jazz. Over two-thirds of the work is devoted to biographies of jazz musicians.

————— —————. London: A. Barker, 1956.

————— —————. 2nd ed. New York: Horizon Press, 1960.

In addition to biographies, it also contains essays, a list of jazz organizations, a list of record companies, and a bibliography.

——— ———. London: A. Barker, 1961.

———. *The Encyclopedia of Jazz in the Sixties*. New York: Horizon Press, 1967.

Supplements the earlier encyclopedia, and is particularly strong on the younger musicians.

———. *Encyclopedia Yearbook of Jazz*. New York: Horizon Press, 1956.

——— ———. London: A. Barker, 1957.

———. *The New Edition of the Encyclopedia of Jazz: Completely Revised, Enlarged and Brought up to Date*. New York: Bonanza Books, 1970.

———. *New Yearbook of Jazz*. New York: Horizon Press, 1958.

——— ———. London: A. Barker, 1959.

———, and Gitler, Ira. *The Encyclopedia of Jazz in the Seventies*. New York: Horizon Press, 1976.

Primarily biographies of performers coming to prominence since 1966. Also contains a brief history of jazz, college jazz offerings, a discography, and a bibliography.

——— ———. London: Quartet Books, 1978.

Hayes, Mileham; Scribner, Ray; and Magee, Peter. *The Encyclopedia of Australian Jazz*. Eight Mile Plains, Australia: The Author, 1976.

Heerkens, Adriaan. *Jazz: Picture Encyclopedia*. Alkmaar, Holland: Arti, 1954.

Text in Dutch, French, English, and German.

Kinkle, Roger D. *The Complete Encyclopedia of Popular Music and Jazz, 1900–1950*. Four vols. New Rochelle, N.Y.: Arlington House, 1974.

A listing of important singers, orchestra leaders, musicians, arrangers, composers, and lyricists. Not included are artists whose careers began after 1950.

Rose, Al, and Souchon, Edmond. *New Orleans Jazz: A Family Album*. Baton Rouge: Louisiana State University Press, 1967.

Guide to New Orleans musicians, bands, and places where the bands played.

——— ———. Baton Rouge: Louisiana State University Press, 1977.

Shapiro, Nat. *An Encyclopedia of Quotations about Music*. Garden City, N.Y.: Doubleday, 1978.

Includes a number of quotations about jazz.

Stambler, Irwin. *Encyclopedia of Pop, Rock and Soul*. New York: St. Martins Press, 1974.

   Includes brief biographies of some jazz and blues musicians.

Walker, Leo. *The Big Band Almanac*. Pasadena, Calif.: Ward Ritchie Press, 1978.

   Factual information about over 1,000 big bands of the 1930s, 1940s and 1950s. An excellent study.

Dictionaries and Glossaries

Burley, Dan. *Dan Burley's Original Handbook of Harlem Jive*. New York: The Author, 1944.

   A glossary of the hip language associated with bebop and parodies of some literary works.

Calloway, Cab. *The New Cab Calloway's Hepsters Dictionary; Language of Jive*. New York: The Author, 1944.

Filmer, Vic. *Jive and Swing Dictionary*. Penzance, England: The Author, 1947.

Gammond, Peter, and Clayton, Peter. *A Guide to Popular Music*. London: Phoenix House, 1960.

——— ———. *Dictionary of Popular Music*. New York: Philosophical Library, 1961.

Gold, Robert S. "A Jazz Lexicon." Ph.D. dissertation, New York University, 1962.

   A collection of words and phrases that have been a part of the jazz musicians' vocabulary since 1900.

———. *Jazz Lexicon: An A-Z Dictionary of Jazz Terms in the Vivid Idiom of America's Most Successful Non-Conformist Minority*. New York: Knopf, 1964.

———. *Jazz Talk*. Indianapolis: Bobbs-Merrill, 1975.

   A dictionary of slang.

Gonzales, Babs. *Be-Bop Dictionary and History of Its Famous Stars*. New York: Arlan, 1947.

Panassie, Hugues, and Gautier, Madeleine. *Dictionary of Jazz*. Translated by Desmond Flower. London: Cassell, 1956.

———. *Guide to Jazz*. Boston: Houghton Mifflin, 1956.

   American version of *Dictionnaire du Jazz*.

——— ———. Westport, Conn.: Greenwood Press, 1973.

Shaw, Arnold. *Lingo of Tin-Pan Alley*. New York: Broadcast Music, 1950.

   A dictionary of terms used by musicians, radio program directors, and recording executives.

Shelly, Low. *Hepcats Jive Talk Dictionary*. Derby, England: T.W.O. Charles, 1945.

Townley, Eric. *Tell Your Story: A Dictionary of Jazz and Blues Recordings 1917 to 1950*. London: Storyville, 1976.

>Investigates the meanings of some 270 tune titles from 1917 to 1950.

Indexes

Armitage, Andrew D., and Tudor, Dean. *Popular Music Record Reviews*. Metuchen, N.J.: Scarecrow Press, 1973.

>An index of record reviews from over sixty periodicals including *Coda, Different Drummer, Downbeat, Jazz Journal, Jazz New England, Jazz Report*, etc.

Blackstone, Orin. *Index to Jazz*. Four vols. New Orleans: Gordon Gullickson, 1947.

———— ————. New Orleans: The Author, 1950s.

———— ————. London: University Microfilms, 1960s.

————. *The Jazz Finder '49*. New Orleans: The Author, 1949.

Gullickson, Gordon. *Numerical Index to Delaunay's "Hot Discography."* Washington, D.C.: The Author, 1941.

Handy, William C. *Negro Authors and Composers of the United States*. New York: Handy Brothers, 1938.

>A selective listing of Negro composers and their works. Includes some ragtime, blues, and jazz composers.

———— ————. New York: AMS Press, 1976.

Shapiro, Nat, ed. *Popular Music: An Annotated Index of American Popular Songs*. New York: Adrian Press. Vol. I: 1950–1959, 1964; vol. II: 1940–1949, 1965; vol. III: 1960–1964, 1967; vol. IV: 1930–1939, 1968.

>Comprehensive coverage of the field including rhythm and blues, jazz, and film, theater and television tunes. Each entry includes copyright dates; full names of authors, composers, and current publishers; details of first and best-selling records and performers who introduced or became identified with the songs. Arrangement is alphabetical by year with indexes of titles and publishers.

Tudor, Dean, and Tudor, Nancy. *Popular Music Periodicals Index, 1973*. Metuchen, N.J.: Scarecrow Press, 1974.

>An index to a number of jazz-oriented periodicals.

Tuft, Harry M. *The Denver Folklore Center Catalogue and 1966 Almanac of Folk Music*. Denver: Denver Folklore Center, 1965.

>Contains listings of black folk music and early jazz records.

Biographical Dictionaries

The Ascap Biographical Dictionary of Composers, Authors and Publishers. New York: Cromwell, 1948.

————— —————. New York: Crowell, 1952.

————— —————. Enlarged ed. New York: Crowell, 1966.

Baker, David; Belt, Lida; and Hudson, Herman; eds. *The Black Composer Speaks*. Metuchen, N.J.: Scarecrow Press, 1978.

Career biographies of selected black composers and a listing of their works.

Berg, I., and Yeomans, I. *Trad: An A–Z Who's Who of the British Traditional Jazz Scene*. London: Foulsham, 1962.

Covers the period 1947–62, but of little permanent value.

Cotterrell, Robert, ed. *Jazz Now: The Jazz Centre Society Guide*. See p. 57.

Granholm, Ake, ed. *Finnish Jazz: History, Musicians, Discography*. Helsinki: Foundation for the Promotion of Finnish Music, 1974.

Slim guide devoted to brief biographical details of Finnish jazz musicians.

Harris, Sheldon. *Blues Who's Who: A Biographical Dictionary of Blues Singers*. New Rochelle, N.Y.: Arlington House, 1979.

Discographies

Aaslund, B. H. *The "Wax Works" of Duke Ellington*. Stockholm: Foliotryck, 1954.

Asman, James, and Kinnell, Bill. *Jazz on Record*. Nottingham, England: Jazz Appreciation Society, 1944.

Avakian, George. *Jazz from Columbia: A Complete Jazz Catalog*. New York: Columbia Records, 1956.

Lists jazz records linked by brief essays on various jazz styles.

Bakker, Dick. *Billie and Terry on Microgroove, 1932/44*. Alphen aan den Rijn, Holland: Micrography, 1975.

—————. *Clarence Williams on Microgroove*. Alphen aan den Rijn, Holland: Micrography, 1977.

—————. *Duke Ellington on Microgroove*. Alphen aan den Rijn, Holland: Micrography, 1977.

Bruyninckx, Walter. *Fifty Years of Recorded Jazz 1917–1967*. Mechelen, Belgium: The Author, 1969.

————. *60 Years of Recorded Jazz*. Belgium: The Author, (published in six sections, two each in 1978, 1979, and 1980).

Complete discography of jazz and blues from the early 1900s to 1977.

Carey, Dave, and McCarthy, Albert J. *The Directory of Recorded Jazz and Swing Music*. Vol. I—Fordingbridge, England: Delphic Press, 1950; 2nd ed.—London: Cassell, 1955. Vol. III—Fordingbridge, England: Delphic Press, 1951; 2nd ed.—London: Cassell, 1956. Vol. IV—Fordingbridge, England: Delphic Press, 1952; 2nd ed.—London: Cassell, 1957. Vol. V—London: Cassell, 1955. Vol. VI—London: Cassell, 1957.

Castelli, Vittoiro, et al. *The Bix Bands*. Milna, Italy: Raretone, 1972.

A discography with photos and a chronology.

Cherrington, G., and Knight, B., eds. *Jazz Catalogue: A Discography of All Jazz Releases Issued in Great Britain*. London: Jazz Journal, 1960– (annual).

Includes a complete bibliography by Colin A. Johnson.

Cusack, Thomas. *Jelly Roll Morton: An Essay in Discography*. London: Cassell, 1952.

Dain, Bernice, and Nevin, David, compilers. "The Black Record: A Selective Discography of Afro-Americana on Audio Discs Held by the Audio/Visual Department, John M. Olin Library." St. Louis: Washington University Library Studies, 1973.

Davies, J. R. T. *The Music of Thomas "Fats" Waller*. London: Friends of Fats, 1953.

Davis, Brian. *John Coltrane Discography*. London: The Author, 1976.

Decca Record Company Ltd. *Complete Catalogue of London Origins of Jazz Records*. London: Decca Record Co. Ltd., 1957.

————. *Complete Catalogue of R.C.A. Victor, R.C.A. Victoria, R.C.A. Camden Records*. London: Decca Record Co. Ltd., annual.

Supplemental catalogs issued every four months.

————. *Complete Catalogue: Records Issued by the Decca Record Company Ltd. and Vogue Records Ltd*. London: Decca Record Co. Ltd., annual.

Supplementary catalogs issued every four months.

————. *Jazz on L.P.'s: A Collector's Guide to Jazz*. London: Decca Record Co., 1956.

―――. *Jazz on 78's: A Guide to the Many Examples of Classic Jazz*. London: Decca Record Co., 1954.

Delaunay, Charles. *Hot Discography*. New York: Commodore Record Co., 1943.
    Discographer's "bible" for early jazz.

―――. *New Hot Discography: The Standard Directory of Recorded Jazz*. Edited by Walter E. Schaap and George Avakian. New York: Criterion Music Corp., 1948.

――― ―――. New York: Wehman, 1963.

Demarey, Bertrano, and Fluchiger, Otto. *Arnette Cobb with Discography*. (Location unknown): Jazz Publications, 1962.

A *Discography of Dizzy Gillespie: 1953/68*, Denmark: Karl Knudsen, 1969.

Edwards, Ernest. *Big Bands*. Whittier, Calif.: Jazz Discographies Unlimited, 1960s.

―――. *Bill Harris Discography*. Whittier, Calif.: Jazz Discographies Unlimited, 1966.

―――. *Dizzy Gillespie Big Bands 1945–1950*. Whittier, Calif.: Jazz Discographies Unlimited, 1966.

―――. *Jimmie Lunceford*. Whittier, Calif.: Jazz Discographies Unlimited, n.d.

―――. *Jimmy Dorsey and His Orchestra*. Whittier, Calif.: Erngeobil Publications, 1968.

―――. *Les Brown and His Band of Renown*. Whittier, Calif.: Jazz Discographies Unlimited, n.d.

―――; Hall, G.; and Korst, B.; eds. *Charlie Barnet and His Orchestra*. Whittier, Calif.: Jazz Discographies Unlimited, n.d.

Electrical and Musical Industries Ltd. *Alphabetical Catalogue of E.M.I. Records: Available and Issued up to and Including―*. London: E.M.I., annual.

Evensmo, Jan. Jazz Solography Series. Vol. I: *The Tenor Saxophone of Leon Chu Berry;* vol. II: *The Tenor Saxophones of Henry Bridges, Robert Carroll, Hershchal Evans and Johnny Russell;* vol. III: *The Tenor Saxophone of Coleman Hawkins, 1929–1942;* vol. IV: *The Guitars of Charlie Christian, Robert Normann and Oscar Aleman;* vol. V: *The Tenor Saxophone and Clarinet of Lester Young 1936–1942;* vol. VI: *The Tenor Saxophone of Ben Webster 1931–1942;* vol. VII: *The Tenor Saxophones of Cecil Scott, Elmer Williams and Dick Wilson;* vol. VIII: *The Trumpet of Henry Red Allen;* vol. IX: *The Trumpets of Bill Coleman 1929/1945 and Frankie Newton;* vol. X: *The*

Alto Saxophone of Benny Carter; vol. XI: *The Trumpet of Roy Eldridge.* Hosle, Norway: The Author, n.d.

In addition to the discography are brief biographies and a critical assessment of recordings and broadcasts. An excellent series.

Fairchild, R. *Discography of Art Hodes.* Ontario, Calif.: The Author, 1962.

Fry, John G., compiler. *Benny Goodman: An English Discography.* Bristol, England: The Author, 1957.

Supplements issued in 1957 and 1958.

Gardner, Mark. *Horace Silver Discography.*

May be found at the Detroit Public Library.

Garrod, Charles. *Bob Chester Orchestra/Teddy Powell Orchestra.* Spotswood, N.J.: Joyce, 1974.

————. *Charlie Barnet and His Orchestra.* Spotswood, N.J.: Joyce, 1973.

———— ————. Laurel, Md.: Jazz Discographies Unlimited, 1970.

————. *Claude Thornhill and His Orchestra.* Spotswood, N.J.: Joyce, 1975.

————. *Elliot Lawrence and His Orchestra.* Spotswood, N.J.: Joyce, 1973.

————. *Larry Clinton and His Orchestra.* Spotswood, N.J.: Joyce, 1973.

————. *Les Brown and His Orchestra.* Spotswood, N.J.: Joyce, 1974.

————. *Tex Beneke and His Orchestra.* Spotswood, N.J.: Joyce, 1973.

————. *Tony Pastor and His Orchestra.* Spotswood, N.J.: Joyce, 1973.

————, and Johnston, Peter. *Harry James and His Orchestra.* Zephyr Hills, Fla.: Joyce, 1975.

Godrich, John, and Dixon, R. M. W. *Blues and Gospel Records, 1902–1942.* London: Brian Rust, 1964.

Basic discography in its field.

———— ————. 2nd ed. London: Storyville, 1969.

———— ————. London: Storyville, 1977.

Goldman, Elliott. *Clarence Williams Discography.* London: Jazz Music Books, 1947.

Hall, George. *Charlie Spivak and His Orchestra.* Laurel, Md.: Jazz Discographies Unlimited, 1972.

————. *Harry James and His Orchestra*. Laurel, Md.: Jazz Discographies Unlimited, 1971.

————. *Jan Savitt and His Orchestra*. (No location): Joyce, 1974.

————. *Jan Savitt and His Top Hatters*. Whittier, Calif.: Jazz Discographies Unlimited, n.d.

————. *Nat "King" Cole*. Whittier, Calif.: Jazz Discographies Unlimited, n.d.

————, and Kramer, Stephen. *Gene Krupa and His Orchestra*. Laurel, Md.: Jazz Discographies Unlimited, 1975.

Harris, Rex, and Rust, Brian. *Recorded Jazz: A Critical Guide*. London: Penguin Books, 1958.

Traditional jazz only is covered.

Harvey, C. M., and Rust, Brian. *The Al Bowlly Discography*. London: Brian Rust, 1965.

Hayes, Cedric. *A Discography of Gospel Records 1937–1971*. Denmark: Karl Knudsen, 1973.

Hibbs, Leonard, ed. *A Short Survey of Modern Rhythm on Brunswick Records*. London: Brunswick Records, 1934.

————. *21 Years of Swing Music on Brunswick Records*. London: The Author, 1937.

Jackson, Jack. *Jack Jackson's Record Round-Up*. London: Max Parrish, 1955.

Jasen, David A. *Recorded Ragtime, 1897–1958*. Hamden, Conn.: Archon Books, 1973.

Stresses the importance of composition and composer rather than performer. Includes a brief essay on ragtime, a section on composers, and an index of performers.

Jepsen, Jorgen. *A Discography of Miles Davis*. Denmark: Knudsen, 1969.

————. *A Discography of Billie Holiday*. Denmark: Knudsen, 1969.

————. *A Discography of Dizzy Gillespie: 1937–1952*. Copenhagen, Denmark: Knudsen, 1969.

————. *A Discography of Dizzy Gillespie: 1953–1968*. Copenhagen, Denmark: Knudsen, 1969.

————. *A Discography of Louis Armstrong: 1923–1971*. Denmark: Knudsen, 1973.

The only complete discography of Armstrong.

————. *Jazz Records: A Discography*. Vol. I—Holte, Denmark: Knudsen, 1966; vol. II—Holte, Denmark: Knudsen, 1966; vol. III—Holte, Denmark: Knudsen, 1967; vol. IV—Holte, Denmark: Knudsen, 1968; vol. V—Copenhagen: Nordisk Tidskrift Forlag, 1963; vol. VI—Copenhagen: Nordisk Tidskrift Forlag, 1963; vol. VII—Holte, Denmark: Knudsen, 1964; vol. VIII— Holte, Denmark: Knudsen, 1965.

Major discographical reference work.

Jones, Cliff. *The Bob Crosby Band*. London: Discographical Society, 1946.

—————. *Hot Jazz*. London: Discographical Society, 1944.

—————. *Jazz in New York*. London: Discographical Society, 1944.

—————. *J. C. Higginbotham*. London: Discographical Society, 1944.

—————. *New Orleans and Chicago Jazz*. London: Discographical Society, 1944.

—————, and Venables, R. G. *Black and White*. London: Discographical Society, 1945.

Korst, Bill, and Garrod, Charles. *Artie Shaw and His Orchestra*. Spotswood, N.J.: Joyce, 1974.

Koster, Piet, and Bakker, Dick M. *Charlie Parker*. Vol. I: 1940–47; vol. II: 1948–50; vol. III: 1951–54; vol. IV: 1940–55. Alphen aan den Rijn, Holland: Micrography, Vol. I—1974; vol. II—1975; vol. III—1975; vol. IV—1976.

Kraner, Dietrich Heinz, and Schulz, Klaus. *Jazz in Austria*. Graz, Austria: Universal Edition, 1972.

A discography of jazz in Austria with a very brief history of Austrian jazz.

Lange, Horst. *The Fabulous Fives*. Essex, England: Storyville Publications, 1978.

Discographical work on the Original Dixieland Jazz Band, the Louisiana Five, New Orleans Jazz Band, Earl Fuller's Famous Jazz Band, the Original Georgia Five, the Original Indiana Five, the Original Memphis Five, and the Southern Five.

Leadbitter, Mike, and Slaven, Neil. *Blues Records, January 1943 to December 1966*. London: Hanover Books, 1968.

————— —————. New York: Music Sales, 1969.

McCarthy, Albert J. *Jazz Discography: An International Discography of Recorded Jazz Including Blues, Gospel and Rhythm and Blues*. Part I, 1958. London: Cassell, 1960.

An attempt to continue the work started in *Directory of Recorded Jazz*. Part I is the only part published, but McCarthy published discographical material in a supplement to his journal *Jazz Monthly*.

Massagli, Luciano, et al. *Duke Ellington's Story on Records*. Milan: Raretone, 1978.

Mello, Edward J., and McBride, Tom. *Bing Crosby, a 1926–1946 Discography*. San Francisco: Anthony Simeone, 1947.

Meriwether, Doug. *The Buddy Rich Orchestra and Small Groups*. Spotswood, N.J.: Joyce, 1974.
    Covers the period 1945 to 1973.

Mitchell, Jack. *Australian Discography*. Melbourne: Australian Jazz Quarterly, 1950.

Neill, Billy, and Gates, E. *Discography of the Recorded Works of Django Reinhardt and the Quintette du Hot Club de France*. London: Clifford Essex Music Co., 1944.

The Okeh Record Catalog, Circa 1920. London: Storyville, 1976.

Personeault, Ken, and Sarles, Carl. *Jazz Discography*. Jackson Heights, N.Y.: The Needle, 1944.

Rowe, John, and Watson, Ted. *Junkshoppers Discography*. London: Jazz Tempo Publications, 1945.
    Guide to pseudonymous jazz bands.

Rowe, John, ed. *Recorded Information*. London: Jazz Tempo Publications, 1945.

Ruppli, Michel. *A Discography of Prestige Jazz Records—1949–1971*. Denmark: Knudsen, 1972.

Rust, Brian A. L. *The American Dance Band Discography 1917–42*. New Rochelle, N.Y.: Arlington House, 1975.
    A very thorough work that lists all the known recorded work of the dance bands between 1917 and 1942.

————— —————. New Rochelle, N.Y.: Arlington House, 1976.

—————. *The HMV Studio House Bands*. London: Storyville, 1976.

—————. *Jazz Records A–Z 1897–1931*. London: The Author, 1961.
    Basic reference work of this period.

————— —————. 2nd ed. London: The Author, 1963.

—————. *Jazz Records A—Z 1932–1942*. London: The Author, 1965.
    Basic reference work of this period.

—————. *Jazz Records 1897–1942*. 4th ed. New Rochelle, N.Y.: Arlington House, 1978.

————— —————. London: Storyville, 1970.

—————. *The Victor Master Book*. Highland Park, N.J.: W. C. Allen, 1970.
    Vol. II: 1925–1936; no vol. I.

—————. *The Zonophone Studio House Bands*. London: Storyville, 1976.

Sanfilippo, Luigi. *General Catalogue of Duke Ellington's Record-ed Music*. Palermo: New Jazz Society, 1964.

Lists 1,472 titles arranged in alphabetical order and referred back to the discographical section. Also included are sections on transcription, both radio and television, v-discs and film.

Schleman, H. R. *Rhythm on Record: A Who's Who and Register of Recorded Dance Music, 1906–1936*. London: Melody Maker, 1936.

Smith, Jay. *Big Gate, a Chronological Listing of the Recorded Works of Jack Teagarden from 1928 to 1950*. Washington, D.C.: The Author, 1951.

Soderbergh, Peter A. *78 RPM Records and Prices*. Des Moines, Iowa: Wallace-Homestead Book Co., 1977.

Lists a number of jazz records with brief discographical notes.

Sparke, Michael, et al. *Kenton on Capitol: A Discography Com-piled with the Co-operation of Capitol Records, Inc*. Middle-sex, England: The Author, 1966.

Comprehensive listing of Kenton's recorded work arranged chronologically from 1941 to date.

Stagg, Tom, and Crump, Charlie, eds. *New Orleans: The Revival. A Tape and Discography of Traditional Jazz Recorded in New Orleans or by New Orleans Bands, 1937–72*. Dublin, Ireland: Bashall Eaves, 1973.

Stilwell, Arnold B. *Record Dating Chart, Part I (up to 1930)*. New York: The Record Changer, 1948.

Topping, Ray. *New Orleans Rhythm and Blues: Record Label Listings*. Bexhill, England: Flyright Records, 1978.

Tudor, Dean, and Tudor, Nancy. *Black Music*. Littleton, Colo.: Libraries Unlimited, 1979.

———. *Jazz*. Littleton, Colo.: Libraries Unlimited, 1979.

For each of the two preceding volumes about 1,300 record-ings were selected. Information provided for each recording in-cludes from where it may be ordered and why it is significant.

Venables, R. G. V., and Jones, Clifford. *Bix*. London: Clifford Jones, n.d.

——— ———. London: Discographical Society, 1945.

———. *Eye Witness Jazz*. London: Discographical Society, 1946.

———, and White, Langston C. W. *A Complete Discography of Red Nichols and His Five Pennies*. Melbourne, Australia: Aus-tralian Jazz Quarterly, 1946.

———— ————. 2nd ed. Melbourne: Australian Jazz Quarterly, 1947.

Venudor, Pete, and Sparke, Michael. *The Standard Stan Kenton Directory, Volume I 1937–1949*. Amsterdam, Holland: Pete Venudor, 1968.

An excellent work.

Vreede, Max E. *Paramount 12000/13000 Series*. London: Storyville, 1971.

Walker, Edward S., and Walker, Steven. *English Ragtime: A Discography 1898–1920*. Derbyshire, England: E. S. Walker, 1971.

Whiteman, Paul. *Records for the Millions*. New York: Hermitage, 1948.

Contains a listing of Whiteman's recordings as well as a listing of popular dance band recordings.

Bio-Discographies

Allen, Walter C. *Hendersonia: The Music of Fletcher Henderson and His Musicians*.

See p. 97.

————, and Rust, Brian A. L. *King Joe Oliver*. Stanhope, N.J.: Walter C. Allen, 1955.

———— ————. London: Jazz Book Club, 1957.

———— ————. London: Sidgwick and Jackson, 1958.

Bedwell, Stephen F. *A Glenn Miller Discography and Biography*. London: Glenn Miller Appreciation Society, 1955.

———— ————. Rev. ed. London: Glenn Miller Appreciation Society, 1956.

Connor, Donald R. *B. G.—Off the Record, a Bio-Discography of Benny Goodman*. Fairless Hills, Pa.: Gaildonna, 1958.

————, and Hicks, Warren W. *B. G.: On the Record*. New Rochelle, N.Y.: Arlington House, 1969.

Flower, John. *Moonlight Serenade: A Bio-Discography of the Glenn Miller Civilian Band*.

See p. 101.

Jepsen, J. G., and Mohr, Kurt. *Hot Lips Page*. (No location): Jazz Publications, 1961.

Waters, H. J. *Jack Teagarden's Music: His Career and Recordings*. Stanhope, N.J: W. C. Allen, 1960.

An excellent work.

Wilbraham, Roy. *Milt Jackson: A Discography and Biography*. London: Frognal Bookshop, 1968.

Bibliography—Filmography—Discography

Agostinelli, Anthony, ed. *The Newport Jazz Festival in Rhode Island 1954 to 1971*. Providence, R.I.: The Author, 1977.

Lonstein, Albert, and Marino, Vito. *The Compleat Sinatra*. Ellenville, N.Y.: Cameron, 1970.

Meeker, David. *Jazz in the Movies: A Guide to Jazz Musicians 1917–1977*. London: Talisman Books, 1977.

Lists in title order and briefly evaluates over 2,200 films in which jazz musicians either appeared or in which they performed on the soundtrack. A well-organized reference book illustrated with "stills" from many films.

Jazz Record Collecting

Anderson, A. *Helpful Hints to Jazz Collectors: Combined with Jazz Men and Their Records*. Baraboo, Wisc.: Andoll, 1957.

Includes discography and biography.

Bannister, L. H. *International Jazz Collector's Directory*. Malvern, England: The Author, 1948.

Brown, Ken, et al. *Collector's Catalogue*. Glasgow, Scotland: Ken Brown, 1943.

Cooper, David E. *International Bibliography of Discographers, Classical Music and Jazz and Blues, 1962–1972: A Reference Book for Record Collectors, Dealers, and Libraries*. Littleton, Colo.: Libraries Unlimited, 1975.

Deitch, Gene. *The Cat*. New York: The Record Changer, 1948.

Fox, Charles; Gammond, Peter; and Morgan, Alun. *Jazz on Record: A Critical Guide: With Additional Material by A. Korner*. London: Hutchinson, 1960.

Useful for collecting the basic records, but now out of date. See entry under McCarthy below.

Fry, A., Kaplan, M., and Love, W. C. *Who's Who in Jazz Collecting*. Nashville: Hemphill Press, 1942.

Harrison, Max. *Modern Jazz, the Essential Records*.

See p. 123.

Langridge, Derek Wilton. *Your Jazz Collection*. London: Bingley, 1970.

A comprehensive guide to the collecting of jazz records, books, and other materials and to their classification, cataloging, and arrangement.

——— ———. Hamden, Conn.: Archon Books, 1970.

Love, W. C., and Rich, Bill. *Who's Who in Jazz Collecting.* Nashville: The Authors, 1949.

Lucas, J. *Basic Jazz on Long Play.* Northfield, Minn.: Carleton College, 1954.

————. *The Great Revival on Long Play.* Northfield, Minn.: Carleton Jazz Club, Carleton College, 1957.

McCarthy, Albert J.; Oliver, Paul; Morgan, Alun; and Harrison, Max. *Jazz on Record: A Critical Guide to the First 50 Years, 1917–1967.* London: Hanover Books, 1968.

Updates *Jazz on Record* (1960).

———— ————. New York: Oak Publications, 1968.

Panassie, Hugues. *144 Hot Jazz Bluebird and Victor Records.* Camden, N.J.: Radio Corp. of America, 1939.

Ramsey, Frederic. *A Guide to Long Play Jazz Records.* New York: Long Player Publications, 1954.

————, and Smith, Charles E. *The Jazz Record Book.* New York: Smith and Durrell, 1942.

Valuable guide to earlier recordings.

Seidel, Richard. *Basic Record Library of Jazz.* Boston: Schwann, 1974.

Semeonoff, B. *Record Collecting: A Guide for Beginners with a Chapter on Collecting Jazz Records by Alexander Ross.* Kent, England: Oakwood Press, 1949.

———— ————. 2nd ed. Surrey, England: Oakwood Press, 1951.

Wilson, J. *Collector's Jazz: Modern.* Philadelphia: Lippincott, 1959.

Critical discography of long-playing records.

————. *Collector's Jazz: Traditional and Swing.* Philadelphia: Lippincott, 1958.

Critical discography.

Photographic Albums

Oliver, J., ed. *Jazz Classic: An Album of Personalities from the World of Jazz.* London: Tolgate Press, 1962.

Album of photographs.

Rosenkrantz, Timme. *Swing Photo Album.* Copenhagen: The Author, 1939.

———— ————. 2nd ed. Suffolk, England: Scorpion Press, 1964.

Stock, D. *Jazz Street: With an Introduction from and Commentary by Nat Hentoff.* New York: Doubleday, 1960.

———— ————. London: Deutsch, 1960.

———— ————. London: Jazz Book Club, 1961.

Chapter 7

Jazz Education

Within the past twenty years, there has been a tremendous growth in the number of books written to train both the educator and student in the area of jazz. One reason for the demand for these books is the acceptance and growth of jazz in the school curriculum, including both high schools and colleges. Another reason for the increased use of instructional books and for the need for formalized jazz instruction has been a decrease in the number of jam sessions that were especially prevalent in the 1940s, and were perhaps most important in the development of bebop. In these jam sessions, a young musician would go to a club where a professional group was performing and ask to "sit in" with the group. After the regular job was over, around 1:00 A.M. or so, the young musician would have an opportunity to play with the professional members of the group. In Kansas City during the 1930s and 1940s, it was not uncommon for these sessions to last all night. These experiences of course allowed a great learning experience for the young musician, and the contacts made with professional musicians could also be quite useful in procuring playing jobs later on. A third reason for the increase in formalized jazz instruction and materials stems from the increased demands and requirements made of the professional musician.

For a comprehensive annotated listing of books on improvisation and arranging, the reader is referred to two periodicals. In the *NAJE Educator*, beginning with volume 7, number 4, April/May 1975, John Kuzmich has written a continuing series of articles that name and describe a wide variety of improvisation methods. Kuzmich has also written a similar series on jazz theory, composition, and arranging books that appears in *The Instrumentalist* magazine of April and May 1977; an update appears in the October and December issues of 1979.

Most of the earliest writings on jazz education were aimed at potential professional dance bandleaders, and tried to depict how a band was organized and how it continued a successful existence. D. K. Antrim's *Secrets of Dance Band Success* (1936) offers a very interesting insight into the organization and administration of a number of popular bands at that time. *How to Build a Dance Band and Make It Pay* (1940) by Ralph Williams discusses a wide array of topics pertaining to both leading and playing in a professional dance band. Another similar work is *How to Be a Band Leader* (1941) by Paul Whiteman and Leslie Lieber. Whiteman was, of course, one of the most successful leaders of the day and was also known for his close relationship with George Gershwin.

The 1940s, and to a lesser extent the late 1930s, saw in print, at least in other than periodical articles, the first recognition of jazz as a potential area of study in the school curriculum. This was first represented by a number of master's theses written by college graduate students. Since jazz was far from being accepted as an art form in those days, and since it was held in some disrepute by the general public, and particularly so by educational institutions, these initial writings were quite remarkable. The first two works of this nature were John Chickaneff's "Popular Dance Music in High School Instrumental Teaching" (1938) and Clifford Weiser's "Popular Music as a Medium of Instrumental Instruction in Secondary Schools" (1938). One of the first educators to recognize the disparity between the demands of professional music and the goals of music education was Gardner Benedict in his "An Analysis of the Commercial Music Field and Its Relation to Music Education" (1942), while probably the first really significant work was "The Place of the Dance Band in the School Music Program" (1942) by Milton Parman. Morris E. Hall, who was probably the most influential educator in starting jazz instruction in the college curriculum, wrote "The Development of a Curriculum for the Teaching of Dance Music at a College Level" (1944). Hall developed the jazz program at North Texas State University, which is one of the most outstanding collegiate jazz programs in the United States. In 1961, Hall also wrote *Teacher's Guide to the High School Stage*

Band, an outstanding guide for jazz band directors. Another well-written thesis written at North Texas State was James Johnson's "The Status and Administration of Student Dance Bands in Colleges and Universities in the United States" (1947). This paper also describes how the jazz program at North Texas was developed. Harry Apetz's "The Place of the Dance Band in the High School Educational Program" (1949) offered advice for administering the school dance band. Clarence Lambrecht, in his "A Survey of Texas High School Dance Bands" (1949), provides a good source of information on the origin of school dance bands. Of similar content is Gene Midyett's "The Place of the Dance Band in the High School Program" (1949), which was written at the University of Southern California. Another early attempt to encourage training in dance music within the school music program was Gene Cronenwett's "The Contribution of Dance Bands to Music Education in the High Schools of Ohio" (1951).

One of the first published works explaining how to organize and direct a school dance band was Ted Hunt's *Organizing and Conducting the Student Dance Orchestra* (1941). Of similar content and including material on the history of the school stage band is Don McCathren's *Organizing the School Stage Band* (1960), which was published by Southern Music Company. Alfred Music Company has also participated in publishing educational guides, and one of their publications, *Jazz-Rock Ensemble: A Conductor's and Teacher's Guide* (1976), by Tom Ferguson and Saul Feldstein, is of immense benefit to the music educator with little or no experience in jazz. It provides a comprehensive account of information pertaining to the organization and development of a school jazz ensemble. Two music instrument companies that have published educational guides are Selmer and F. E. Olds. The former has published *Jazz Education in the 70's. A High School Teacher's Guide* (1973), which is a superb compendium of articles pertaining to many areas of jazz performance, and can be of immense benefit to both educator and student. All of the articles were written by outstanding jazz educators and professional musicians. The latter has published *Factors Associated with the Rise of the Stage Band in the Public Secondary Schools of Colorado* (1962) by Jess Gerardi, and *The Educational Validity of Stage Band Literature in High School Music Education* (1962) by Tim Jones. Both of these were originally written as master's theses. Another paper particulary valuable for the educator with no jazz experience is Ronald Logan's "The Stage Band in the Secondary School" (1966). This provides a brief history of the school stage band, and suggests solutions to the principle problems involved in directing the high school stage band. James Reed's "A Guideline for Teaching Stage Band Concepts to Instrumental Music Students in Grades Seven through Twelve" (1971) is also a source of information for the band director who has been inadequately trained in jazz music. A slightly different approach is taken by Alexander Sample in "A Plan for Stimulating Interest and Motivation in High School Instrumental Music through the Utilization of the Dance Orchestra" (1955). This excellent work provides a plan to promote the musical growth of the school dance band, and was particularly appropriate considering the date of its writing.

Two papers of a more specialized nature are Harold McCarter's "Contemporary Jazz Improvisation: A Source Book for the Music Educator" (1973) and Bruce Brummond's "Developing the High School Vocal Jazz Ensemble" (1974). The former provides an excellent source of information pertaining to techniques of modern jazz improvisation and also gives brief biographies of selected jazz musicians. The latter perhaps helped to spark an interest in vocal jazz that is now of much interest in many school vocal music programs. This is an excellent study of organizational and performance techniques for the high school vocal jazz ensemble.

One of the first and still possibly the best book dealing with techniques of jazz performance is George Wiskirchen's *Developmental Techniques for the School Dance Band Musician* (1961). This should be required reading for any jazz student, and is also of immense benefit to the educator. Two books written especially for the jazz educator and student are David Baker's *A Comprehensive Method of Jazz Education for Teacher and Student* (1978) and Graham Collier's *Jazz: A Student's and Teacher's Guide* (1975). The latter is a text designed to assist the teacher in covering jazz. It has two main parts: part one is a history of jazz, while part two deals with the techniques of playing jazz. Of a somewhat similar nature is Jerry Coker's *The Jazz Idiom* (1975), which covers all areas of jazz including history, styles, improvisation, and arranging, and includes a survey of literature available in each area. This book is perhaps too brief and diverse to be of real value, and certainly does not compare to his outstanding *Listening to Jazz* (see p. 118), which should be required study for any student of jazz improvisation.

A most unique book by Allen Scott, *Jazz Educated, Man* (1973) discusses opportunities for jazz study. It also includes a brief history of jazz and a history of jazz in education. It is a bit dated, however, because of the tremendous increase in jazz education opportunities that have been engendered since its writing.

BIBLIOGRAPHY

Aitken, Allan Eugene. "A Self-Instructional Audio-Imitation Method Designed to Teach Trumpet Students Jazz Improvisation in the Major Mode." Ph.D. dissertation, University of Oregon, 1975.

Part one describes the need for this method, part two gives a brief history of jazz, part three is a review of improvisation literature, and part four is the improvisational method.

Allen, Walter C., ed. *Studies in Jazz Discography.* New Brunswick, N.J.: Institute of Jazz, 1971.

A collection of lectures and discussions about discographical research and preservation of jazz-related materials.

Alrutz, Louis W. "A Study of Popular Music and Reactions to Its Use in High Schools." Master's thesis, Northwestern University, 1939.

Popular music means swing and dance band music. This work is of little value because of its publication date and writing style.

Anderson, Edgar W. "An Investigation of Jazz Instruction in Texas Secondary Schools." Master's thesis, Sam Houston State Teachers College, 1959.

Examines employment opportunities in jazz and how high schools are preparing music students for work in this area. Not well written.

Anderson, Lawrence Edmund. "The Effects of Divergent Musical Literature Used in High School Performance Organizations in Developing Aesthetic Sensitivity to Music." Ph.D. dissertation, University of California at Berkeley, 1972.

Examines the effect of the music literature of the stage band and concert band on the development of musicality.

Antrim, D. K., ed. *Secrets of Dance Band Success*. New York: Famous Stars, 1936.

Although dated, this book does offer interesting insight into the organization and administration of some of the older dance bands.

Apetz, Harry B. "The Place of the Dance Band in the High School Educational Program." Master's thesis, Texas Christian University, 1949.

Examines the evolution of dance music, determines the values and dangers of dance band work, and offers suggestions for administering the school dance band. One of the first formal works on the dance band in the schools.

Appleton, Clyde Robert. "The Comparative Preferential Response of Black and White College Students to Black and White Folk and Popular Music Styles." Ph.D. dissertation, New York University, 1970.

Asman, James, and Kinnell, Bill. *Jazz Today*. Nottingham, England: Jazz Appreciation Society, 1945.

Baker, David. *A Comprehensive Method of Jazz Education for Teacher and Student*. Chicago: Downbeat, 1978.

Baker, Mickey. *Jazz and Rhythm 'n Blues Guitar*. New York: AMSCO Music, 1969.

Barr, Walter Laning. "The Jazz Studies Curriculum." Ed.D. dissertation, Arizona State University, 1974.

Structures a college curriculum for a major in jazz and studio music.

Barritt, Hugh G. "Developing a High School Stage Band." Master's thesis, Manhattan School of Music, 1958.

Barton, Charles Wynne. "The Development and Musical Objectives of the School Stage Band." Master's thesis, Texas Tech University, 1964.

Educational validity, methods, and contributions of the school stage band. Of limited value because of poor writing style.

Bauman, Dick. "Jazz Education in the Public School Music Program." Master's paper, Northwest Missouri State University, 1970.

Benedict, Gardner. "An Analysis of the Commercial Music Field and its Relation to Music Education." Master's thesis, Northwestern University, 1942.

Comments on the music business as it pertains to dance bands and radio broadcasts. The author points out the separation between the world of professional music and the world of music education.

Berk, Lee Eliot. *Legal Protection for the Creative Musician*. Boston: Berkley Press, 1970.

An important book but now of lesser value because of the recent changes in the copyright law.

Bonsanti, Neal J. "A Survey of Stage Band Curricula in the High Schools of Florida." Master's thesis, University of Miami, 1968.

Concerned with the need for high school training for those wishing to become professionals in the commercial music field. Musicians and educators are surveyed to determine their feelings.

Bowlin, Margie N. "A Guide to Teaching Jazz Rhythms in the Instrumental Program." Master's thesis, Texas Woman's University, 1972.

A rather inexperienced approach.

Branch, London Grigsby. "Jazz Education in Predominantly Black Colleges." Ph.D. dissertation, Southern Illinois University, 1975.

A study to determine the level of development of jazz education in twenty-three black colleges.

Briscuso, Joseph James. "A Study of Ability in Spontaneous and Prepared Jazz Improvisation Among Students Who Possess Different Levels of Musical Aptitude." Ph.D. dissertation, University of Iowa, 1972.

Brummond, Bruce E. "Developing the High School Vocal Jazz Ensemble." Master's thesis, Central Washington State College, 1974.

A discussion of organizational and performance techniques for the high school vocal jazz ensemble. An excellent work.

Bryce, O., and McLaren, A. *Let's Play Jazz: A Beginner's Guide to Jazz*. Bushey, England: The Authors, 1965.

Burnsed, Charles V. "The Development and Evaluation of an Introductory Jazz Improvisation Sequence for Intermediate Band Students." Ph.D. dissertation, University of Miami, 1978.

   The author concludes that improvisatory experience has a positive effect on student's attitude toward band.

Carratello, John. "An Eclectic Choral Methodology and Its Effect on the Understanding, Interpretation, and Performance of Black Spirituals." D.M.A. dissertation, California State University, Fullerton, 1976.

   An investigation of the black spiritual in terms of its historical and organic development.

Chickaneff, John L. "Popular Dance Music in High School Instrumental Teaching." Master's thesis, Eastman School of Music, 1938.

Chilton, John. *Teach Yourself Jazz*. London: Hodder and Stoughton, 1979.

   Very much improved version of Martin Lindsay's original work in the Teach Yourself series published in 1958 (see below).

Coker, Jerry. *The Jazz Idiom*. Englewood Cliffs, N.J.: Prentice-Hall, 1975.

   Covers all areas of jazz study: history, styles, improvisation, and arranging. Also includes a brief survey of available literature in each area.

———. *Listening to Jazz*.

   See p. 118.

Collier, Graham. *Jazz: A Student's and Teacher's Guide*. London: Cambridge University Press, 1975.

   A text designed to assist the teacher in covering jazz. Section 1 deals with the history of jazz, and section 2 deals with the practical aspects of playing jazz.

Colnot, Cliff. "Instrumental Ensemble—Stage Band Music." Miami, Dade County Public Schools, 1971.

   A nine-week course in stage band performance.

Cronenwett, Gene. "The Contribution of Dance Bands to Music Education in the High Schools of Ohio." Master's thesis, Ohio State University, 1951.

   An examination of dance band participation as to its worth in adult life. An early attempt to encourage training in dance music within the school music program.

Damron, Bert Lee. "The Development and Evaluation of a Self-Instructional Sequence in Jazz Improvisation." Ph.D. dissertation, Florida State University, 1973.

Dance, Stanley. *Jazz Notebook*. Notts, England: Jazz Appreciation Society, 1945.

Dankworth, Avril. *Jazz: An Introduction to Its Musical Basis*.
See p. 119.

Davis, Sarah G. "A Creative Instructional Method in Popular and Jazz Music Using Fake Books for Third and Fourth Grade Piano Students." Master's thesis, Texas Woman's University, 1973 or 1974.

Learning piano improvisation through the use of fake books.

Dedrick, Art, and Polhamus, Al. *How the Dance Band Swings*. East Aurora, N.Y.: Kendor Music, 1958.

de Lerma, Dominique-Rene. *Black Music in Our Culture*. Kent, Ohio: Kent State University Press, 1970.

Lectures and discussions from a seminar, "Black Music in College and University Curricula," held at Indiana University in 1969.

————. *Reflections on Afro-American Music*.
See p. 22.

————; Baker, David; and Caswell, Austin B. *Black Music Now: A Source Book on Twentieth Century Black-American Music*. Kent, Ohio: Kent State University Press, 1974.

Deshore, Thomas Jake. "Dance Bands and Public School Music." Master's thesis, Northwestern University, 1954.

Duke, John R. "Teaching Musical Improvisation: A Study of 18th and 20th Century Methods." Ph.D. dissertation. George Peabody College, 1972.

Early, Robert B. "Assessment of Selected High School Instrumental Students: The Effect of Jazz Band Experience on Certain Rhythmic Skills." Ph.D. dissertation, Michigan State University, 1978.

Ferguson, Tom, and Feldstein, Saul. *Jazz-Rock Ensemble: A Conductor's and Teacher's Guide*. Port Washington, N.Y.: Alfred, 1976.

Primarily for the music educator with little jazz experience.

Ferriano, Frank. "A Study of the School Jazz Ensemble in American Music Education." Ed. D. dissertation, Columbia University, 1974.

Included is a survey of the practices of some outstanding jazz educators.

Fly, Benton G. "Rapid Development of Stylistic Techniques in Secondary School Stage Band Drummers." Master's thesis, Texas Tech University, 1970.

Primarily deals with the transfer of drumming skills to their actual usage in playing music.

Fox, Sidney. *The Origins and Development of Jazz*. Chicago: Follett Educational Corp., 1968.

Freundlich, Douglas A. "The Development of Musical Thinking: Case Studies in Improvisation." Ed. D. dissertation, Harvard University, 1978.

Gee, John, and Wadsley, Michael, eds. *Jazzography*. Herts, England: Society of Jazz Appreciation in the Younger Generation, 1944.

Gerardi, Jess L. "Factors Associated with the Rise of the Stage Band in the Public Secondary Schools of Colorado." Master's thesis, University of California at Los Angeles, 1961.

Examines the characteristics of a good stage band, how to organize and maintain a stage band, and the educational values associated with the stage band.

————— —————. Fullerton, Calif.: F. E. Olds, 1962.

Good, Melvin Lee. "A Study of the Effectiveness of Public School Music in the Opinions of Selected Dance Band Musicians." Master's thesis, Northwestern University, 1954.

Hall, Morris E. "The Development of a Curriculum for the Teaching of Dance Music at a College Level." Master's thesis, North Texas State University, 1944.

A well-written paper and one of the earliest on jazz in the curriculum.

—————. *Teacher's Guide to the High School Stage Band*. Elkhart, Ind.: Selmer Inc., 1961.

An excellent work recommended for any school jazz band director.

Hepworth, Loel Thomas. "The Development of a Course of Study in Stage Band Techniques at the University of Utah for Inclusion in the Preparation of Secondary Instrumental Music Teachers." Ph. D. dissertation, University of Utah, 1974.

Hilligoss, C. Adair. "Materials and Methods for High School

Stage-Dance Bands." Master's thesis, Washington State University, 1961.

Hinds, Bobbie M. "An Investigation of the Stage Band Program in the Missouri Public High Schools." Master's thesis, Central Missouri State College, 1969.

Statistics on the organization and administration of stage bands.

Hinkle, William J. "A Survey-Appraisal of Jazz-Oriented Curriculum in Higher Education in the State of Florida." Ph.D. dissertation, Florida State University, 1977.

Hores, Robert. "A Comparative Study of Visual- and Aural-Oriented Approaches to Jazz Improvisation with Implications for Instruction." D.M.A. dissertation, Indiana University, 1977.

Hunt, Ted. *Organizing and Conducting the Student Dance Orchestra*. Chicago: Rubank, 1941.

Jacobs, Gordon. *A Study of Jazz*. Staffs, England: The Author, 1944.

Jazz Education in the 70's. A High School Teacher's Guide. Elkhart, Ind.: Selmer Inc., 1973.

An excellent collection of articles on jazz education written by outstanding educators and professional musicians.

Johnson, Bill. "An Analysis of Jazz and the Jazz Ensemble as It Pertains to the Music Curriculum of the Public Schools." Master's thesis, Kansas State College at Pittsburg, 1974.

Reviews available literature on the subject of jazz in the curriculum. A somewhat unorganized and naïve approach.

Johnson, James W. "The Status and Administration of Student Dance Bands in Colleges and Universities in the United States." Master's thesis, North Texas State Teachers College, 1947.

A systematic survey of the usages of school dance bands. Also includes a brief history of jazz in schools and a history of the development of the North Texas State stage band. A well-written study.

Jones, Geraldine Wells. "The Negro Spiritual and Its Use as an Integral Part of Music Education." Master's thesis, Hartt College of Music, 1953.

Jones, Tim R. "The Educational Validity of Stage Band Literature in High School Music Education." Master's thesis, Hardin-Simmons University, 1961.

———— ————. Fullerton, Calif.: F. E. Olds, 1962.

Keathley, Kenneth E. "A Proposed Guitar Method for High School Dance Bands." Master's thesis, Sam Houston State Teachers College, 1955.

A text written for the band director to teach the dance band guitar player.

Kemp, Barbara Ann. "The Comparative Effectiveness of Contemporary Youth Music and Traditional Folk Music in the Development of Music Comprehension in Sixth Grade Students." Master's thesis, American University, 1976.

King, Jeffrey Michael. "Developing a Guide to the Techniques of Imitating Select Commercial Music Styles." Master's thesis, North Texas State University, 1975.

Different musical aspects are examined from a variety of commercial music styles.

Konowitz, Bertram L. "Jazz Improvisation at the Piano—A Textbook for Teachers." Ed.D. dissertation, Columbia University, 1969.

A valuable method.

Lambrecht, Clarence J. "A Survey of Texas High School Dance Bands." Master's thesis, University of Texas, 1949.

A good source of information on the origin of school dance bands.

Lindsay, Martin. *Teach Yourself Jazz*. London: English Universities Press, 1958.

Little value as a manual of jazz.

Logan, Ronald F. "The Stage Band in the Secondary School." Master's thesis, University of California at Los Angeles, 1966.

Suggests solutions to the principal problems involved in directing the high school stage band. Gives a brief history of the school stage band. This serves as a good reference source for the educator with no knowledge of jazz.

Lomakin, Nicholas. *Lomakin Pocket Fake List for Leaders, Musicians and Singers*. Pittsburgh: The Author, 1944.

Lowris, George. "The Teaching of Jazz in Junior High School General Music Classes through Keyboard and Listening Experiences: A Source Book for Teachers." Ed.D. dissertation, Columbia University Teachers College, 1977.

Serves as an aid to the teaching of jazz in junior high music.

McCarter, Harold D. "Contemporary Jazz Improvisation: A Source Book for the Music Educator." Master's thesis, Kansas State College at Pittsburg, 1973.

Section 1 deals with the techniques of improvisation, and section 2 contains brief biographies of some modern jazz musicians. Highly recommended for the educator.

McCathren, Don. *Organizing the School Stage Band.* San Antonio, Tex.: Southern Music Co., 1960.

Describes the history of the school stage band and gives suggestions on its organization.

McCauley, John W. "Jazz Improvisation for the B-Flat Soprano Trumpet: An Introductory Text for Teaching Basic Theoretical and Performance Principles." Ph.D. dissertation, Louisiana State University, 1973.

Information for study at all levels of improvisation.

McCormick, Todd D. "A Proposed Listening Course on Ten Styles of Jazz Using Call Charts for Use in the General Music Class." Master's thesis, Mankato State University, 1977.

Uses jazz to aid in the perception of basic musical elements and emotional responses. An excellent educational aid.

McDaniel, William T. "Differences in Music Achievement, Musical Experience, and Background between Jazz-Improvising Musicians and Non-Improvising Musicians at the Freshman and Sophomore College Levels." Ph.D. dissertation, University of Iowa, 1974.

It was found that improvisers have better musical awareness.

McKinney, John E. "The Pedagogy of Lennie Tristano." Ed.D. dissertation, Fairleigh Dickinson University, 1978.

Midyett, Gene H. "The Place of the Dance Band in the High School Program." Master's thesis, University of Southern California, 1949.

Nanry, Charles. *The Jazz Text.* New York: Van Nostrand Reinhold, 1979.

Noice, Albert H. "A Survey and Analysis of Teacher-Training and Experience in Relation to the Stage Band Movement in the Public Secondary Schools of Minnesota with Implications for Teacher Education." Ed.D. dissertation, Colorado State College, 1965.

Ostransky, Leroy. *Understanding Jazz.*
See p. 126.

Owens, Thomas. "Charlie Parker: Techniques of Improvisation."
See p. 126–27.

———. "Improvisation Techniques of the Modern Jazz Quartet."
See p. 127.

Parman, Milton C. "The Place of the Dance Band in the School
Music Program." Master's thesis, Ohio State University, 1942.

An excellent work noted for being perhaps the earliest writing on jazz in the curriculum.

Payne, Jerry R. "Jazz Education in the Secondary Schools of
Louisiana: Implications for Teacher Education." Ed.D. dissertation, Northwestern State University of Louisiana, 1973.

A survey of school band directors to determine recommendations for teacher training.

————. "A Manual for Teaching Interpretation of the Intricacies
of Jazz Rhythm, Styling, Articulation, and Phrasing to the Entire School Band." Master's thesis, Northwestern State University of Louisiana, 1968.

Read, Danny L. "A Selective Bibliography of Periodical Literature in Jazz Education.

See p. 147.

Reagon, Bernice. "A History of the Afro-American through His
Songs. Part of a Packet with Audiotape." New York, Educational Department—Albany. Division of Humanities and Arts, 1969.

Suggests ways to show children how to appreciate the musical contributions of blacks.

Reed, James R. "A Guideline for Teaching Stage Band Concepts
to Instrumental Music Students in Grades Seven through Twelve." Master's thesis, Wisconsin State University at Platteville, 1971.

This is a "how to" book for the inexperienced school jazz band director.

Ricker, Ramon Lee. "A Survey of Published Jazz-Oriented Clarinet Study Materials: 1920–1970." D.M.A. dissertation, Eastman School of Music, 1973.

Rizzo, Jacques C. "Written Jazz Rhythm Patterns: A Series of
Original, Accompanied Wind Instrument Duets of an Intermediate Degree of Difficulty with Suggestions for Their Performance." Ed.D. dissertation, New York University, 1979.

Designed to help classically trained musicians play jazz rhythms.

Rodgers, Virgil. "The Role of Black Music in the Los Angeles
School District." Master's thesis, California State University at Los Angeles, 1972.

Rulli, Joseph. "The Stage Band as a Teaching Tool for the Performance of Contemporary Band Literature." Master's thesis, University of Wyoming, 1971.

A rather meaningless study.

Sample, Alexander C. "A Plan for Stimulating Interest and Motivation in High School Instrumental Music through the Utilization of the Dance Orchestra." Master's thesis, Texas Southern University, 1955.

Provides a plan to promote the musical growth of the school dance orchestra. An excellent work.

Scott, Allen. *Jazz Educated, Man*. Washington, D.C.: American International, 1973.

A discussion of opportunities for study in jazz. Also includes a brief history of jazz and a history of jazz in education.

Scotti, Joe. *Jazz*. St. Louis: Community Music Schools, 1973.

A basic primer on the history and fundamentals of jazz.

————— —————. St. Louis: Entropy Productions, 1974.

Seibert, Bob. *Making a Good Stage Band Recording*. Dallas: KSM Publishing, 1965.

A brief pamphlet describing the techniques of recording a stage band.

Silverman, Herbert. *Units in the Study of Modern Jazz Music*. Boston: The Author, 1946.

Smith, Hugh L. "The Literary Manifestation of a Liberal Romanticism in American Jazz."

See p. 129.

Specht, Paul L. *How They Became Name Brands*.

See p. 129.

Standifer, James A., and Reeder, Barbara. *Source Book of African and Afro-American Materials for Music Educators*.

See p. 147.

Stanley, John W. "An Analysis and Comparison of Four Tests on Arranging and Composing for Jazz Orchestra." Master's thesis, Sam Houston State Teachers College, 1964.

Stephans, Michael L. "Delineating the Process of Curriculum Development in Higher Education: The Development of Jazz as a Part of the Music Curriculum." Ph.D. dissertation, University of Maryland, 1976.

A study of the factors that contributed to the inclusion of jazz studies in the college curriculum.

Stuart, Mary L. "Unit Organization of the Topic Jazz in the Senior High School." Master's thesis, Boston University, 1953.

The application of procedures developed by Roy O. Billett to the high school general music class unit in jazz.

Thomas, Richard. "A Proposed Plan for the Integration of the Dance Orchestra into the High School Music Program." Master's thesis, Texas Southern University, 1954.

Points out the values of the dance band. A poorly written paper.

Traill, S. *Play That Music: A Guide to Playing Jazz*. London: Faber, 1956.

Contributions by leading British jazz musicians.

——— ———. London: Jazz Book Club, 1958.

Turnbull, Stanley. *How to Run a Small Dance Band for Profit*. London: Nelson and Sons, 1932.

Weiser, Clifford. "Popular Music as a Medium of Instrumental Instruction in Secondary Schools." Master's thesis, University of Southern California, 1938.

Weitz, Lowell E. "The Stage Band as a Part of the High School Music Program." D.M.A. dissertation, University of Missouri at Kansas City, 1964.

White, Constance E. "A Suggested Curriculum for Utilizing Jazz Music in the High School Program." Master's thesis, San Francisco State College, 1969.

Whiteman, Paul, and Lieber, Leslie. *How to Be a Band Leader*. New York: Robert M. McBride, 1941.

——— ———. New York: McBride, 1948.

Williams, Ralph. *How to Build a Dance Band and Make It Pay*. Chicago: Downbeat, 1940.

A thorough "how to" book covering every aspect of information needed by the sideman and leader.

Williams, Thomas G. "The Evolution of Jazz Performance and Study in High Schools and Colleges." D.A. dissertation, University of Mississippi, 1972.

Lacking in research and of little value.

Williamson, Ken. *Jazz Quiz I*. Durham City, England: Panda Publications, 1945.

———. *Jazz Quiz II*. Durham City, England: Panda Publications, 1946.

Wiskirchen, George. *Developmental Techniques for the School Dance Band Musician*. Boston: Berkley Press, 1961.

A most valuable book that should be mandatory study for all jazz students. Highly recommended.

Wucher, Jay R. "Jazz Band and Concert Band Performance Skills of Selected Undergraduate Instrumental Music Education Majors at the University of Southern Mississippi." Master's thesis, University of Southern Mississippi, 1972.

Tries to determine if there are performance deficiencies between music majors with jazz experience and those without jazz experience. Not an important study.

Wylie, Floyd E. "An Investigation of Some Aspects of Creativity of Jazz Musicians." Ph.D. dissertation, Wayne State University, 1962.

Investigates the influence of musical training and experience on creativity.

Chapter 8

Jazz in Novels, Poetry, Plays, and Films

Since the 1930s when jazz writing began to make an impact, there have been many examples of the influence of this musical form upon creative artists in all the main spheres. As far as films are concerned, the connection dates from the invention of talking motion pictures in 1928. For a comprehensive listing of jazz in motion pictures, the reader is referred to David Meeker's *Jazz in the Movies: A Guide to Jazz Musicians 1917–1977* (1977). There are a substantial number of works of fiction with a jazz theme, about a jazz-playing character, or set within a jazz environment. We have not set out to identify and list all of these and, indeed, many are either ephemeral works or have a very tenuous link to jazz. Our list is selective and includes references to jazz poetry and the few plays with a jazz theme.

One of the earliest jazz novels is Dorothy Baker's *Young Man with a Horn*, written eight years after the death of Chicago-style jazz cornet player Leon "Bix" Beiderbecke and loosely based on his brief but colorful career. Although by no means a major work of fiction, it has some interest, and since its original publication in 1938 has reappeared in many editions including book club and paperback up to 1962. In the early 1950s, it was filmed (not very successfully) under the title in Britain of *Young Man of Music*. It is doubtful if any existing jazz novels stand in the first rank of literature and, just as the definitive jazz film has yet to be made, the definitive jazz novel remains to be written.

John A. Williams, a black author, has written *Night Song* (1961), which is perhaps the most believable of all the attempts to make fictional sense of a black jazz musician's life. British writer Roland Gant's book *World in a Jug*

(1959) had its share of faults but did provide a realistic picture of a jazz pianist who lived an unnatural life out of a suitcase. This world of the one night stand—traveling long distances each day and performing in a different town each night—is a common factor in the lives of practicing jazz musicians, as indeed of other entertainers. Other novels refer to this situation and the stresses and strains it produces on those who live this way. Another British writer, better qualified than most to write this type of book, is Benny Green, who gave up playing professionally as a musician to earn his living as a writer. An example is his *Blame It on My Youth* (1967), even though the actual amount of jazz itself in the book is limited.

Many authors seek authenticity by mentioning the famous names in jazz, and liberally using the picturesque terminology associated with jazz musicians. This can easily be detected by the real expert, and sometimes affects any appreciation of the work, even when the literary standard is high. Nat Hentoff does not fall into this category. He understands the feelings of black musicians extremely well, and his *Jazz Country* (1965), aimed at a youthful readership, is outstanding. John Clellon Holmes's *The Horn* (1958) was described by a reviewer in *Jazz Journal* as the "best jazz novel to date." Another book of the same period well reviewed in the jazz press was Garson Kanin's *Blow Up a Storm* (1959). Kanin is a skillful author, but the work is only partially successful since the characterization is weak. Ross Russell's *The Sound* (1961) fictionalizes the life of leading modern jazz saxophonist Charlie Parker, and is one of the most successful of its genre. Another claimant to the title of "the best novel written on jazz" is Herbert Simmons's *Man Walking on Eggshells* (1962). This received considerable critical acclaim on publication. Other American authors writing jazz fiction include Langston Hughes and Harold Flender. Hughes's *Tambourines to Glory* (1958) is the story of two black women gospel singers, while Flender's *Paris Blues* (1957) explores the relationship between two American jazz musicians (one black and one white) living and working in Paris. Their creative work is distracted by the presence of two female tourists who attempt to get them to return to the United States. The film version of this book featured the playing of Louis Armstrong and other jazz musicians and Duke Ellington's fine musical score. Mary Weik's *The Jazz Man* (1966) is a brief forty-two-page fable unusually illustrated by Ann Grifalioni's woodcuts.

Few stage plays have had jazz themes, but one outstanding exception was *The Connection* (1960), by J. Gelber, which ran in New York before being made into a successful film directed by Shirley Clarke in 1961. The plot involves a group of heroin addicts who are waiting for their "connection" to arrive with the drug. The score was written by pianist Freddie Redd and played on stage by him and other musicians, including saxophonist Jackie McLean, in both the stage and film versions. The quality of the music was excellent and, in some ways, it provides the most serious presentation of jazz in a feature film. Edward Albee's play *Death of Bessie Smith* (1960) has tenuous links with jazz, although the legend on which it was based has been effectively disproved by recent books on the famous blues singer.

Jazz has enjoyed a considerable affinity with modern poetry although, on the whole, the literary content has often little connection with jazz music. Poets like Christopher Logue were associated with the linking of jazz to poetry readings. Poetry on jazz themes has appeared in various collections. Black poet Langston Hughes produced an early anthology in 1926 entitled *The Weary Blues,* and other more recent collections include Jake Trussell's *After Hours Poetry* (1958), Rosey Pool's *Beyond the Blues* (1962), and John Sinclair's *This Is Our Music* (1965).

One of the best critical discussions on the subject of jazz and films appeared in the *Downbeat Yearbook 1967.* In this, Dan Morgenstern points out that jazz and the cinema are "the two arts truly indigenous to our time." They have a great deal in common, including humble and obscure origins in the later years of the nineteenth century, and belated recognition as legitimate forms of artistic expression. The ironic fact is that although conditions appear ideal for mutual inspiration, real achievements are extremely rare. The Original Dixieland Jazz Band appeared soundless in the 1917 film *Good for Nothing* filmed at Reisenweber's Restaurant in New York and thus recorded another "first" performance paralleling their first gramophone record. It was with the coming of sound movies in 1928 that jazz musicians were able to make an impact, and over the fifty years to date they have appeared in many films and have composed and performed background music for many others. Unfortunately not a single jazz film—fictional or documentary—that could be called a masterpiece has yet been made. There have been some praiseworthy efforts however, dating back to director Dudley Murphy's *St. Louis Blues* and *Black and Tan Fantasy,* which were both made in 1929. In many cases, the mere preservation of some of the incomparable jazz artists of the 1920s and 1930s is sufficient to make the films of real value to the jazz historian.

The pattern of relationships between jazz and the film developed over the years and the following broad categories can be defined:

1. Commercial shorts.
2. The use of jazz musicians in cameo performances within the basic framework of film musicals.
3. The dramatic feature film with a jazz theme including "biographies" of famous musicians.
4. The jazz documentary presenting its subject in a straightforward or possibly "arty" way.
5. The all-black film—made with an all-star cast either for the general audience or for the black audience exclusively.
6. The films using jazz music and musicians on the background score with little or no jazz aspects in their subject content. Impressionist color films can also be included in this category.

A major work published in recent years has greatly assisted in documenting the relationship of jazz to the moving picture industry. David Meeker's *Jazz in the Movies* (1977) lists in title order over 2,200 films in which jazz musicians either appeared or contributed to the score. Brief evaluations help to make this an essential reference book. It is well organized, and includes an index of names of musicians. It is illustrated with stills from many films.

Jazz and the cinema have had a checkered development.

Commerical considerations have almost always intervened and prevented the sympathetic and informed presentation needed to get the best out of the collaboration between these two contemporary and fascinating art forms.

BIBLIOGRAPHY

Albee, Edward. *The Death of Bessie Smith*. New York: Coward-McCann, 1960.

    A play.

———— ————. London: Samuel French, 1968.

Allen, S. *Bop Fables*. New York: Simon and Schuster, 1955.

Avery, R. *Murder on the Downbeat*. New York: Mystery House, 1943.

Baird, J. *Hot, Sweet and Blue*. New York: Fawcett, 1956.

Baker, Dorothy. *Young Man with a Horn*. Boston: Houghton Mifflin, 1938.

———— ————. London: Gollancz, 1938.

———— ————. New York: Readers Club, 1943.

———— ————. New York: Dial Press, 1944.

———— ————. Cleveland: World, 1946.

———— ————. London: Jazz Book Club, 1957.

———— ————. London: Transworld, 1962.

Bird, B. *Downbeat for a Dirge*. New York: Dodd, Mead, 1952.

————. *Dead and Gone*. New York: Dell, n.d.

    Paperback edition of *Downbeat for a Dirge*.

Bontemps, Arna. *Lonesome Boy*. Boston: Houghton Mifflin, 1955.

    A children's novel about a young trumpet player in New Orleans.

Borneman, Ernest. *Tremolo*. New York: Harper, 1948.

———— ————. London: Jarrolds, 1948.

———— ————. London: Four Square Books, 1960.

Brossard, C. *Who Walk in Darkness*. New York: New Directions, 1952.

———— ————. London: John Lehmann, 1952.

———— ————. New York: Signet, 1954.

Bunyan, P. *The Big Blues*. (No location): Magenta Books, Newstand Library, 1958.

    An unintentionally funny jazz novel.

Clapham, W. *Come Blow Your Horn*. London: Cape, 1958.

———— ————. Toronto: Clarke Irwin, 1958.

Curran, D. *Dupree Blues*. New York: Knopf, 1948.

——— ———. New York: Berkley, n.d.

———. *Piano in the Band*. New York: Reynal and Hitchcock, 1940.

Cuthbert, C. *The Robbed Heart*. New York: Fischer, 1945.

——— ———. New York: Dell, n.d.

Duke, O. *Sideman*. New York: Criterion, 1956.

English, R. *Strictly Ding-Dong and Other Swing Stories*. Garden City, N.Y.: Doubleday, 1941.

Ewing, A. *Little Gate*. New York: Rinehart, 1947.

Flender, Harold. *Paris Blues*. New York: Ballantine, 1957.

——— ———. London: Hamilton, 1961.

Foote, S. "Ride Out." In *New Short Novels*, by M. L. Aswell. New York: Ballantine, 1954.

Gant, Roland. *World in a Jug*. London: Cape, 1959.

——— ———. New York: Vanguard Press, 1961.

Garvin, Richard, and Addeo, Edmond G. *The Midnight Special*. (No location): Bernard Geis Associates, 1971.

A novel based on the life of Huddie Ledbetter. A well-written and entertaining book.

Gelber, J. *The Connection: A Play*. New York: Grove Press, 1960.

——— ———. London: Evergreen Books, 1960.

Gilbert, E. *The Hot and the Cool*. Garden City, N.Y.: Doubleday, 1953.

——— ———. New York: Popular Library, 1954.

Green, Benny. *Blame It on My Youth*. London: MacGibbon and Kee, 1967.

Gwinn, W. *Jazz Bum*. New York: Lion Books, 1954.

Hanley, J. *Hot Lips*. New York: Designs, 1952.

Harper, Michael S. *Dear John, Dear Coltrane*. Pittsburgh: University of Pittsburgh Press, 1970.

A book of poems inspired by jazz music and musicians.

——— ———. Pittsburgh: University of Pittsburgh Press, 1972.

——— ———. Pittsburgh: University of Pittsburgh Press, 1975.

Harvey, C., ed. *Jazz Parody: Anthology of Jazz Fiction*. London: Spearman, 1948.

Hentoff, Nat. *Jazz Country*. New York: Harper, 1965.

——— ———. London: Hart-Davis, 1966.

——— ———. New York: Harper and Row, 1976.

Holmes, J. C. *Go*. New York: Scribners, 1952.

———. *The Horn*. New York: Random House, 1958.

———— ————. London: Deutsch, 1959.

———— ————. London: Jazz Book Club, 1961.

Hughes, Langston. *Ask Your Mama: 12 Moods for Jazz.* New York: Knopf, 1961.

> Poetry inspired by blues and jazz.

————. *Tambourines to Glory, A Novel.* New York: J. Day, 1958.

> Story of two black female gospel singers.

———— ————. London: Gollancz, 1959.

————. *The Weary Blues.* New York: Knopf, 1926.

> Poems.

Hunter, E. *Second Ending.* New York: Simon and Schuster, 1956.

———— ————. London: Constable, 1956.

———— ————. London: Transworld, 1956.

Huston, J. *Frankie and Johnny.* New York: Boni, 1930.

> A stage adaptation of this song.

Joans, Ted. *A Black Manifesto in Jazz Poetry and Prose.* London: Calder and Boyers, 1971.

————. *Jazz Poems.* New York: Rhino Review, 1959.

Jones, Le Roi, and Neal, Larry. *Black Fire: An Anthology of Afro-American Writing.* New York: Morrow, 1968.

> Contains some poems about jazz musicians.

Kanin, Garson. *Blow Up a Storm.* New York: Random House, 1959.

———— ————. London: Heinemann, 1960.

———— ————. London: Hamilton, 1961.

Kayton, George. *Swing It High Sweet Saxophones.* Prairie City, Ill.: Press of James A. Decker, 1944.

> Includes a poem about a dancehall.

Kelley, W. M. *A Drop of Patience.* New York: Doubleday, 1965.

Kerouac, Jack. *On the Road.* New York: Viking Press, 1957.

———— ————. London: Deutsch, 1958.

———— ————. London: Pan Books, 1961.

————. *The Subterraneans.* New York: Grove Press, 1958.

———— ————. London: Deutsch, 1960.

Lea, G. *Somewhere There's Music.* Philadelphia: Lippincott, 1958.

Lee, G. *Beale Street Sundown.* New York: House of Field, 1942.

Marks, Jim. *Jazz, Women, Soul.* Millbrae, Calif.: Celestial Arts, 1974.

> Includes poems about jazz musicians.

Martucci, Ida. *Jive Jungle.* New York: Vantage Press, 1956.

> A novel featuring references to jazz musicians.

Meeker, David. *Jazz in the Movies*.
See p. 161.
Millen, G. *Sweet Man*. London: Cassell, 1930.
———— ————. New York: Pyramid, 1952.
Mitchell, A. *If You See Me Comin'*. London: Cape, 1962.
———— ————. New York: Macmillan, 1962.
Ondaatje, Michael. *Coming through Slaughter*. New York: W. W. Norton, 1976.
A novel based on the life of Buddy Bolden.
Pool, R. E. *Beyond the Blues*. Kent, England: Hand and Flower Press, 1962.
Quin, Ann. *Tripticks*.
See p. 128.
Reed, Harlan. *The Swing Music Murder*. New York: E. P. Dutton, 1938.
A novel involving dance bands.
Rieman, T. *Vamp Till Ready*. New York: Harper, 1954.
———— ————. London: Gollancz, 1955.
Rundell, W. *Jazz Band*. New York: Greenberg, 1935.
Russell, Ross. *The Sound*. New York: Dutton, 1961.
A novel based on the life of Charlie Parker.
Shurman, I. *Death Beats the Band*. New York: Phoenix Press, 1943.
Sill, Harold. *Misbehavin' with Fats*. Reading, Mass.: Addison-Wesley, 1978.
An adventure novel for children based on the life of Fats Waller.
Simmons, H. A. *Man Walking on Eggshells*. Boston: Houghton Mifflin, 1962.
———— ————. London: Methuen, 1962.
———— ————. London: Jazz Book Club, 1964.
Simon, G. T. *Don Watson Starts His Band*. New York: Dodd, Mead, 1940.
For children.
Sinclair, H. *Music out of Dixie*. New York: Rinehart, 1952.
———— ————. New York: Perma Books, 1953.
Sinclair, J. *This Is Our Music*. Detroit: Artists Workshop Press, 1965.
Poems.
Sklar, G. *The Two Worlds of Johnny Truro*. Boston: Little, Brown, 1947.
———— ————. Garden City, N.Y.: Sun Dial Press, 1948.

———— ————. New York: Popular Library, 1950.

Smith, R. P. *Plus Blood in Their Veins*. New York: Avon, 1952.

————. *So It Doesn't Whistle*. New York: Harcourt Brace, 1941.

Spicer, B. *Blues for the Prince*. New York: Dodd, Mead, 1950.

———— ————. London: Collins, 1951.

———— ————. New York: Bantam Books, 1951.

Steig, H. *Send Me Down*. New York: Knopf, 1941.

———— ————. New York: Avon, n.d.

———— ————. London: Jarrolds, 1943.

Stephens, E. *Roman Joy*. New York: Doubleday, 1965.

Sylvester, R. *Rough Sketch*. New York: Dial Press, 1948.

Trussell, Jake. *After Hours Poetry*. Kingsville, Tex.: The Author, 1958.

Updyke, J. *It's Always Four O'Clock*. New York: Random House, 1956.

Van Vechten, C. *Nigger Heaven*. New York: Knopf, 1926.

———— ————. London: Knopf, 1926.

———— ————. New York: Avon, n.d.

Wain, J. *Strike the Father Dead*. London: MacMillan, 1962.

Wallop, D. *Night Light*. New York: Norton, 1953.

Weik, Mary Hays. *The Jazz Man*. New York: Atheneum, 1966.
    A children's fable.

Whitmore, S. *Solo*. New York: Harcourt Brace, 1955.

———— ————. London: Gollancz, 1956.

———— ————. London: Transworld, 1958.

Williams, John. *Night Song*. New York: Farrar, Straus and Giroux, 1961.

———— ————. London: Collins, 1962.

———— ————. London: Jazz Book Club, n.d.

Willis, G. *Little Boy Blues*. New York: Dutton, 1947.

————. *Tangleweed*. Garden City, N.Y.: Doubleday, Doran and Co., 1943.

————. *The Wild Faun*. New York: Greenberg, 1945.

Chapter 9

Jazz Periodicals

Many jazz periodicals have led a very brief existence. Often they are produced by a small group of similar-minded individuals, and appear more or less frequently for a few months to a few years. There are many reasons for this brief existence, of which economics is certainly the biggest factor. It is also true that some of these short-lasting periodicals have been of very high quality, having been produced by dedicated jazz enthusiasts and having articles written by top experts in the field. Since institutions such as libraries often wait to see if a journal is going to have significance before seeking to acquire it, the jazz magazine often ceases publication without any files being maintained.

A great service has been done in efforts to reprint some of these magazines. Probably the best jazz periodical yet published in the United States has been the *Jazz Review*, which lasted from 1958 to 1961, and was edited by Nat Hentoff and Martin Williams. The first four volumes have been reprinted by the Kraus Reprint Company in Millwood, New York. Other reprints include Whitney Balliett's *Dinosaurs in the Morning* (1962), *New York Notes* (1976) and *Such Sweet Thunder* (1966), all of whch originally appeared in the *New Yorker* magazine. Martin Williams's *Jazz Panorama* (1962) is also a collection of articles from *Jazz Review*.

The Greenwood Press in Westport, Connecticut, now has available on 35 mm microfilm twenty-two jazz periodicals, including both current and defunct magazines. The collection of defunct periodicals includes *The Needle* (1944–45), published and edited by Robert Reynolds, that lasted only eight months, and *Jazz Hot* (1935–72), founded by Charles Delaunay and Hugues Panassie, and was published in both

189

French and English from 1935 until 1945; after 1945 it was published only in French. Along with *Downbeat* magazine, published in the United States, *Jazz Hot* was the earliest and longest lasting periodical devoted to jazz.

Other now defunct periodicals in the Greenwood Press collection include: *Clef* (1946), which lasted only seven months and included articles on traditional jazz; *Jazz Quarterly* (1942–?), which was published in Chicago by traditional jazz enthusiast Jake Trussell; *Jazz* (1942–43); *Jazz: A Quarterly of American Music* (1958–60), edited by Ralph Gleason; *Jazz Digest* (1972–74), primarily devoted to book and record reviews; *Jazz Information* (1931–41), jointly edited in New York by Ralph de Toledano, Ralph Gleason, and Eugene Williams; *Jazz Session* (1944–46), published by the Hot Club of Chicago, with a very traditional outlook; *Music and Rhythm* (1940–42), originally edited by Paul Edward Miller and later by Carl Cons, and featuring articles by a number of top jazz musicians of the day; *H.R.S. Society Rag* (1938–41); *Ragtime Review* (1914–18), which contained scores of ragtime music; *Playback* (1948–52), originally entitled the *Jazzfinder*, which was edited by Orin Blackstone and was mainly of discographical interest; *The Jazz Record* (1943–47), possibly the only magazine to be edited by a renowned jazz musician—Art Hodes; *Hip: The Jazz Record Digest* (1962–71), primarily concerned with record reviews and information on record releases; *The Discophile: The Magazine for Record Information* (1948–58), primarily of discographical interest; *Australian Jazz Quarterly: A Magazine for the Connoisseur of Hot Music* (1946–57); and *Matrix* (1945–75), also primarily of discographical interest.

Greenwood Press also includes two periodicals currently in publication, the *NAJE Educator* (1968–), which is edited by Matt Betton and is of interest to students and educators, and *The Second Line* (1950–), which is a publication of the New Orleans Jazz Club.

Jazz magazines proper divide broadly into four main categories with some inevitable overlapping between these groups. As might be expected, there is a tremendous variation in quality of production and content. The journals aimed at the widest readership can be loosely grouped together because they usually follow an editorial formula of feature articles, news, book and record reviews, and plenty of photographs, and are perhaps the aristocrats of the jazz magazine world. This group includes the American *Jazz* (now *Jazz and Pop*) and *Downbeat*, the British *Jazz Monthly* and *Jazz Journal*, the Swedish *Orkester Journalen*, the German *Jazz Podium* and the Canadian *Coda*. There are others of a similar quality throughout the world, but these are all good examples of the breed. With the exception of *Downbeat*, most are "pure," in that they exclude coverage of all material outside the jazz sphere. *Downbeat* is subtitled "The Contemporary Music Magazine" and although primarily jazz, it does include some coverage of rock and contemporary "classical" music. It is a monthly magazine (which also appears in a Japanese edition), and has been one of the most influential and reliable magazines in the jazz field since its inception in 1934. It is indexed in *The Music Index*.

Jazz Journal, one of the two leading British journals, has been described as probably the finest all-round jazz magazine in the world. This was the verdict of an editor of a rival American journal. It covers the whole field of jazz in an adult and responsible manner, and many articles of permanent value have appeared in its pages since its commencement in 1948. It is also indexed by *Music Index* and, unusual for a jazz magazine, publishes an annual index to itself. Albert McCarthy's *Jazz Monthly* (now *Jazz and Blues*) (1945 to date), with its scholarly articles, excellent reviews, and regular discographical features, is probably the main reading of the British jazz intellectual and is a first-class journal with an international reputation. Between 1962 and 1966 it included the supplement *Jazz Record*, which listed jazz record releases of the month. Another useful journal is *Storyville*, which first appeared in 1964. Published bimonthly in London, it is neatly produced with a mixture of discographical information and general articles. It has a special trading section paged separately with lists of records for sale.

Canada's leading magazine, *Coda*, has developed over the years since 1958 into a first class publication. It appears bi-monthly and has worldwide correspondents who regularly contribute to its pages.

Another important journal was *Record Changer*, which

flourished in the 1940s and early 1950s. In its May, 1948, issue it included a complete index of all articles appearing in its pages from the first issue in August, 1942, up to December, 1947.

Other magazines that fall under the previous classification and are of more recent origin are *Jazz Magazine* (1976–   ), which is published in the United States, and *Into Jazz,* a British publication that ceased in 1974 after only two fine issues.

A larger group consists of magazines aimed at either a specialized geographic area or a specialized audience. This includes the purely local jazz magazines that cover the activities of local personalities in depth; most of such material is ephemeral and of little permanent significance. The previously mentioned *Second Line* is an excellent example of this species. This has been published since 1950 and includes articles of wider interest as well as the local news items. Other examples are *Hip: The Milwaukee Jazz Letter* (1962–67), *Jazz Times* (1964–   ) from London, and *Just Jass* (1062–   ) from Birmingham, England.

Two magazines aimed primarily at the avant-garde audience are *Bells,* which also includes information on improvisational music in the San Francisco area, and *The Grackle* (1976), which is of similar content and published in Brooklyn, New York.

A third specialized group is formed from the discographical magazines that circulate to a small number of enthusiasts, often spread through many countries. These magazines usually consist of discographical listings and a few articles. They seem to merge and split up very frequently. For example *Matrix,* which incorporated its rival *Discophile* in 1958, is a bi-monthly record research magazine that has approximately twenty pages in each issue and is extremely useful in its specialized field. Like one of its American counterparts, *Record Research* (and its subsidiary *Blues Research*), is indexed in *Music Index*. *Record Research*, subtitled "the magazine of record statistics and information,"appears about nine times each year. It is comprised mainly, though not entirely, of jazz material and usually includes several articles as well as pages of discography and lists of records for auction. *Blues Unlimited,* a British journal, concentrates on the blues field and has a strong list of contributors. According to its editor, "it covers all forms of Negro blues, gospel and rhythm and blues from 1920 to the present day." It publishes an index to itself.

Lastly there are magazines that are purely vehicles for the buying and selling of jazz records. Some are produced by record shops (e.g., *Record Finder* [U.S.A.] and *Goodchild's Jazz Bulletin* [U.K.]) but probably the most used and widest known is *Vintage Jazz Mart*, which appears monthly and contains some eighty pages per issue. It circulates internationally and includes material otherwise unobtainable. It is invaluable to the true collector but, because of the tiny print, is extremely difficult to read.

Another important title that does not fit into any of the above categories is the British *Melody Maker*. It has covered jazz in its pages since 1926 as part of the popular music and entertainment field.

Two other very important jazz periodicals are *The Journal of Jazz Studies* (1973–), published at Rutgers University, and the *NAJE Educator* (1968), published by the National Association of Jazz Educators. The former is perhaps the most scholarly and academic jazz periodical currently published, and is noted for the quality and expertise of its contributors involved in jazz research. The latter is certainly the leading periodical of interest to jazz educators and students. It features articles by experts in a variety of jazz-related fields and offers a great deal of current events news on jazz in the educational system.

The appeal of jazz to a worldwide audience is well demonstrated by a study of the periodical literature, and publications appear regularly in most languages and many countries. Apart from the more obvious ones there are magazines in Polish, Danish, Finnish, Dutch, Norwegian, Icelandic, and Italian. Continental Europe has a long history of an intellectual and semi-intellectual interest in jazz since the early days of Robert Goffin and Hugues Panassie. Journals in French and German particularly have been appearing for many years.

Periodicals are listed in alphabetical order. If known, the title of the periodical is followed by its dates of publication, country of publication, and complete address if currently being published. This is followed by brief comments on the nature of the periodical. Only English language periodicals are included.

LIST OF PERIODICALS

Ad Lib (1944–47). Canada.

American Jazz Review (1944–?). U.S.A.
>   Originated in mimeographed form as the *American Jazz Monthly*.

Australian Jazz Quarterly (1946–57). Australia.
>   "A magazine for the connoisseur of hot music."

Ballroom and Band (1934–36). England.

Band Leaders (1942–?). U.S.A.

Basin Street (1945–?). U.S.A.

The Beat (1949–?). Australia.

Bells. U.S.A. 1921 Walnut #1, Berkeley, Calif. 94704.
>   Primarily deals with the avant-garde.

Billboard (1961–   ). U.S.A. 165 W. 46th Street, New York City, N.Y. 10036.
>   Not primarily devoted to jazz but of interest to jazz musicians.

Black Perspective in Music (1973–   ). U.S.A.
>   Not principally devoted to jazz but does have occasional jazz-related articles.

Blues Research (1959–   ). U.S.A.
>   A subsidiary publication of *Record Research* devoted entirely to blues discography with few articles or record reviews. Consists almost entirely of discographical lists.

Blues Rhythm (1942). Australia.

Blues Unlimited (1963–   ). England.
>   "The journal of the blues appreciation society." Duplicated discographic magazine. According to critic Albert J. McCarthy, "the finest magazine of its type." Contains general articles on the blues plus biographical material on artists and the usual book and record reviews and discographical material. According to its editor, it covers "all forms of Negro blues, gospel and rhythm and blues from 1920 to the present day." It also publishes an index to itself.

Blues World (1965–   ). England.

Brio (1964–). England.
 Occasional articles and book review of jazz interest.
British Institute of Jazz Studies Newsletter (1966–). England.
 Duplicated newssheet designed to report to members of the institute on developments in its activities.
Buffalo Jazz Report. U.S.A. 1335 Main Street; Buffalo, N.Y. 14209.
Cadence (1976–). U.S.A. Route 1, Box 345; Redwood, N.Y. 13679.
 Focuses on oral histories, interviews, and record reviews.
Clef (1946). U.S.A.
 Devoted to traditional jazz.
Climax (1955–). U.S.A.
Coda (1958–). Canada. P.O. Box 87J; Toronto, Ontario M4J 4 X 8 Canada.
 Canada's leading jazz magazine. Includes news articles from various parts of the world plus a good section of record reviews.
Connchord (1958–). U.S.A.
 Contains occasional articles on jazz analysis and instrumental technique.
Consolidated Artist Newsletter (1976–). U.S.A. 290 Riverside Drive, Apartment 11 D; New York City, N.Y. 10025.
 Contains articles and interviews with jazz musicians.
Crescendo (1962–). England. P.O. Box 187; Williston Park, N.Y. 11596.
 Not strictly a jazz magazine, although it contains a good proportion of interest to the jazz enthusiast. Aimed perhaps toward the amateur and semiprofessional musician.
Different Drummer (1973–?) U.S.A. P.O. Box 136; Rochester, N.Y. 14601.
 Consists primarily of record reviews, and is aimed at jazz listeners rather than scholars or professional musicians.
Discographical Forum (1960–61). England.
Discography (1942–46). England.
 "For the jazz student."
The Discophile (1948–58). England.
 An excellent pioneering discographical journal.
Dis-Counter (1948–). U.S.A.
Downbeat (1934–). U.S.A. 222 W. Adams Street; Chicago, Ill. 60606.
 A magazine with an international circulation which contains

news, feature articles, and reviews. One of the longest-established journals, it is also one of the most influential and reliable American magazines in the jazz field.

Ethnomusicology (1955–). U.S.A.
   Occasional research articles in the area of jazz.

Eureka (1960). England.

Footnote (1969–). England. Flat 3, 37 High Street; Cherry Hilton, Cambridge, England.
   Focuses on New Orleans jazz.

Goodchild's Jazz Bulletin (196?). England.

The Grackle (1976–). U.S.A. P.O. Box 244; Vanderveer Station; Brooklyn, N.Y. 11210.
   Primarily deals with avant-garde music and musicians.

Guitar Player (1967–). U.S.A.
   Contains many articles on instrumental technique and jazz theory for the jazz guitarist.

Hip: The Jazz Record Digest (1962–71). U.S.A.
   Originally published as *Hip: The Milwaukee Jazz Letter*.

Hot News (1935–?). England.

Hot Notes (1946–48). Ireland.

Hot Notes (1969–). U.S.A.
   A newsletter of the New York Jazz Museum.

H.R.S. Society Rag (1938–42). U.S.A.
   A publication of the Hot Record Society.

Impetus. England.
   Devoted to new music.

The Instrumentalist (1946–). U.S.A.
   Includes very informative articles of interest to the jazz educator and student.

International Art of Jazz. U.S.A. 5 Saywood Lane; Stony Brook, N.Y. 11790.

International Association of Jazz Record Collectors Journal. P.O. Box 50440; Nashville, Tenn. 37205.
   Deals with association activities and some research on traditional jazz.

International Discophile. U.S.A.

Into Jazz (1974). England.
   The two issues of this magazine were well written and promised much for the future.

Jazz. (1942–45). U.S.A.
   Focuses on traditional jazz.

Jazz (1958–60). U.S.A.
"A quarterly of American music."
Jazz and Blues. England.
Originally titled *Jazz Monthly*. Contains important articles on jazz history and analysis. One of the better magazines for the jazz educator and student.
Jazz and Pop (1962–   ). U.S.A.
Originally titled *Jazz Magazine*. Before becoming *Jazz and Pop*, it was one of the best jazz periodicals, containing intructional articles, and lead sheets; emphasis on education.
Jazz Beat (1964–66). England.
Originally titled *Jazz News*.
Jazz Catalogue (1960–   ). England.
A discographical magazine listing all jazz records issued in Great Britain.
Jazz Circle News (1978–   ). England.
Jazz Commentary (1944–45). Scotland.
Jazz Digest (1972–74). U.S.A.
Primarily concerned with record and book reviews.
Jazz Fan (195?–?). England.
Jazz Forum (1946–47). England.
"Quarterly review of jazz and literature." Contains some well-written articles by distinguished contributors. An unusual venture combining literature with jazz.
Jazz Forum (1968–   ). Poland. P.O. Box 671; A-1011; Vienna, Austria.
Printed in English and Polish, this is the magazine of the European Jazz Federation.
Jazz Guide (1964–   ). England.
Jazz Hot (1935–72). France.
Published in both French and English from 1935 to 1945. Published only in French from 1945.
Jazz Illustrated (1949–?). England.
All pictures and current news with a few record reviews.
Jazz Index (1977–   ). West Germany.
Indexes 32 important jazz periodicals using approximately 60 main subject headings.
Jazz Information (1939–41). U.S.A.
Jazz Journal (1948–   ). England. 7 Carnaby Street; London WIVIPG England.
Covers the whole field of jazz in a responsible and adult

manner, and is indispensable to the jazz student. Many articles of permanent value have appeared in it since its inception and its record reviews are by recognized authorities. It also issues an annual index.

Jazz Junction Jive (1943–45). England.

Jazz Magazine (1946–47). England.

Jazz Magazine (1976–). U.S.A. Box 212; Northport, N.Y. 11768.

Jazz Monthly (1945–). England.

 See *Jazz and Blues*.

Jazz Music (1944–60). England.

 This was the most influential of the British magazines published during the war years—a period of great jazz activity.

Jazz New England (1976–?). U.S.A.

 Deals with local jazz activities in the New England states.

Jazz News (1956–64). England.

Jazz Notes (1941–). Australia.

Jazz Notes and Blue Rhythm (1940–?). Australia.

Jazz Orchestras (1946–?). England.

 A short printed magazine with articles on various jazz artists.

Jazz Panorama (1946–48). Canada.

Jazz Quarterly (1942–45). U.S.A

 Concentrates on jazz in Chicago.

Jazz Record (1943–44). England.

The Jazz Record (1943–47). U.S.A

 Edited by pianist Art Hodes.

Jazz Register (1965–). England.

Jazz Report (1958–). U.S.A. 357 Leighton Drive; Ventura, Calif. 93001.

Jazz Review (1948–?). England.

Jazz Review (1958–61). U.S.A.

 Probably the best jazz periodical produced in the United States. Authoritative, academic, and maintained a very high standard of journalism, producing much of permanent value.

Jazz, Rhythm and Blues (1967–). Switzerland.

 Published in English, French, and German.

Jazz Scene (1962–). England.

Jazz Session (1944–46). U.S.A.

 Publication of the Hot Club of Chicago.

Jazz Studies (1964–). England.

Jazz Tempo (1943–44). England.

Jazz Tempo (1946). U.S.A.
   Edited by Ross Russell.
Jazz Times (1964–?). England.
   "Bulletin of the West London Jazz Society." Of local interest focusing primarily on traditional jazz.
Jazz Today (1956–57). U.S.A.
Jazz Wax (1948). England.
Jazz World (1957). U.S.A.
Jazz Writings (1936–?). England.
Jazzette (1944–?). U.S.A.
The Jazz Finder (1948). U.S.A.
Jazzmen News (1945). England.
Jazznocracy (1975–   ). England. Milton Keynes, The Old Rectory; Wavenden, MK 17 8LT England.
Jazzography. England.
Jazzologist. U.S.A. P.O. Box 1225; Kerrville, Tex. 78020.
   A magazine focusing on New Orleans jazz. It is the official journal of the New Orleans Jazz Club of California.
Jazzology (1944–47). England.
Jazzways (1946). U.S.A.
   Its one issue contained excellent articles on jazz history.
Jersey Jazz. U.S.A. 51 Woodland Avenue; Verona, N.J. 07044.
   One of the best regional jazz magazines.
Journal of Jazz Discography (1976–   ). England.
Journal of Jazz Studies (1973–   ). U.S.A. Transaction Periodicals Consortium; Rutgers University; New Brunswick, N.J. 08903.
   Certainly the only American magazine devoted exclusively to serious jazz research.
Just Jass (1962). England.
   Duplicated local newssheet on the Birmingham jazz scene, and thus mainly of local interest to fans in that area.
Keynote (1945–47). England.
Mainstream. England.
   Edited by Albert McCarthy.
Matrix (1954–75). Published in Australia to 1959, from then on in England.
   Of discographical interest.
Melody Maker (1926–   ). England.
Metronome (1885–1961). U.S.A.

The Mississippi Rag. (1974–   ). U.S.A. P.O. Box 19068; Minneapolis, Minn. 55419.

Focuses on Dixieland and traditional jazz.

Music and Rhythm (1940–42). U.S.A.

Includes articles written by outstanding musicians of the day.

Music Maker (1966–   ). England.

Not exclusively material of jazz interest.

Music Memories and Jazz Report (1961–   ). U.S.A

It is primarily discographical and a vehicle for the exchange, buying, and selling of jazz records.

Musical Express (1946–52). England.

Musigram (1963–?). U.S.A.

NAJE Educator (1968–   ). U.S.A. P.O. Box 724; Manhattan, Kans. 66502.

Essential reading for the jazz educator and student. It contains, among many other things, various "how to" articles, information on happenings, equipment and literature in jazz, and feature articles dealing with aspects of jazz education.

National Society for Jazz Study (1943–46). England.

The Needle (1944–45). U.S.A.

New Jazz Tempo. U.S.A.

New Musical Express (1952–?). England.

Only the earlier issues are of jazz interest.

Note (1946). U.S.A.

Oh Play That Thing (1938). U.S.A.

Published by the San Francisco Record Society.

Percussionist (1964–   ). U.S.A.

Contains occasional articles of interest to the jazz drummer.

Percussive Notes (1963–   ). U.S.A.

Contains occasional articles of interest to the jazz drummer.

Pickup (1946–47). England.

"The record collector's guide."

Pieces of Jazz (196?–?). England.

Platter Chatter (1945–?). U.S.A.

Playback (1948–52). U.S.A.

Of interest to discographers and record collectors.

R and B Monthly (196?–66). England.

Discographical magazine of value in its field although some material included is outside the strictly jazz field.

R.S.V.P.: The Record Collectors Journal (1966–   ). England.

Lists some records of interest to the jazz collector.

Ragtime Review (1914–18). U.S.A.

Published in Chicago with news of ragtime music and actual ragtime scores.

Ragtime Society (1962–?). Canada.

The Record Advertiser (1948–?). England.

The Record Changer (1942–57). U.S.A.

One of the finer jazz magazines containing many articles of educational interest.

The Record Exchange (1948–?). Canada.

Record Finder (1958–?). U.S.A.

Duplicated periodical issued by a California jazz record shop. Consists of items for sale and auction from collectors in the United States, Canada and England.

Record Research (1955–?). U.S.A.

Discographical research periodical comprised primarily, but not entirely, of jazz material. Includes several articles in addition to the usual pages of discography and lists of records for auction.

Record Review (1976–   ). U.S.A. P.O. Box 91878; Los Angeles, Calif. 90009.

Recordiana (1944). U.S.A.

Reprints and Reflections (1945–?). Australia.

Rhythm (1926–39). England.

Rhythm and Blues (?–1965). U.S.A.

Printed magazine of only limited interest to the jazz enthusiast.

Rhythm and Soul (1966–?). England.

Royal Notes from the House of Kings. U.S.A.

A newsletter published by the King Instrument Company containing articles on jazz instrumental technique.

Sabin's Radio Free Jazz. U.S.A. 3212 Pennsylvania Avenue, S.E.; Washington, D.C. 20020.

Includes information on jazz radio programs and articles on musicians.

The Second Line (1950–   ). U.S.A. 833 Conti Street; New Orleans, La. 70112.

An excellent publication of the New Orleans Jazz Club.

Selmer Bandwagon (1952–   ). U.S.A.

Published by the Selmer Instrument Company; contains regular articles of interest to the jazz educator and student.

Sheffield University Jazz Club Magazine (1966–?). England.

Shout (1968–   ). England.

A comprehensive journal covering rhythm and blues.

Solid Set (1943–45). U.S.A.

Published in St. Joseph, Mo.

Song Hits (1937–   ). U.S.A.

Soul (1965– .). Canada.

Soul Music Monthly (1967–68). England.

Sounds Magazine (1976–?). U.S.A. P.O. Box 2918; .New York City, N.Y. 10019.

Information on jazz activities in New York.

Storyville (1965–   ). England. 1 Cecil Court; London Road, Enfield; Middlesex EN 2 6DB, England.

A well-produced journal, neatly organized with a mixture of discographical information and general articles. Also has a special section of lists of records for sale.

Swing (1938–40). U.S.A.

"The guide to modern music."

Swing Music (1935–36). England.

Swing Shop Mag-List (1952–55). England.

A supplement to Carey and McCarthy's *Directory of Recorded Jazz and Swing Music*.

Swinging Newsletter. Austria. P.O. Box 671; A-1011 Vienna, Austria.

A publication of the European Jazz Federation.

Tempo (1933–40). U.S.A.

"The modern musical magazine."

Tempo (1936–   ). Australia.

"The Australian musical news magazine."

Theme (1953–   ). U.S.A.

Universal Jazz (1946). England.

Vibrations (1967–   ). U.S.A.

"The sound of the jazz community."

Vintage Jazz Mart, England. Dollis Hill, London NW2, England.

This magazine is purely a vehicle for buying, selling, and exchanging jazz records. Circulates internationally and includes much unobtainable material. Invaluable to the true collector, although a bit difficult to read.

Vox Pop (1945). England.

The Wheel (1948). U.S.A.

"A record collectors rag."

Name Index

Aaronson's Commanders, 136
Aaslund, B. H., 142, 152
Abdul, Raoul, 9
Abrahams, R. D., 9
Abrams, Max, 83, 103
Addeo, Edmond G., 185
Adderley, Cannonball, 22
Agostinelli, Anthony, 161
Aitken, Allan E., 167
Albee, Edward, 182, 184
Albertson, Chris, 31, 34, 82, 104
Aleman, Oscar, 154
Allen, Henry "Red," 60, 114, 154
Allen, Richard B., 59
Allen, S., 62, 184
Allen, Walter C., 97, 116, 142, 160, 167
Allen, William, 3, 11
Allsopp, Kenneth, 8, 21, 56
Alrutz, Louis W., 167
Ames, Russell, 11
Ammons, Albert, 65
Anderson, A., 161
Anderson, Edgar W., 167–68
Anderson, Ernest, 63, 111, 120
Anderson, Lawrence E., 168
Ansermet, Ernst, 111
Antrim, D. K., 164, 168
Apetz, Harry B., 165, 168
Appleton, Clyde R., 168
Ardley, Neil, 54
Armitage, Andrew D., 151
Armitage, Merle, 95
Armstrong, Louis, 6, 9, 21, 44, 45, 47, 58, 60, 61, 67, 72–73, 77, 84, 85, 86, 87–88, 93, 104, 105, 112, 137, 156, 182
Arundel, P., 116
Asbury, Herbert, 7, 26
Asch, Moses, 30–31, 34
Asher, Don, 81, 97
Asman, James, 116, 145, 152, 168
Aswell, M. L., 185
Avakian, George, 152, 154
Avery, R., 184
Ayler, Albert, 23, 61

Babbitt, Milton, 119
Backus, Rob, 68
Baggelaar, Kristin, 17
Bailey, Mildred, 104
Bailey, Pearl, 89, 104
Baird, J., 184
Baker, Barbara, 11
Baker, David, 22, 34, 84, 116, 152, 166–67, 168, 171
Baker, Dorothy, 74–75, 89, 180, 184
Baker, Mickey, 168
Bakker, Dick, 142, 152, 157
Balliett, Whitney, 56, 71–72, 84, 103, 113–14, 116–17, 189
Bannister, L. H., 161
Barker, Danny, 7, 21–22, 57
Barnes, Ken, 92, 104
Barnet, Charlie, 67, 154, 155
Barnouw, Erik, 25
Baron, Stanley, 96
Barr, Walter L., 168
Barritt, Hugh G., 168

Barton, Charles W., 168–69
Basie, William "Count," 59, 67, 80, 81, 85, 89, 110, 112, 130
Baskerville, David R., 117
Baston, Bruce, 31–32, 34
Bauman, Dick, 99, 117, 169
Baxter, Derrick Stewart, *see* Stewart-Baxter, Derrick
Bebey, Francis, 27
Bechet, Sidney, 60, 76, 84, 89, 111
Becker, Howard S., 21
Bedwell, Stephen, 160
Beiderbecke, Leon "Bix," 47, 61, 72, 74–75, 80, 83, 89–90, 113, 121, 122, 137, 153, 159, 180
Bellocq, Ernest, 26
Bellson, Louie, 84
Belt, Lida, 84, 152
Belton, Geneva R., 9, 60
Benedict, Gardner, 164, 169
Beneke, Tex, 67, 155
Benford, R. J., 144, 147
Bennett, Carolyn L., 12
Bennett, Josephine, 27
Bennett, Tony, 61
Bennington, Billy D., 50
Benson, Kathleen, 6, 19
Berendt, Joachim, 47, 50, 62, 113, 117
Berg, I., 152
Berigan, Bunny, 90
Berk, Lee E., 169
Berry, Leon "Chu," 154
Berton, Ralph, 75, 89
Bethell, Tom, 78, 99
Betton, Matt, 190
Bezou, James, 88
Bilk, Bernard "Acker," 90
Billett, Roy O., 177
Bird, B., 184
Blackstone, Orin, 138–39, 151, 190
Blake, Blind, 30, 86
Blake, Eubie, 84, 86, 90
Blakey, Art, 47, 60
Blancq, Charles C., 62, 117
Bland, Bobby, 32
Blandford, Edmund L., 104

Blesh, Rudi, 5, 7, 12, 18, 45–47, 50, 62, 72, 84
Blocher, Arlo, 69
Boeckman, Charles, 19, 69
Bokelman, Marina, 18, 34
Bolcom, William, 86
Bolden, Buddy, 59, 77, 90, 125
Bonsanti, Neal J., 169
Bontemps, Arna, 184
Borenstein, Larry, 56, 84
Borneman, Ernest, 47, 52, 117, 184
Botkin, B. A., 9, 56
Boulton, David, 49, 56
Bowlin, Margie N., 169
Bowlly, Al, 156
Boyar, J., 93
Boyd, William C., 62
Bradford, Perry, 30, 34, 90
Braff, Ruby, 84
Branch, London G., 169
Brask, Ole, 54
Breeden, Leon, 84
Bridges, Henry, 154
Briscuso, Joseph J., 169
Britt, Stan, 148
Broonzy, William "Big Bill," 29, 30, 34, 35, 86, 90, 132
Brossard, C., 184
Broven, John, 33, 34–35, 56–57
Brown, Clifford, 129
Brown, Ken, 161
Brown, Les, 67, 154, 155
Brown, Robert L., 117–18
Brown, Sandy, 118
Brown, Theodore D., 118
Bruccoli, Matthew J., 72, 84
Brummond, Bruce E., 166, 169
Brunn, H. O., 43, 57
Bruyninckx, Walter, 152–53
Bruynoghe, Yannick, 30, 34, 35, 90
Bryce, O., 170
Budds, Michael, 60, 118
Buerkle, Jack V., 7, 21–22, 57
Bunyan, P., 184
Burley, Dan, 150
Burnsed, Charles V., 170

Burton, Gary, 90
Burton, Roger V., 22

Calabrese, Anthony, 75, 105–6
Calloway, Cab, 80, 90–91, 150
Carey, Dave, 139, 140, 153, 202
Carmichael, Hoagy, 83, 91
Carr, Ian, 34, 57, 114–15, 118
Carr, Leroy, 29
Carratello, John, 12, 170
Carroll, Robert, 154
Carter, Albert E., 12
Carter, Benny, 155
Case, Brian, 148
Castelli, Vittorio, 153
Caswell, Austin B., 171
Cerulli, D., 118
Charles, Ray, 61, 85, 91, 111
Charters, Ann, 6, 18
Charters, Samuel B., 29–30, 35,
    48, 57, 84, 98, 134, 148
Chase, Gilbert, 4, 20
Cherrington, G., 112, 153
Cherry, Don, 61
Chester, Bob, 155
Chickaneff, John L., 164, 170
Chilton, John, 73, 82, 88, 97, 134,
    142, 148, 170
Christian, Charlie, 84, 154
Clapham, W., 184
Clark, C. E., 72, 84
Clarke, John, 9
Clarke, Kenny, 60
Clarke, Shirley, 182
Claxton, William, 57
Clayton, Peter, 5, 20, 115, 121,
    150
Clinton, Larry, 155
Clooney, Rosemary, 91
Cobb, Arnette, 154
Coin, Gregory M., 62, 118
Coker, Jerry, 118, 167, 170
Cole, Maria, 81, 91
Cole, Nat "King," 61, 81, 91, 104,
    156
Cole, William S., 74, 80–81, 91,
    92, 118
Coleman, Bill, 154

Coleman, Ornette, 61, 86, 87, 92,
    111, 114, 125
Colin, S., 66
Collier, Graham, 62, 82, 92, 115,
    118–19, 166, 170
Collier, James L., 47, 51, 69
Collins, Lee, 77, 91
Collins, Mary, 77, 91
Colnot, Cliff, 170
Coltrane, Alice, 86
Coltrane, John, 23, 36, 47, 61, 72,
    74, 80, 86, 91–92, 114, 118, 153
Condon, Eddie, 49–50, 57, 62, 78–
    79, 82, 92, 119
Cone, James H., 12, 31, 35
Connor, Anthony, 32, 39, 86
Connor, Donald R., 142, 160
Cons, Carl, 62, 190
Cook, Bruce, 31, 35–36
Cook, Will Marion, 111
Cooper, David, 145, 161
Cornell, Jean G., 82, 88, 98
Coryell, Julie, 148
Cotterrell, Roger, 57, 135, 152
Courlander, Harold, 2, 12, 27
Cowley, M., 10
Crane, Genevieve, 119
Cronenwett, Gene, 165, 170–71
Crosby, Bing, 82–83, 92, 158
Crosby, Bob, 157
Crosby, E. J., 82, 92
Crump, Charlie, 159
Cunard, N., 9
Curran, D., 185
Cusack, Thomas, 76, 153
Cuthbert, C., 185

Dachs, David, 8, 20
Dain, Bernice, 153
Dameron, Tadd, 60
Damron, Bert L., 171
Danca, Vince, 90
Dance, Stanley, 60, 66, 73–74, 77,
    81, 93, 94, 97, 119, 171
Dankworth, Avril, 62, 116, 119,
    171
Dankworth, John, 82, 92
Darrell, R. D., 93

Davies, J. H., 145
Davies, J. R. T., 75, 105, 153
Davis, Brian, 153
Davis, Gary, 37, 86
Davis, J. P., 9, 148
Davis, Miles, 47, 60, 73, 80, 85, 86, 92, 132, 156
Davis, Nathan Tate, 22, 102
Davis, Sammy, 93
Davis, Sarah G., 171
Decca Record Company, 153–54
Dedrick, Art, 171
Deitch, Gene, 161
Delaunay, Charles, 83, 103, 136, 139, 140–41, 151, 154, 189–90
De Lerma, Dominique-Rene, 3, 22, 171
Demarey, Bertrand, 154
Denisoff, R. S., 22
Deshore, Thomas J., 171
Desmond, Paul, 61
de Toledano, Ralph, 111, 119, 190
Dexter, Dave, 25, 51
Dixon, Christa K., 12
Dixon, Robert, 36, 140, 155
Dixon, William, 9
Dodds, Baby, 77, 93
Dodds, Johnny, 77, 93, 137
Dodge, R. P., 45
Dolphy, Eric, 61, 80, 81, 93, 114
Dorsey, Jimmy, 67, 80, 93, 137, 154
Dorsey, Tommy, 48, 67, 80, 93, 137
Dowling, Eleanor, 127
Dowling, Lyle, 127
Downey, John, 119
Driggs, Frank, 52, 62
Duffty, W., 38, 97
Duke, John R., 171
Duke, O., 185
Dupree, "Champion" Jack, 32, 38

Early, Robert B., 171–72
Easton, Carol, 80, 99
Eaton, J., 88
Eckstine, Billy, 61
Edison, Thomas, 9

Edwards, Ernest, 154
Eldridge, Roy, 154
Electrical and Musical Industries, 154
Elkins, S. M., 10
Ellington, Duke, 6, 9, 10, 36, 48, 52, 58, 72, 73–74, 80, 85, 86, 94, 111, 112, 117, 120, 132, 137, 142, 159, 182
Ellington, Mercer, 73, 94
Elliott, Rudwick, 11
Ellis, Don, 85
Ellison, R., 120
Emett, Dan, 15
English, R., 185
Epstein, Dena J., 3–4, 12
Erlich, Lillian, 51, 115, 120
Europe, James Reese, 10
Evans, David, 31, 36, 98
Evans, Herschal, 154
Evans, Mark, 18
Evans, Mary, 63
Evans, Philip R., 75, 89
Evans, Tom, 63
Evensmo, Jan, 154–55
Ewen, David, 4–5, 20, 85, 95
Ewing, A., 185

Fahey, John, 31, 36, 103
Fairchild, R., 155
Farrell, Jack, 58, 63, 122
Faulkner, Robert R., 22
Feather, Leonard, 9, 25, 51, 60, 72, 85, 94, 112, 115, 120, 124, 133–34, 136, 148–49
Feldstein, Saul, 165, 171
Ferguson, Tom, 165, 171
Fernett, Gene, 48, 66
Ferriano, Frank, 171–72
Ferris, William, 31, 36, 146
Filmer, Vic, 150
Finkelstein, Sidney, 12, 109, 120–21
Fisher, Miles M., 3, 12
Fitzgerald, Ella, 21, 58, 85, 132
Flender, Harold, 181, 185
Flower, Desmond, 150
Flower, John, 101, 142, 160

Fluchiger, Otto, 154
Fly, Benton G., 172
Fong-Torres, Ben, 20
Foote, S., 185
Foreman, Ronald C., 60, 121
Foster, George M. "Pops," 78, 95
Foster, William P., 13
Fountain, Pete, 95
Fox, Charles, 51, 63, 75, 105, 143, 161
Fox, Roy, 95
Fox, Sidney, 51, 172
Frabizio, William, 130
Francis, A., 51
Frankenstein, Alfred, 63
Franklin, Aretha, 36, 86
Fraser, Al, 95
Frazier, E. F., 10
Freeman, Bud, 79, 95, 121
Freundlich, Douglas A., 172
Friedman, Laura, 148
Fry, A., 161
Fry, John G., 155
Fuller, Blind Boy, 30, 31, 34
Fuller, Earl, 157

Gammond, Peter, 5, 18–19, 20, 63, 73, 94, 115, 121, 150, 161
Ganfield, J., 146
Gant, Roland, 180–81, 185
Gara, L., 93
Gardner, Mark, 155
Garland, Phyl, 33, 36
Garlick, George, 75, 89–90
Garon, Paul, 31, 32, 36, 106
Garrison, L. M., 11
Garrod, Charles, 155, 157
Garvin, Richard, 185
Garwood, Donald, 36, 121
Gaskin, L. J. P., 146
Gates, E., 158
Gautier, Madeleine, 135, 136, 150
Gee, John, 172
Gehman, R., 119
Gelatt, Roland, 8–9, 25–26
Gelber, J., 182, 185
Gerardi, Jess L., 166, 172
Gerlach, Horace, 88

Gerow, Maurice, 55–56, 112–13, 130
Gershwin, George, 44, 95, 164
Gert zur Heide, Karl, 31, 36, 101
Getz, Stan, 86
Gilbert, E., 185
Gillenson, L. W., 63, 120
Gillespie, Dizzy, 48, 60, 74, 80, 81, 84, 85, 86, 95–96, 114, 154, 156
Gillett, Charlie, 33, 37
Gillis, Frank, 77, 91, 146
Gitler, Ira, 47–48, 60, 134, 149
Gleason, Ralph J., 85, 121, 190
Glover, Tony, 33, 37
Godbolt, Jim, 58, 84, 95, 121
Goddard, Chris, 121
Godrich, John, 36, 140, 155
Goffin, Robert, 44–45, 51–52, 72, 88, 193
Gold, Robert S., 135, 150
Goldberg, Isaac, 95, 121
Goldberg, Joe, 47, 60–61
Goldblatt, Burt, 49, 63
Goldkette, Jean, 48
Goldman, Elliott, 155
Gonzales, Babs, 121, 150
Good, Melvin L., 172
Goodman, Benny, 48, 67, 79, 85, 96, 111, 113, 122, 137, 142, 155, 160
Gordon, Dexter, 60
Goreau, Laurraine, 81–82, 98
Gottlieb, William, 63
Grady, Edythe R., 13
Graettinger, Robert, 96, 126
Graham, A. P., 85
Graham, Charles, 9, 25
Granholm, Ake, 58, 135, 152
Granz, Norman, 85
Grauer, B., 49, 53
Graves, Charles, 66
Gray, James M., 122
Gray, Wardell, 86
Green, Benny, 49, 58, 79, 85, 113, 122, 181, 185
Green, Jonathan, 80, 101
Greenfield, Edward, 103

Greenway, John, 3, 18, 146
Gridley, Mark, 52, 112–13, 122
Grifalioni, Ann, 182
Griffin, Nard, 61, 122
Grime, Kitty, 122
Grofe, Ferdie, 64
Groom, Bob, 32, 37
Grossman, Stefan, 33, 37
Grossman, William, 58, 63, 122
Guckin, John, 27
Gulledge, O. L., 16
Gullickson, Gordon, 151
Gumina, Michael J., 22
Guralnick, Peter, 37
Gutman, Bill, 94
Guttridge, L., 78, 105
Gwinn, W., 185
Gwynn-Jones, P., 90

Hackett, Bobby, 84
Hadlock, Richard, 47, 61
Hagelstein, Robert, 136
Hall, George, 153, 155–56
Hall, Jim, 114
Hall, Morris E., 164–65, 172
Hall, S., 20
Hammond, John, 26, 84, 96
Handy, D. Antoinette, 122
Handy, W. C., 10, 30, 37, 39, 76,
    85, 96, 151
Hanley, J., 185
Hansen, Chadwick C., 13, 37, 85
Haralambos, Michael, 22, 33, 37
Hare, Maud C., 2–3, 13
Harper, Michael S., 185
Harris, Bill, 154
Harris, Rex, 47, 52, 69, 115, 123,
    143, 156
Harris, Sheldon, 152
Harrison, Max, 52, 74, 102, 113,
    123, 143, 161, 162
Harvey, C. M., 156, 185
Haselgrove, J. R., 146
Haskins, James, 6, 19, 26, 58
Haupt, Lois Von, *see* Von Haupt,
    Lois
Hawes, Hampton, 80, 81, 97
Hawkins, Coleman, 81, 97, 154

Hayes, Cedric, 156
Hayes, Mileham, 135, 149
Heath, Ted, 97
Heaton, P., 64, 123
Heckman, Don, 11
Heerkens, Adriaan, 149
Hefti, Neal, 141
Heide, Karl, *see* Gert zur Heide,
    Karl
Heilbut, Tony, 13, 33, 37
Henderson, Fletcher, 9, 61, 79,
    97, 137, 142, 160
Hennessey, Thomas J., 52, 123
Hentoff, Nat, 7–8, 22–23, 46–47,
    52–53, 55, 71, 86–87, 112, 123,
    129, 162, 181, 185, 189
Hepworth, Loel T., 172
Herman, Woody, 67
Herzog zu Mecklenburg, Carl G.,
    145, 146
Hibbs, Leonard, 66, 156
Hicks, Warren W., 160
Higginbotham, J. C., 157
Hill, Richard, 27
Hilligoss, C. A., 172
Hinds, Bobbie M., 173
Hines, Earl, 47, 61, 77, 97, 114
Hinkle, William J., 173
Hoare, Ian, 33, 37
Hobsbawn, Eric, 8
Hobson, Wilder, 53, 109, 123
Hodeir, Andre, 53, 110, 123–24
Hodes, Art, 37, 85, 155, 190, 198
Hoeffer, George, 105
Holiday, Billie, 21, 38, 81, 82, 84,
    85, 86, 97, 112, 113, 122, 132,
    156
Hollander, B., 10
Holmes, J. C., 181, 185–86
Hopkins, Lightnin', 29
Hores, Robert, 173
Horn, David, 145, 146
Horne, Lena, 58, 82, 97–98, 104
Horricks, Raymond, 65, 71, 80,
    85, 89, 114, 124, 126
Howe, Martin, 38
Howlin' Wolf, 37
Hoyt, Charles A., 13

Hsio Wen Shih, 52
Huber, Leonard, 26, 58
Hudson, Herman, 84, 152
Huggins, Nathan I., 10
Hughes, Langston, 4, 10, 70, 85, 181, 182, 186
Hughes, Patrick C., 83, 98
Hughes, W. E., 99
Hunt, Ted, 165, 173
Hunter, E., 186
Huon, H. E., 73
Huston, J., 186
Hylton, Jack, 136
Hyman, S. E., 10

Iverson, Genie, 88

Jablonski, Edward, 95
Jackson, Arthur, 49, 66
Jackson, Bruce, 4, 13
Jackson, Clyde O., 13
Jackson, Edgar, 66
Jackson, George P., 18
Jackson, Jack, 156
Jackson, Mahalia, 3, 21, 81, 86, 98
Jackson, Milt, 98, 160–61
Jacobs, Gordon, 173
James, Burnett, 75, 89, 124
James, Harry, 67, 98, 155
James, Michael, 71, 80, 81, 85, 92, 96, 103, 114
James, Skip, 37
Janis, Harriet, 5, 18
Jasen, David A., 6, 19, 142–43, 156
Jefferson, Blind Lemon, 29
Jenkins, Mildred L., 27
Jensen, Robert A., 53
Jepsen, J. G., 102, 140, 156–57, 160
Jewell, Derek, 73, 94
Joans, Ted, 186
Johnson, Bill, 173
Johnson, Colin A., 153
Johnson, Frank, 66
Johnson, G., 102
Johnson, G. B., 3, 4, 13, 16
Johnson, J. J., 60

Johnson, J. W., 165, 173
Johnson, James P., 61
Johnson, James Weldon, 10
Johnson, Pete, 65, 78, 98
Johnson, Robert, 30, 35, 98
Johnson, Tommy, 31, 36, 98
Johnson, Willie Geary "Bunk," 77, 99
Johnston, Peter, 155
Jones, A. M., 27
Jones, Cliff, 157, 159
Jones, Elvin, 23, 86
Jones, Geraldine W., 13, 173
Jones, Hettie, 86
Jones, Le Roi, 7, 23, 61, 68, 124, 186
Jones, Max, 14, 31, 38, 49, 53, 73, 88, 124, 125
Jones, P. Gwynn, see Gwynn-Jones, P.
Jones, R. P., 70, 115, 124
Jones, Tim R., 166, 173
Joplin, Scott, 5, 6, 18, 19
Jost, Ekkehard, 61, 114, 124
Jungleers, 9

Kahn, Ely J., 104
Kamin, Ira, 64
Kaminsky, Max, 79, 86, 99
Kane, Harnett, 26, 58
Kanin, Garson, 181, 186
Kaplan, M., 161
Kaufman, Fredrich, 27
Kaufmann, Helen L., 20
Kayton, George, 186
Keathley, Kenneth E., 174
Keepnews, Orrin, 49, 53
Keil, Charles, 32, 38
Kelley, W. M., 186
Kemp, Barbara A., 174
Kennedy, R. E., 14
Kennington, Donald, 146
Kenton, Stan, 67, 80, 96, 99, 117, 159, 160
Kerouac, Jack, 186
Kimball, Robert, 86
King, B. B., 32, 36, 39, 61, 99
King, Jeffrey M., 124, 174

King, Nel, 101
Kinkle, Roger D., 134, 149
Kinnell, Bill, 116, 145, 152, 168
Kirkeby, W. T. E., 75, 105
Kitt, Eartha, 99
Kloss, Eric, 84
Kmen, Henry, 7, 18
Knight, B., 112, 153
Kofsky, Frank, 23, 68, 114, 124
Kolodin, Irving, 96
Konitz, Lee, 60, 86
Konowitz, Bertram L., 174
Korner, A., 161
Korst, Bill, 154, 157
Koster, Piet, 142, 157
Kramer, Stephen, 156
Kraner, Dietrich, 157
Krehbiel, Henry E., 14, 124
Kriss, Eric, 32–33, 38, 125
Krupa, Gene, 67, 84, 156
Kunstadt, L., 48, 57
Kupferman, Mayer, 130
Kuzmich, John, 163–64

Ladnier, Tommy, 137
Laine, Cleo, 82, 92
Lambert, C., 23
Lambert, G. E., 73, 77, 93, 94
Lambrecht, Clarence J., 165, 174
Landeck, Beatrice, 14
Lang, Eddie, 47, 61, 137
Lang, I., 38
Lange, Horst, 157
Langridge, Derek W., 144, 161
Larkin, P., 125
Lascelles, Gerald, 112, 130
Lawrence, Elliot, 155
Lea, G., 186
Leadbelly, *see* Ledbetter, Huddie
Leadbitter, Mike, 32, 38, 140, 157
Leaf, Earl, 27
Ledbetter, Huddie, 15, 30–31, 33, 34, 38–39, 41, 85, 185
Lee, Edward, 5, 20–21, 53–54
Lee, G., 186
Lee, G. W., 38
Lee, Peggy, 104
Leecan, Bobby, 136

Lefkowits, Judith W., 14
Leonard, Neil, 7, 23, 68, 125
Lerma, Dominique-Rene de, *see* de Lerma, Dominique-Rene
Leslie, P., 90
Lessner, John, 63
Levin, Robert, 8, 24, 69, 86, 90, 129
Levy, Louis H., 23
Lewis, Furry, 30
Lewis, George, 77–78, 99–100
Lewis, Jerry Lee, 37
Lewis, John, 86
Lewis, Meade Lux, 65, 85
Lieber, Leslie, 164, 178
Lindsay, Martin, 125, 170, 174
Livengood, Karen S., 14
Locke, Alain, 14
Logan, Ronald F., 166, 174
Logue, Christopher, 182
Lomakin, Nicholas, 174
Lomax, Alan, 3, 14–15, 18, 30–31, 34, 38–39, 75–76, 101–2
Lomax, John, 3, 14–15, 18, 30, 38–39
Lombardo, Guy, 100
Longstreet, Stephen, 26, 64, 91, 125
Lonstein, Albert, 161
Lord, Tom, 78, 107
Louisiana Five, 157
Love, W. C., 143–44, 161, 162
Lovell, John, 15
Lowris, George, 174
Lucas, John S., 15, 162
Lunceford, Jimmie, 154
Lydon, Michael, 39, 99
Lyons, Jimmy, 64
Lyttleton, Humphrey, 64, 83, 100

McBride, Mary, 107
McBride, Tom, 158
McCarter, Harold D., 166, 174–75
McCarthy, Albert J., 31, 38, 46–47, 48, 52–53, 64, 66–67, 72, 81, 88, 90, 97, 111, 124, 125, 139, 140, 141, 153, 157, 162, 191, 194, 199, 202

McCathren, Don, 165, 175
McCauley, John W., 175
McCormick, Todd D., 175
McCue, George, 23
McDaniel, William T., 175
McGhee, W. G., 39, 100
McIlwaine, Shields, 39
McKinney, John E., 175
McKinney's Cotton Pickers, 137, 142
McLaren, A., 170
McLean, Jackie, 87, 114, 182
MacLeod, Bruce, 24
McLuhan, Marshall, 54, 128
McPartland, Jimmy, 84
McPartland, Marian, 84
McRae, B., 114, 125
McTell, Willie, 30, 86
Magee, Peter, 135, 149
Mann, Woody, 39, 86
Mannix, D. P., 10
Manone, Wingy, 100
Marino, Vito, 161
Markewich, Reese, 147
Marks, Jim, 186
Marquis, Donald, 77, 90, 125
Martin, P., 92
Martinez, Raymond J., 15, 58
Martucci, Ida, 186
Massagli, Luciano, 142, 158
Matthew, B., 58, 125
Mattin, Leonard, 134
Maurerer, H. J., 78, 98
Mecklenburg, Carl Gregor Herzog zu, *see* Herzog zu Mecklenburg, Carl Gregor
Meeker, David, 161, 180, 183, 187
Meier, August, 11
Mellers, Wilfred, 54, 109, 125
Mello, Edward J., 158
Melly, George, 83, 100
Meltzer, Milton, 4, 10
Memphis Minnie, 86
Mendl, R. W. S., 44, 64
Meriwether, Doug, 158
Merriam, Alan P., 64, 126, 144, 146, 147
Meryman, Richard, 72, 87

Mezzrow, Milton, 78, 100–1
Middleton, Richard, 24, 33–34, 39
Midyett, Gene H., 165, 175
Miles, Barry, 84
Miles, Lizzie, 136
Millen, G., 187
Miller, E. W., 147
Miller, Glenn, 67, 80, 101, 142, 160
Miller, Paul E., 62, 64–65, 111, 119, 120, 126, 190
Miller, W. R., 24, 68, 126
Miller, William H., 86
Milton, Donald, 17
Miner, John W., 77, 91
Mingus, Charles, 47, 61, 80, 101
Mitchell, A., 187
Mitchell, George, 15, 39
Mitchell, Jack, 158
Modern Jazz Quartet, 61, 114, 127
Mohr, Kurt, 102, 140–41, 160
Mole, Miff, 137
Monk, Thelonius, 47, 60, 86
Montgomery, Elizabeth R., 74, 94, 96
Montgomery, Little Brother, 31, 32, 37, 38, 101
Moore, Bill, 106
Moore, Carmen, 82, 104–5
Moore, Thurston, 39
Mordden, Ethan, 24
Morgan, Alun, 65, 89, 114, 126, 161, 162
Morgan, Robert, 96, 126
Morgenstern, Dan, 23–24, 54, 182
Morton, Ferdinand "Jelly Roll," 52, 59, 72, 75–76, 85, 101–2, 111, 132, 153
Moten, Benny, 110
Muccini, Peter, 54
Mulligan, Gerry, 47, 60, 86
Mulligan, Mick, 100
Murphy, Dudley, 183
Murray, Albert, 39
Murray, Sunny, 86
Myers, Helen, 16
Mylne, David, 76, 89
Myrus, D., 39, 70, 126

Nanry, Charles A., 24, 68, 175
Nathan, Hans, 4, 15
Neal, Larry, 124, 186
Neely, Bill, 95
Neff, Robert, 32, 39, 86
Neill, Billy, 158
Nelson, Oliver, 86
Nelson, S. R., 44, 58
Nettl, Bruno, 15
Nettl, Paul, 19
Nevin, David, 153
New Orleans Jazz Band, 157
New Orleans Rhythm Kings, 59,
    111, 137
Newton, Francis, 8, 24, 126
Newton, Frankie, 154
Nichols, Herbie, 87, 114
Nichols, Loring "Red," 102, 137,
    159
Niemoeller, Adolph F., 54
Niles, Abbie, 30, 37
Nketia, J. H. K., 27
Noakes, David, 53
Noble, Peter, 65
Noice, Albert H., 175
Normann, Robert, 154

Oakley, Giles, 31, 39
Oathout, Melvin C., 147
O'Brien, Floyd, 86
Odum, Howard W., 3, 16
Oliver, J., 162
Oliver, Joseph "King," 44, 59, 77,
    85, 102, 111, 114, 137, 142, 160
Oliver, Paul, 27, 28–29, 30, 40,
    52, 82, 90, 105, 162
Oliver, Sy, 84
Olsen, George, 136
Olsson, Bengt, 31, 40
Ondaatje, Michael, 187
O'Neal, Hank, 62, 92
Original Dixieland Jazz Band, 43–
    44, 57, 59, 137, 157, 182–83
Original Georgia Five, 157
Original Indiana Five, 157
Original Memphis Five, 157
Ory, Edward "Kid," 60
Osgood, Henry O., 44, 54
Oster, Harry, 11, 40–41

Ostransky, Leroy, 58, 68, 109–10,
    126, 175
Ottley, Roi, 58
Owens, Thomas, 126–27, 175

Page, Oran "Hot Lips," 102
Palmer, Bob, 20
Palmer, Tony, 5, 21
Panassie, Hugues, 44–45, 67, 72,
    88, 108–9, 110, 127, 133, 135–
    36, 137, 150, 162, 189–90, 193
Parker, Charlie, 6, 22, 48, 52, 59,
    60, 72, 74, 80, 85, 86, 102–3,
    110, 112, 113, 114, 122, 126–27,
    142, 157, 175, 181
Parman, Milton C., 164, 176
Pastor, Tony, 155
Patton, Charley, 31, 36, 103
Paul, E., 127
Payne, Jerry R., 176
Pearsall, Ronald, 21
Pearson, Boyce, 16
Pease, Sharon, 65, 127
Pepin, M. N., 127
Pepper, Art, 103
Pernet, Robert, 49, 58
Personeault, Ken, 158
Peterson, Oscar, 85
Peterson, Richard A., 22
Pettiford, Oscar, 60
Phillips, Sam, 37
Physter, George Von, *see* Von
    Physter, George
Pleasants, Henry, 21, 127
Polhamus, Al, 171
Polillo, A., 54
Poling, James, 63, 120
Pool, R. E., 182, 187
Postgate, John, 54, 116, 127–28
Powell, Bud, 60, 86
Powell, Teddy, 155
Previn, André, 103
Pyke, Launcelot A., 128

Quin, Ann, 128, 187
Quinn, James J., 54, 128
Quintet of the Hot Club of France,
    83, 158

Raim, W., 17, 41
Rainey, Gertrude "Ma," 31, 41–42, 86, 103, 137
Ramsay, Jean P., 128
Ramsey, Frederic, 24, 45, 54, 59, 143, 162
Ravel, Maurice, 127, 128
Read, Danny L., 147, 176
Reagon, Bernice, 16, 176
Redd, Freddie, 182
Redman, Don, 61
Reed, Addison, 19
Reed, Harlan, 187
Reed, James R., 166, 176
Reed, Lawrence N., 41
Reeder, Barbara, 147–48
Reinhardt, Django, 83, 103, 136, 158
Reisner, Robert G., 46, 71, 74, 86, 102, 144–45, 147
Reynolds, Robert, 189
Rich, Bill, 144, 162
Rich, Buddy, 103, 158
Rich, Charlie, 37
Ricker, Ramon L., 176
Ricks, George R., 16
Ridgway, John, 104
Riedel, Johannes, 5–6, 16, 19
Rieman, T., 187
Ritz, David, 91
Rivelli, Pauline, 86, 90
Rizzo, Jacques C., 176
Roach, Hildred, 3, 16, 86, 128
Roach, Max, 60
Rober, Robert W., 128
Roberts, John S., 3, 27
Robertson, A., 104
Robinson, Louie, 81, 91
Rock, John, 16
Rockmore, Noel, 84
Rodgers, Virgil, 176
Rollins, Bryant, 90
Rollins, Charlemae, 86
Rollins, Sonny, 47, 61, 114
Rooney, James, 106
Rose, Al, 7, 26, 59, 90, 134–35, 149
Rosenkrantz, Timme, 86, 162
Rosenthal, G. S., 64, 124

Ross, Alexander, 162
Ross, Diana, 82
Routley, E., 24
Rowe, John, 65, 158
Rowe, Mike, 32, 41
Rublowsky, John, 16
Rulli, Joseph, 176–77
Rundell, W., 187
Ruppli, Michel, 158
Rushing, Jimmy, 104
Russell, Bill, 56, 84
Russell, George, 119
Russell, Johnny, 154
Russell, Ross, 59, 74, 103, 110, 128, 181, 187, 199
Russell, Tony, 16, 32, 41
Russo, Bill, 117
Rust, Brian, 60, 67, 68, 78, 139–40, 142, 143, 156, 158, 160

Sablosky, Irving L., 65
Sackheim, Eric, 33, 41
Sample Alexander C., 166, 177
Samuels, C., 106
Sanders, Pharaoh, 86
Sanders, Ruby, 73, 88
Sanfilippo, Luigi, 142, 159
Sanford, Herb, 80, 93
Sargeant, Winthrop, 54, 109, 128
Sarles, Carl, 158
Sartre, Jean Paul, 111
Savitt, Jan, 156
Scarborough, Dorothy, 11, 16
Schaap, Walter E., 154
Schafer, William J., 5–6, 19, 59
Schaun, George, 65
Schickel, R., 98
Schiedt, Duncan, 49, 59
Schiffman, Jack, 4, 11, 59
Schleman, H. R., 136, 159
Scholes, Percy, 44
Schuller, Gunther, 34, 47, 52, 65, 104, 110, 117, 119, 129, 130
Schulz, Klaus, 157
Scobey, Bob, 103
Scobey, Jan, 103

Scott, Allen, 167, 177
Scott, Cecil, 154
Scott, Ronnie, 49, 58, 104, 122
Scotti, Joe, 177
Scribner, Ray, 135, 149
Seibert, Bob, 177
Seidel, Richard, 162
Seldes, G. V., 65
Semeonoff, B., 162
Shacter, James D., 105
Shapiro, Nat, 21, 46, 55, 71, 86–
    87, 112, 129, 149, 151
Shaw, Arnold, 16–17, 41, 49, 59,
    61, 104, 150
Shaw, Artie, 67, 79–80, 104, 157
Shaw, George, 24
Shaw, Kirby H., 129
Sheatsley, Paul, 135–39
Shelly, Low, 151
Shelton, R., 17, 41
Shepp, Archie, 61, 86
Sherock, Shorty, 86
Shih, Hsio Wen, *see* Hsio Wen
    Shih
Shines, Johnny, 37
Shirley, K., 33, 41
Shockett, Bernard I., 41, 129
Shurman, I., 187
Sidran, Ben, 68–69, 129
Sill, Harold, 105, 187
Silver, Horace, 155
Silverman, Herbert, 177
Silverman, Jerry, 33, 41
Simmons, H.A., 181, 187
Simon, George T., 48, 67, 80,
    101, 129, 187
Simone, Nina, 36
Simosko, Vladimir, 81, 93
Simpkins, Cuthbert O., 74, 91–92
Sinatra, Frank, 61, 104, 161
Sinclair, H., 187
Sinclair, John, 8, 24, 69, 129, 182,
    187
Singleton, Zutty, 60, 136
Sissle, Noble, 86
Sklar, G., 187
Slaven, Neil, 140, 157
Smith, Bessie, 21, 31, 34, 40, 47,
    61, 73, 81, 82, 83, 85, 86, 104–
    5, 137, 182
Smith, Charles E., 45, 52, 54,
    102, 143, 162
Smith, Hugh L., 69, 129, 177
Smith, J. D., 78, 105
Smith, Jay, 159
Smith, R. P., 188
Smith, Stephen, 45
Smith, Willie, 78, 105
Soderbergh, Peter A., 159
Sonnier, Austin M., 77, 99
Souchon, Edmond, 59, 134–35,
    149
Southern, Eileen, 3, 17, 55
Southern Five, 157
Spaeth, S. G., 4, 21
Spann, Otis, 32, 38
Sparke, Michael, 159, 160
Specht, Paul L., 129, 177
Speckled Red, 32, 38
Spellman, A. B., 87, 114, 124, 129
Spicer, B., 188
Spivak, Charlie, 84, 155
Spivey, Victoria, 136
Stacy, Frank, 98
Stacy, Jess, 114
Stagg, Tom, 159
Stambler, Irwin, 150
Stampp, K. M., 11
Standifer, James A., 147–48, 177
Stanley, John W., 177
Stearns, Jean, 4, 11
Stearns, Marshall, 4, 11, 46, 47,
    55
Stebbins, Robert A., 25
Steig, H., 188
Steiner, John, 52
Stephans, Michael L., 177
Stephens, E., 188
Stewart, Lawrence, 95
Stewart, Milton L., 129
Stewart, Rex W., 47–48, 61
Stewart-Baxter, Derrick, 31, 41–
    42, 103
Stilwell, Arnold B., 159
Stock, D., 162
Strait, Raymond, 91

Stravinsky, Igor, 119
Stuart, Jay Allison, 78, 99–100
Stuart, Mary L., 177–78
Suber, Charles, 134
Sudhalter, Richard M., 75, 89
Sudnow, David, 129
Sugrue, Thomas, 57, 92
Sullivan, Franklin D., 65, 130
Summerfield, Maurice J., 65, 130
Sun Ra, 61, 91
Surge, Frank, 42, 87
Sutton, Ralph, 105
Swingle, John, 57
Sydeman, William, 130
Sykes, Roosevelt, 32, 38
Sylvester, R., 188
Szwed, John, 11, 25

Tait, Dorothy, see Stuart, Jay Allison
Tallmadge, William H., 55
Tanner, Paul, 55–56, 112–13, 130
Taylor, Billy, 84
Taylor, Cecil, 61, 87, 114
Taylor, John E., 17
Taylor, William E., 65, 130
Teagarden, Jack, 47, 61, 78, 84, 105, 110, 132, 137, 142, 159, 160
Tepperman, Barry, 81, 93
Terkel, Studs, 87
Terry, Richard R., 27
Thomas, J. C., 74, 92
Thomas, Richard, 178
Thompson, Charles, 82–83, 92
Thornhill, Claude, 155
Thurman, Howard, 17
Tichenor, Trebor, 6, 19
Tirro, Frank, 47, 56
Titon, Jeff, 42
Toledano, Ralph de, see de Toledano, Ralph
Toll, Robert C., 4, 11
Topping, Ray, 159
Torme, Mel, 104
Torres, Ben Fong, see Fong-Torres, Ben
Townley, Eric, 151

Townsend, A. O., 17
Tracy, Jack, 115, 120
Traill, Sinclair, 111, 130, 178
Treadwell, Bill, 67, 87
Tristano, Lennie, 60, 175
Trone, Dolly G., 69, 130
Trussell, Jake, 182, 188, 190
Tudor, Dean, 151, 159
Tudor, Nancy, 151, 159
Tuft, Harry M., 151
Tuozzolo, James M., 130
Turnbull, Stanley, 178
Tyner, McCoy, 23

Ulanov, Barry, 46, 56, 73, 82, 92, 94, 112, 130
Ullman, Michael, 130
Updyke, J., 188

Van Vechten, C., 188
Vance, Joel, 75, 105
Vandervoort, P., 100
Vaughan, Sarah, 61, 104, 132
Vechten, C. van, see Van Vechten, C.
Venables, R. G. V., 65, 126, 139, 157, 159–60
Venudor, Pete, 160
Venuti, Joe, 137
Von Haupt, Lois, 56, 130
Von Physter, George, 62
Vreede, Max E., 160

Wadsley, Michael, 172
Wain, J., 188
Walden, Jean E., 17
Waldo, Terry, 6, 19
Walker, Edward S., 143, 160
Walker, Leo, 48, 67–68, 150
Walker, Steven, 143, 160
Waller, Maurice, 75, 106
Waller, Thomas "Fats," 47, 61, 72, 75, 86, 105–6, 153
Wallop, D., 188
Walton, Ortiz, 8, 25, 69
Ware, C. P., 11
Wareing, Charles H., 75, 89–90
Washington, Dinah, 104

Waterman, Guy, 5, 47, 52
Waters, Ethel, 3, 81, 104, 106
Waters, H. J., 142, 160
Waters, Muddy, 33, 37, 41, 61, 106
Watson, Ted, 158
Wayne, Bennett, 87
Weaver, Sylvester, 136
Webster, Ben, 154
Weik, Mary H., 182, 188
Weiser, Clifford, 164, 178
Weitz, Lowell E., 178
Welk, Lawrence, 106
Wells, Dicky, 81, 106
Weston, Paul, 121
Whannel, P., 20
Wheaton, Jack, 25, 69, 131
Wheatstraw, Peetie, 31, 36, 106
White, Constance E., 178
White, Josh, 17, 41
White, Langston C. W., 159–60
White, Mark, 56, 68, 116, 131
White, N. L., 17
Whiteman, Paul, 48, 64, 80, 85, 95, 107, 160, 164, 178
Whitmore, S., 188
Whitten, Norman E., 25
Wickins, Robert, 86
Wilberforce, Christopher, 16
Wilbraham, Roy, 98, 101, 160
Wilk, Max, 5, 21
Williams, Anne S., 127
Williams, Clarence, 78, 107, 155
Williams, Elmer, 154
Williams, Eugene, 190
Williams, John, 180, 188
Williams, Martin T., 5, 19, 47–48,

51, 52, 53, 59–60, 61, 76, 77, 87, 102, 111, 115, 123, 131, 189
Williams, Mary Lou, 65, 114
Williams, Peter, 131
Williams, Ralph, 164, 178
Williams, Robert Pete, 37
Williams, Stewart, 60
Williams, Thomas G., 178
Williamson, Ken, 131–32, 178
Willis, G., 188
Wills, Ron, 66
Wilmer, Valerie, 61, 63, 87, 114, 122, 132
Wilson, C., 132
Wilson, Dick, 154
Wilson, Earl, 104
Wilson, John S., 62, 112, 132, 143, 162
Winick, Steven, 145, 148
Wiskirchen, George, 166, 178
Wolfe, B., 100–1
Woods, Phil, 84
Woodward, W., 56
Work, J. W., 17
World's Greatest Jazz Band, 105
Wucher, Jay R., 179
Wyler, Michael, 9, 26, 66
Wylie, Evan McLeod, 98
Wylie, Floyd E., 179

Yaged, Sol, 84
Yancey, Jimmy, 32, 38
Yeomans, I., 152
Young, Lester, 59, 84, 85, 112, 113, 122, 154

Zeiger, Albert L., 132

Title Index

"The Acceptance of Jazz by Whites in the United States, 1918–1942," 23, 68, 125

Adventures of a Ballad Hunter, 14

Africa Sings and the Psychology of Jazz, 16

African Music: A People's Art, 27

African Roots of Jazz, 27

"African Survivals in the Religious Music Tradition of the United States Negro," 12

Afro-American Anthology, 25

Afro-American Folksongs, 14, 124

"The Afro-American—His Literature and Music," 14

Afro-American Music, 55

After Hours Poetry, 182, 188

"The Ages of Jazz: A Study of Jazz in Its Cultural Context," 13

Ah-One, Ah-Two!, 106

Ain't Misbehavin': The Story of Fats Waller, 75, 105

The Al Bowlly Discography, 156

Alec Wilder and His Friends, 72, 84, 113, 116

All about Jazz, 44, 58

All the Years of American Popular Music, 20

All This and 10%, 58, 84, 96, 121

All What Jazz: A Record Diary, 1961–68, 125

All You Need Is Love: The Story of Popular Music, 5, 21

Alone with Me: A New Autobiography, 99

Alphabetical Catalogue of E.M.I. Records, 154

The Alto Saxophone of Benny Carter, 155

American Ballads and Folksongs, 3, 14–15

The American Dance Band Discography, 1917–42, 158

"The American Folk-Song and Its Influence on the Works of American Composers," 17

American Folk Songs of Protest, 3, 18, 146

American Jazz, 116

American Jazz Music, 53, 109, 123

American Music, 65

American Music: From Storyville to Woodstock, 68

American Negro Folk-Songs, 17

The American Negro Reference Book, 9–10, 148

American Negro Songs and Spirituals: A Comprehensive Collection of 230 Folk Songs, Religious and Secular, 17

American Popular Songs, 5, 20

American Singers, 116

America's Music: From the Pilgrims to the Present, 4, 20

"An Analysis of the Commercial Music Field and Its Relation to Music Education," 164, 169

"An Analysis of the Jazz Influence in Each of the Following Contemporary Works," 119

The Anatomy of Jazz, 109, 126
And the Bands Played On, 66
And the Beat Goes On: A Survey of Pop Music in America, 19
André Previn, 103
Anything Goes: The World of Popular Music, 8, 20
The Appeal of Jazz, 44, 64
Arnette Cobb with Discography, 152, 154
The Art of Jazz: Essays on the Nature and Development of Jazz, 5, 19, 111, 131
The Art of Ragtime, 6, 19
Artie Shaw, 104
Artie Shaw '36–'55, 104
Artie Shaw and His Orchestra, 157
As Serious as Your Life: The Story of the New Jazz, 61, 114, 132
The ASCAP Biographical Dictionary of Composers, Authors and Publishers, 152
Ask Your Mama: 12 Moods for Jazz, 186
Aspects of the Blues Tradition, 40
"Assessment of Selected High School Instrumental Students," 171
Auld Acquaintance, 100
Australian Discography, 158

B. B. King, 99
Be-Bop Dictionary and History of Its Famous Stars, 150
B. G.—Off the Record, A Bio-Discography of Benny Goodman, 160
B. G.: On the Record, 160
The Baby Dodd's Story, 77, 93
Background of the Blues, 38
Ballads, Blues and the Big Beat, 39, 126
Barrelhouse and Boogie Piano, 125
Basic Jazz on Long Play, 162
Basic Record Library of Jazz, 162
Beale Street Sundown, 186
Beale Street, Where the Blues Began, 38

Been Here and Gone, 24
Beneath the Underdog, 80, 101
Benny Goodman: An English Discography, 155
Benny, King of Swing, 96
Bessie, 34, 82, 104
Bessie Smith, 82, 105
Bessie Smith, Empress of the Blues, 34, 40, 104
The Best of Jazz, 64
Beyond the Blues, 182, 187
Bibliography of Jazz, 147
A Bibliography of Jazz, 144, 147
Bibliography of Jazz and Pop Tunes Sharing the Chord Progressions of Other Compositions, 147
The Big Band Alamnac, 67, 150
Big Band Jazz, 48, 66
The Big Bands, 48, 67, 154
The Big Bands Songbook, 67
Big Bill Blues, 30, 34, 35, 90
The Big Blues, 184
Big Book of Swing, 67, 87
Big Gate, A Chronological Listing of the Recorded Works of Jack Teagarden from 1928 to 1950, 159
Big Star Fallin' Mama, 86
Bill Harris Discography, 154
Billie and Terry on Microgroove, 1932/44, 152
Billie's Blues, 82, 97
Bing: The Authorized Biography, 82, 92
Bing Crosby, a 1926–1946 Discography, 158
Bird Lives, 74, 103
Bird: The Legend of Charlie Parker, 74, 102
The Birdland Story, 62
Bix, 159
The Bix Bands, 153
Bix Beiderbecke, 75, 89
Bix: Man and Legend, 75, 89
Black America, 11
Black American Music—Past and Present, 3, 16, 86, 128

Black and White, 157
Black Beauty, 93
Black Cargoes: A History of the Atlantic Slave Trade, 1518–1865, 10–11
The Black Composer Speaks, 84, 152
Black Fire: An Anthology of Afro-American Writing, 124, 186
The Black Giants, 86
"Black Gospel Music Styles," 11
Black Magic: A Pictorial History of the Negro in American Entertainment, 4, 10,
Black Manhattan, 10
A Black Manifesto in Jazz Poetry and Prose, 186
Black Music, 7, 23, 61
Black Music (Handy), 122
Black Music (Tudor), 159
Black Music, Four Lives, 87, 114, 129
Black Music in America, 16
Black Music in Our Culture, 171
Black Music Now, 171
Black Music of Two Worlds, 3, 27
Black Nationalism and the Revolution in Music, 23, 68, 114, 124
Black Odyssey, 58
"The Black Record," 153
Black Song: The Force and the Flame, 15
Black Talk, 68–69, 129
Blacking Up: The Minstrel Show in Nineteenth Century America, 9, 11
Blacks in Classical Music, 9
Blacks, Whites and Blues, 16, 41
Blame It on My Youth, 181, 185
Blow My Blues Away, 15, 39
Blow Up a Storm, 181, 186
Blue Jazz, 38
Blues (Handy), 30
Blues (Neff), 32, 39
Blues: An Anthology, 37
Blues and Gospel Records, 1902–1942, 140, 155

Blues and the Poetic Spirit, 32, 36
Blues Fell This Morning, 28, 40
Blues from the Delta, 31, 36
Blues for the Prince, 188
Blues Harp, 33, 37
The Blues Line, 33, 41
Blues People: Negro Music in White America, 7, 23, 68
The Blues Project: The Sound, 34
Blues Records, January 1943 to December 1966, 140, 157
The Blues Revival, 32, 37
Blues Who's Who, 152
The Bluesmen, 29, 35
Bluff Your Way in Folk and Jazz, 131
Bob Chester Orchestra/Teddy Powell Orchestra, 155
The Bob Crosby Band, 157
Boogie Woogie Fundamentals, 127
Boogie-Woogie Piano Styles, 65
Book of Bilk, 90
The Book of Django, 83, 103
The Book of Jazz, 51, 112, 126
The Book of Jazz from Then Till Now, 51, 120
The Book of the Blues, 33, 41
Books and Periodical Articles on Jazz in America, 1926–1934, 146
The Bootleggers, 8, 21, 56
Bop Fables, 184
Boptionary: What Is Bop?, 121
Born with the Blues, 30, 34, 90
Bossmen: Bill Moore and Muddy Waters, 106
Bourbon Street Black: The New Orleans Black Jazzman, 7, 21, 57
Brandy of the Damned: Discourses of a Musical Eclectic, 132
Brass Bands and New Orleans Jazz, 59
"A Brief History of Jazz," 50
British Dance Bands, 68, 140
Brother Ray, 91
The Buddy Rich Orchestra and Small Groups, 158
Bugles for Beiderbecke, 75, 89

Bunny, 90

Call Him George, 78, 99

Call Me Lucky, 82, 92

"A Cantometric Analysis of Three Afro American Songs," 16

The Cat, 161

Celebrating the Duke, 85

Charles Mingus—A Biography and Discography, 101

Charley Patton, 31, 36, 103

Charlie Barnet and His Orchestra, 154, 155

Charlie Parker, 74, 102

Charlie Parker (Koster), 157

"Charlie Parker: Techniques of Improvisation," 126, 175

"Charlie Parker's Kansas City Environment and Its Effect on His Later Life," 22, 102

Charlie Spivak and His Orchestra, 155

Chasin' the Trane, 74, 92

Chicago Breakdown, 32, 41

Chicago Documentary: Portrait of a Jazz Era, 24, 59

Chords and Discords, 132

Clarence Williams, 78, 107

Clarence Williams Discography, 155

Clarence Williams on Microgrove, 152

Claude Thornhill and His Orchestra, 155

Cleo and John: A Biography of the Dankworths, 82, 92

A Closer Walk: The Pete Fountain Story, 95

Coleman Hawkins, 81, 97

Collector's Catalogue, 161

Collector's Jazz: Modern, 143, 162

Collector's Jazz: Traditional and Swing, 143, 162

Coltrane: A Biography, 74, 91

Combo: USA, 72, 84

Come Blow Your Horn, 184

Coming Though Slaughter, 187

"The Comparative Effectiveness of Contemporary Youth Music and Traditional Folk Music in the Development of Music Comprehension in Sixth Grade Students," 174

"The Comparative Preferential Response of Black and White College Students to Black and White Folk and Popular Music Styles," 168

"A Comparative Study of Visual- and Aural-Oriented Approaches to Jazz Improvisation with Implications for Instruction," 173

The Compleat Sinatra, 161

Complete Catalogue of London Origins of Jazz Records, 153

Complete Catalogue of R.C.A. Victor. . . , 153

Complete Catalogue. . ., 153

A Complete Discography of Red Nichols and His Five Pennies, 159

The Complete Encyclopedia of Popular Music and Jazz, 1900–1950, 134, 149

Composer and Nation: The Folk Heritage of Music, 12

Compositional Devices Based on Songs for My Father, 118

A Comprehensive Method of Jazz Education for Teacher and Student, 166, 168

Concerning Jazz, 130

The Connection: A Play, 182, 185

"Contemporary Jazz Improvisation: A Source Book for the Music Educator," 166, 174

"The Contribution of Dance Bands to Music Education in the High Schools of Ohio," 165, 170

"The Contribution of Negro Music and Musicians in World War II," 9, 60

Conversation with the Blues, 29, 40

Conversations with Jazz Musicians, 72, 84

Cool, Hot, and Blue: A History of Jazz for Young People, 69

"The Coon Con Game: A Blues Ballad Tradition," 18, 34

The Cotton Club, 58

Count Basie and His Orchestra, 80, 89

The Country Blues, 29, 35

The Country Blues Guitar, 33, 37

"A Creative Instructional Method in Popular and Jazz Music Using Fake Books for Third and Fourth Grade Piano Students," 171

The Creoles of Color of New Orleans, 26

The Crosby Years, 92

Crying for the Carolinas, 32, 34

Dan Burley's Original Handbook of Harlem Jive, 150

Dan Emett and the Rise of Early Negro Minstrelsy, 4, 15

"Dance and Jazz Elements in the Piano Music of Maurice Ravel," 127

The Dance Band Era: The Dancing Decades from Ragtime to Swing, 48, 67

The Dance Bands, 67

"Dance Bands and Public School Music," 171

Dance Music Annual, 66

Dead and Gone, 184

Dear John, Dear Coltrane, 185

Death Beats the Band, 186

Death of a Music? The Decline of the European Tradition and the Rise of Jazz, 127

The Death of Bessie Smith, 182, 184

The Decca Book of Jazz, 63

Deep Down in the Jungle, 9

Deep River, 17

Deep South Piano: The Story of Little Brother Montgomery, 31, 37, 101

"Delineating the Process of Curriculum Development in Higher Education," 177

Delta Country Blues, 32, 38

The Denver Folklore Center Catalogue and 1966 Almanac of Folk Music, 151

Destiny, a Study of Swing Musicians, 62

"Developing a Guide to the Techniques of Imitating Select Commercial Music Styles," 124, 174

"Developing a High School Stage Band," 168

"Developing the High School Vocal Jazz Ensemble," 166, 169

"The Development and Evaluation of an Introductory Jazz Improvisation Sequence," 170

"The Development and Evaluation of a Self-Instructional Sequence in Jazz Improvisation," 171

"The Development and Musical Objectives of the School Stage Band," 168

"The Development of a Course of Study in Stage Band Techniques at the University of Utah," 172

"The Development of a Curriculum for the Teaching of Dance Music at a College Level," 164, 172

"The Development of Musical Thinking," 172

"Developmental Parallels in the Evolution of Musical Styles," 31, 62, 118

Developmental Techniques for the School Dance Band Musician, 166, 178

The Devil's Music: A History of the Blues, 39

Devil's Son-in-Law: The Story of Peetie Wheatstraw and His Songs, 31, 36, 106

Dictionary of Jazz, 135, 136, 150

Dictionary of Popular Music, 20, 150

"Differences in Music Achievement," 175

Dinosaurs in the Morning, 113, 116, 189

The Directory of Recorded Jazz and Swing Music, 138, 153

Discography of Art Hodes, 155

A Discography of Billie Holiday, 156

A Discography of Dizzy Gillespie, 154

A Discography of Dizzy Gillespie: 1937–1952, 156

A Discography of Dizzy Gillespie: 1953–1968, 156

A Discography of Gospel Records, 1937–1971, 156

A Discography of Louis Armstrong: 1923–1971, 156

A Discography of Miles Davis, 156

A Discography of Prestige Jazz Records—1949–1971, 158

Discography of the Recorded Works of Django Reinhardt and the Quintette du Hot Club de France, 158

"A Dissection of the History and Musical Product of Stan Kenton," 99

Dizzy, Duke, the Count and Me, 64

Dizzy Gillespie, 81, 96

Dizzy Gillespie Big Bands, 1945–1950, 154

Django Reinhardt, 83, 103

Don Watson Starts His Band, 187

Downbeat for a Dirge, 184

Downbeat's Yearbook of Swing, 64, 65, 119

A Drop of Patience, 186

The Drum and the Hoe: Life and Lore of the Haitian People, 2, 27

Drums in My Ears: Jazz in Our Time, 113

Duke: A Portrait of Duke Ellington, 73, 94

Duke Ellington (Lambert), 73, 94

Duke Ellington (Montgomery), 74, 94

Duke Ellington (Ulanov), 73, 94

Duke Ellington: His Life and Music, 73, 94

Duke Ellington in Person: An Intimate Memoir, 73, 94

Duke Ellington on Microgroove, 152

Duke Ellington's Story on Records, 142, 158

Duke: The Musical Life of Duke Ellington, 94

Dupree Blues, 185

Early Down Home Blues, 42

Early Jazz: Its Roots and Early Development, 65, 110, 129

Echoes of Africa, 14

"An Eclectic Choral Methodology and Its Effect on the Understanding, Interpretation, and Performance of Black Spirituals," 12, 170

Ecstasy at the Onion, 113, 116

The Eddie Condon Scrapbook of Jazz, 50, 62

Eddie Condon's Treasury of Jazz, 119

"Educational Validity of Stage Band Literature in High School Music Education," 166, 173

"The Effects of Divergent Musical Literature," 168

Elliot Lawrence and His Orchestra, 155

The Encyclopedia of Australian Jazz, 135, 149

The Encyclopedia of Jazz, 133, 136, 148

The Encyclopedia of Jazz in the Seventies, 134, 149

The Encyclopedia of Jazz in the Sixties, 134, 149

Encyclopedia of Pop, Rock and Soul, 150

The Encyclopedia of Quotations about Music, 149

Encyclopedia of Swing, 66

Encyclopedia Yearbook of Jazz, 133, 149

English Ragtime, 143, 160

Enjoying Jazz, 69, 115, 123

Eric Dolphy, 81, 93

Esquire's Jazz Book, 62, 120

Esquire's 1945 Jazz Book, 62, 120

Esquire's 1946 Jazz Book, 62, 120

Esquire's 1947 Jazz Book, 63, 120

Esquire's World of Jazz, 63, 111, 120

Essays on Jazz, 124

Ethnomusicology and Folk Music, 146

"Ethnomusicology of Downhome Blues Phonograph Records, 1926–30," 42

Eubie Blake, 90

"The Evolution of Jazz Performance and Study in High School and Colleges," 178

"The Evolution of Slave Songs in the United States," 12

"An Examination of the Evolution of Jazz as It Relates—," 54, 128

Eye Witness Jazz, 159

The Fabulous Fives, 157

The Fabulous Phonograph: 1877–1977, 8, 26

Fabulous Phonograph: From Edison to Stereo, 26

The Fabulous Phonograph: From Tin Foil to High Fidelity, 25

The Fabulous Phonograph: The Story of the Gramaphone from Tin Foil to High Fidelity, 25–26

"Factors Associated with the Rise of the Stage Band in the Public Secondary Schools of Colorado," 165–66, 172

Famous Negro Entertainers, 86

Famous Negro Musicmakers, 10, 85

Father of the Blues, 30, 37, 76, 96

Fats Waller (Fox), 75, 105

Fats Waller (Waller), 75, 106

Fats Waller, His Life and Times, 75, 105

Feel Like Going Home, 37

The Feeling of Jazz, 129

52nd Street, 49, 59

Fifty Years of Recorded Jazz, 1917–1967, 152

Finding Buddy Bolden, 125

Finnish Jazz: History, Musicians, Discography, 58, 135, 152

Firemusic: A Political History of Jazz, 68

The First Book of Jazz, 70

The Five Pennies: The Biography of Jazz Band Leader Red Nichols, 102

Folk and Traditional Music of Western Continents, 15

Folk Blues, 33, 41

Folk Music, More Than a Song, 17

Folk: Review of People's Music, 14

Folk Song of the American Negro, 17

Folk Song U.S.A., 3, 18

Folk Songs of North America, 3, 18

"The Formalization of New Orleans Jazz Musicians," 23

Four Lives in the Bebop Business, 87, 114

Fourteen Miles on a Clear Night, 115, 121

Frankie and Johnny, 186

Free Jazz, 61, 114, 124

The French Quarter: An Informal History of the New Orleans Underworld, 7, 26

"From Jazz to Swing: Black Jazz Musicians and Their Music, 1917–1935," 52, 123

From Jehovah to Jazz, 20

From Satchmo to Miles, 72, 85, 112, 120

Frontiers of Jazz, 111, 119

Gene Krupa and His Orchestra, 156

General Catalogue of Duke Ellington's Recorded Music, 142, 159
George Gershwin, 95
George Gershwin, A Study in American Music, 95
George Gershwin, Man and Legend, 95
George Lewis, a Jazzman from New Orleans, 78, 99
The Gershwin Years, 95
Giants of Jazz, 87
Glenn Miller and His Orchestra, 80, 101
Glenn Miller and the Age of Swing, 80, 101
A Glenn Miller Discography and Biography, 160
A Glimpse at the Past, 9, 26, 66
Go, 185
The Goldern Age of Jazz, 63
The Gospel Sound, Good News and Bad Times, 13, 33, 37
The Great American Popular Singers, 21
The Great Jazz Artists, 69
The Great Music of Duke Ellington, 94
The Great Revival on Long Play, 162
Guide to Jazz, 135, 150
A Guide to Long Play Jazz Records, 143, 162
A Guide to Popular Music, 5, 20, 150
"A Guide to Teaching Jazz Rhythms in the Instrumental Program," 169
"A Guideline for Teaching Stage Band Concepts to Instrumental Music Students in Grades Seven through Twelve," 166, 176
The Guitar Player Book, 64
Guitar Styles of Brownie McGhee, 39, 100
Guitars, from the Renaissance to Rock, 63
The Guitars of Charlie Christian, Robert Normann and Oscar Aleman, 154

Haiti Singing, 2, 27
Handbook of Jazz, 112, 130
Harlem Renaissance, 10
Harlem, U.S.A., 9
Harry James and His Orchestra, 156
Harry James' Pin-up Life Story, 98
Hear Me Talkin' to Ya, 46, 55
The Heart of Jazz, 58, 122
Helpful Hints to Jazz Collectors, 161
Hendersonia: The Music of Fletcher Henderson and His Musicians, 97, 142, 160
Hepcats Jive Talk Dictionary, 151
His Eye Is on the Sparrow, 3, 81, 106
"A History and Analysis of Jazz Drumming to 1942," 118
"The History and Development of Jazz Piano," 65, 130
"The History, Development, and Contribution of the Negro Folk Song," 17
"A History of American Jazz Music Illustrated with Stone Lithography," 53
A History of Broadcasting in the United States to 1933, 25
A History of Jazz in America, 46, 56
"The History of Jazz Orchestration," 62
A History of Popular Music in America, 4, 21
"A History of the Afro-American through His Songs," 16, 176
The HMV Studio House Bands, 140, 158
Hollywood, Mayfair and All That Jazz, 95
Honkers and Shouters, 41
Horace Silver Discography, 155
The Horn, 181, 185
Horn of Plenty, 45, 72, 88
The Hot and the Cool, 185
Hot Discography, 136, 137, 154
Hot Jazz (Jones), 157

Hot Jazz: The Guide to Swing Music, 67, 108, 127

Hot Lips, 185

Hot Lips Page, 102, 160

Hot, Sweet and Blue, 184

How the Dance Band Swings, 171

How They Became Name Bands, 129, 177

How to Be a Band Leader, 164, 178

How to Build a Dance Band and Make It Pay, 164

How to Run a Small Dance Band for Profit, 178

I Like Jazz, 70, 126

I Paid My Dues: Good Times—No Bread, 121

I Play as I Please, 83, 100

If You Know of a Better Life, Please Tell Me, 79, 95, 121

If You See Me Comin', 187

The Illustrated Encyclopedia of Jazz, 148

The Illustrated Yearbook of Jazz, 1946, 65

"The Impact of African Music upon the Western Hemisphere," 127

"Improvisation Techniques of the Modern Jazz Quartet," 127, 175

Improvising: Sixteen Jazz Musicians and Their Art, 113, 117

In Person, Lena Horne, 82, 97

In Search of Buddy Bolden, 77, 90, 125

The Incredible Crosby, 82, 92

Index to Jazz, 138, 151

"Inflections for the Jazz Choir: A Practical Guide," 129

"The Influence of the Negro on Music in America," 13

"The Influence of the World War (1917) on the Art of Music in America," 69, 130)

Inside Bebop, 60, 112

Inside Jazz, 60, 69, 112, 115, 118, 120

"Instrumental Ensemble—Stage Band Music," 170

"Instruments and Instrumental Usages in the History of Jazz," 64, 126

International Bibliography of Discographers, 145, 161

International Jazz Bibliography, 146

International Jazz Collector's Directory, 161

An Introduction to Folk Music in the United States, 15

"An Investigation of Jazz Instruction in Texas Secondary Schools," 167

"An Investigation of Some Aspects of Creativity of Jazz Musicians," 179

"An Investigation of the Stage Band Program in the Missouri Public High Schools," 173

Is Jazz Music Christian?, 24

Isles of Rhythm, 27

It's Always Four O'Clock, 188

J. C. Higginbotham, 157

Jack Jackson's Record Round-up, 156

Jack Teagarden: The Story of a Jazz Maverick, 78, 105

Jack Teagarden's Music: His Career and Recordings, 142, 160

Jam: An Annual of Swing Music, 66

Jam Session, 121

Jan Savitt and His Orchestra, 156

Jan Savitt and His Top Hatters, 156

Jan Scobey Presents: He Rambled! 'til Cancer Cut Him Down, 103

Jazz (Asman), 116

Jazz (Blocher), 69

Jazz (Francis), 51

Jazz (Harris), 47, 52

Jazz (Heaton), 64, 123

Jazz (Jones), 70, 115, 124

Jazz (Scotti), 177

Jazz (Tudor), 159

Jazz (Whiteman), 80, 107

Jazz: A Selection of Books, 147

Jazz: A Student's and Teacher's Guide, 62, 119, 166–67, 170

Jazz Ambassador: Louis Armstrong, 73, 88

Jazz Americana, 56

Jazz: A Guide to the History and Development of Jazz and Jazz Musicians, 54

Jazz: A History (Sargeant), 55, 128

Jazz: A History (Tirro), 47, 56

Jazz: A History of the New York Scene, 48, 57

Jazz: A Photo History, 62

"Jazz: An Historical and Analytical Study," 56, 130

Jazz: An Introduction, 53

Jazz: An Introduction to Its Musical Basis, 62, 116, 119, 171

"Jazz and Its Origin," 13

"Jazz and Race Records, 1920–32," 60, 121

Jazz and Rhythm 'n Blues Guitar, 168

Jazz and the White Americans, 7, 23, 68

Jazz and Western Culture, 63, 122

Jazz at Ronnie Scott's, 122

Jazz Away from Home, 121

Jazz Band, 45, 187

"Jazz Band and Concert Band Performance Skills," 179

The Jazz Book, 50, 113

Jazz Bum, 185

The Jazz Cataclysm, 114, 125

Jazz Catalogue, 112, 141, 153

Jazz Cavalcade, 51

Jazz City, 58

Jazz Classic, 162

"The Jazz Community: The Sociology of a Musical Subculture," 25

Jazz Country, 181, 185

The Jazz Dance: The Story of American Vernacular Dance, 4, 11

Jazz Decade: Ten Years at Ronnie Scott's, 49, 58

Jazz Discography (McCarthy), 141, 157

Jazz Discography (Personeault), 158

Jazz Educated, Man, 167, 177

"Jazz Education in Predominantly Black Colleges," 169

"Jazz Education in the Public School Music Program," 169

"Jazz Education in the Secondary Schools of Louisiana," 176

Jazz Education in the 70's, 165, 173

"Jazz Elements and Formal Compositional Techniques in 'Third Stream' Music," 119

Jazz Era: The Forties, 60, 119

The Jazz Finder '49, 151

Jazz from Columbia, 152

Jazz, from Congo to Swing, 45, 52

Jazz, from the Congo to the Metropolitan, 45, 51

The Jazz Guitar: Its Evolution and Its Players, 65, 130

Jazz Guitarists: Collected Interviews from "Guitar Player" Magazine, 124

Jazz: Hot and Hybrid, 54, 109, 128

The Jazz Idiom, 167, 170

"Jazz Improvisation for the B-Flat Soprano Trumpet," 175

"Jazz Improvisation at the Piano— a Textbook for Teachers," 174

Jazz in Austria, 157

Jazz in Britain, 49, 56

Jazz in Chicago, 60

Jazz in Little Belgium, 49, 58

Jazz in New Orleans, 60

Jazz in New York, 157

Jazz in Perspective: The Background of the Blues, 38, 51

Jazz in the Movies, 161, 180, 183, 187

Jazz in the Sixties, 60, 118

"Jazz Influence on Art Music to Mid-Century," 117

"Jazz Influences in the Music of Maurice Ravel," 128

Jazz Is, 123
Jazz: Its Evolution and Essence, 53, 110
Jazz Lexicon, 135, 150
"A Jazz Lexicon," 150
The Jazz Life, 7–8, 22
Jazz Lives, 130
The Jazz Makers, 71, 86, 112, 129
The Jazz Man, 182, 188
Jazz Masters in Transition, 1957–69, 47, 61, 111, 131
Jazz Masters of New Orleans, 47, 59
Jazz Masters of the Fifties, 47, 60
Jazz Masters of the Forties, 47, 60
Jazz Masters of the Thirties, 47, 61
Jazz Masters of the Twenties, 47, 61
Jazz Music, What It Is and How to Understand It, 121
Jazz: New Orleans, 1885–1957, 57, 134, 148
Jazz: New Orleans, 1885–1963, 57, 134, 148
Jazz: New Perspectives on the History of Jazz, 47, 52
"Jazz, 1920 to 1927: An Analytical Study," 128
Jazz Notebook, 171
Jazz Now, 57, 135, 152
Jazz on L.P.'s, 153
Jazz on 78's, 154
Jazz on Record, 143, 152
Jazz on Record (Fox), 161
Jazz on Record (McCarthy), 162
Jazz Panorama, 111, 131, 189
Jazz Parody, 185
Jazz People, 54, 87, 114, 132
Jazz: A People's Music, 109, 120
Jazz Photo Album, 49, 53
Jazz: Picture Encyclopedia, 149
Jazz Poems, 186
Jazz Profiles, 86
Jazz Publicity, 147
Jazz Publicity Two, 147
Jazz Quiz I, 178
Jazz Quiz II, 178
The Jazz Record Book, 143, 162

Jazz Records, 1897–1942, 139, 158
Jazz Records A-Z, 1897–1931, 158
Jazz Records A-Z, 1932–1942, 158
Jazz Records: A Discography, 140, 156
A Jazz Retrospect, 113, 123
Jazz Review, 53, 123, 189
Jazz Review: A Miscellany, 124
Jazz-Rock Ensemble: A Conductor's and Teacher's Guide, 165, 171
Jazz-Rock Fusion, 148
The Jazz Scene (Fox), 63
The Jazz Scene (Newton), 8, 24, 126
The Jazz State of Indiana, 49, 59
The Jazz Story: An Outline History of Jazz, 54
The Jazz Story: From the 90's to the 60's, 51
Jazz Street, 162
"The Jazz Studies Curriculum," 168
Jazz Style in Kansas City and the Southwest, 59, 110, 128
Jazz Styles, 52, 112, 122
Jazz Talk, 135, 150
Jazz Text, 175
The Jazz Titans, 71, 86
Jazz Today, 116, 168
The Jazz Tradition, 87, 111, 131
Jazz: The Transition Years, 1940–1960, 62, 112, 132
Jazz West Coast, 57
Jazz, Women, Soul, 186
The Jazz Word, 118
Jazz Writings, 145
Jazzbook: From the Esquire Jazz Books, 1944–1946, 65, 126
Jazzbook 1947, 64, 125
Jazzbook 1955, 64, 125
Jazzmen, 45, 54
Jazzography, 172
Jazzways: A Yearbook of Hot Music, 64, 124
Jelly Roll Morton, 76, 102
Jelly Roll Morton: An Essay in Discography, 153

Jelly Roll Morton's New Orleans Memories, 102

Jimmie Lunceford, 154

Jimmy Dorsey and his Orchestra, 154

Jive and Swing Dictionary, 150

Jive Jungle, 186

John Coltrane, 74, 91

John Coltrane Discography, 153

John Hammond on Record, 26, 84, 96

John Henry: Tracking Down a Negro Legend, 4, 13

Johnny Dodds, 77, 93

The Josh White Song Book, 17, 41

A Journey to Greatness, the Life and Music of George Gershwin, 95

Joy of Boogie and Blues, 38

Junkshoppers Discography, 158

Just Jazz, 111, 130

Just Mahalia, Baby, 82, 98

Kenton on Capitol, 159

King Joe Oliver, 77, 102, 142, 160

The Kingdom of Swing, 79, 96

Know about Jazz, 115, 121

Lady Sings the Blues, 38, 82, 97

Larry Clinton and His Orchestra, 155

Laughter from the Hip, 115, 120

Lawrence Welk's Musical Family Album, 106

The Leadbelly Legend, 15, 38

Leadbelly Songbook, 30–31, 34

The Legacy of the Blues, 30, 35, 84

Legal Protection for the Creative Musician, 169

Lena, 82, 97

Les Brown and His Band of Re-known, 154

Les Brown and His Orchestra, 155

Let's Play Jazz, 170

Life and Death of Tin Pan Alley, 4–5, 20

"The Life and Works of Scott Joplin," 19

Lingo of Tin-Pan Alley, 150

Listen to the Blues, 31, 35–36

Listen to My Music, 97

Listening to Jazz, 118, 167, 170

"The Literary Manifestation of a Liberal Romaniticism in American Jazz," 69, 129, 177

The Literature of American Music in Books and Folk Music Collections, 145, 146

The Literature of Jazz (Kennington), 146

The Literature of Jazz (Reisner), 144, 147

Little Boy Blues, 188

Little Gate, 185

Living Country-Blues, 40

Living Forwards, 124

Lomakin Pocket Fake List for Leaders, Musicians and Singers, 174

Lonesome Boy, 184

Louis Armstrong (Iverson), 88

Louis Armstrong (McCarthy), 72, 88

Louis Armstrong (Panassie), 72, 88

Louis Armstrong: A Self-Portrait, 72, 87

Louis Armstrong: Ambassador Satchmo, 88

Louis: The Louis Armstrong Story 1900–1971, 73, 88

"The Louisiana Negro and His Music," 12

Ma Rainey and the Classic Blues Singers, 31, 41, 103

The McJazz Manuscripts, 117

Mahalia, 81, 98

Mahalia Jackson: Queen of Gospel Song, 82, 98

Making a Good Stage Band Recording, 177

The Making of Black America, 11

The Making of Jazz, 47, 51

Man Walking on Eggshells, 181, 187

"A Manual for Teaching Interpretation," 176

Masters of Instrumental Blues Guitar, 36, 121

"Materials and Methods for High School Stage-Dance Bands," 172

The Meaning of the Blues, 28–29, 40

Mellows: A Chronicle of Unknown Singers, 14

"Melodic Improvisation: Its Evolution in American Jazz 1943–1960," 62, 117

Memory Lane, 5, 21

Memphis Blues and Jug Bands, 31, 40

Memphis Down in Dixie, 39

Men of Popular Music, 85

The Midnight Special, 185

Miles Davis (James), 80, 92

Miles Davis, a Musical Biography, 80, 92

Miller's Yearbook of Popular Music, 65

Milt Jackson, 98, 160

"The Minneapolis Jazz Community," 25

Misbehavin' with Fats, 105, 187

Mississippi Black Folklore, 146

Mister Jelly Roll, 76, 101

Modern Jazz: A Survey of Developments since 1939, 65, 114, 126

Modern Jazz, the Essential Records, 123, 143, 161

Moonlight Serenade, 101, 160

More Mellows, 14

Movin' on Up, 3, 81, 98

Murder on the Downbeat, 184

"The Music and Life of Robert Graettinger," 96, 126

Music: Black, White and Blue, 8, 25, 69

Music Ho!: A Study of Music in Decline, 23

The Music of Africa, 27

"Music for All Occasions," 24

Music in a New Found Land, 54, 109, 125

Music in American Society, 1776–1976, 23

Music in New Orleans: The Formative Years, 1791–1841, 7, 18

Music Is My Mistress, 73, 94

"Music Listening—Jazz Music," 65, 130

Music Makers, 126

Music of Black Americans, 55

The Music of Black Americans: A History, 17

Music on My Mind, 78, 105

Music Out of Dixie, 187

Music Outside: Contemporary Jazz in Britain, 57, 114, 118

Music of the People, 5, 20

Music and Politics, 8, 24, 69, 129

The Music of Thomas "Fats" Waller, 75, 105, 153

Musicalia: Sources of Information in Music, 145

My America, Your America, 106

My Life in Jazz, 79, 99

Nat King Cole, 81, 91

Nat "King" Cole, 156

The Negro and His Music, 14

The Negro and His Songs, 16

Negro Anthology, 1931–33, 9

Negro Authors and Composers of the United States, 151

Negro Folk Music, 12

The Negro in America, 147

The Negro in the United States, 10

"Negro Music and Its Influence on American Music," 14

Negro Musicians and Their Music, 2–3, 13

Negro Slave Songs in the United States, 3, 12

Negro Songs as Sung by Leadbelly, 15, 30, 38–39

"The Negro Spiritual and Its Use as an Integral Part of Music Education," 13, 173

Negro Spirituals, 12

Negro Workaday Songs, 3, 16

The New Cab Calloway's Hipsters Dictionary, 91, 150

The New Edition of the Encyclopedia of Jazz, 134, 149

The New Equality, 7, 23

The New Expanded Bibliography of Jazz Compositions Based on the Chord Progessions of Standard Tunes, 147

New Hot Discography, 154

The New Jazz Book, 50, 113, 117

The New Negro, 14

New Orleans, a Pictorial History, 26, 58

New Orleans and Chicago Jazz, 157

New Orleans Jazz: A Family Album, 59, 134, 149

New Orleans Rhythm and Blues, 159

New Orleans: The Revival, 159

New Yearbook of Jazz, 9, 25, 133, 149

New York Notes, 56, 113, 117, 189

Newport Jazz Festival, 49, 63

The Newport Jazz Festival in Rhode Island, 1954 to 1971, 161

Nigger Heaven, 188

Night Light, 188

The Night People, 81, 106

Night Song, 180, 188

1970 Supplement to International Jazz Bibliography, 146

1971/72/73 Supplement to International Jazz Bibliography, 146

Nothing but the Blues, 32, 38

Numerical Index to Delaunay's "Hot Discography," 151

O Susanna: A Sampler of the Riches of American Folk Music, 12

The Observer's Book of Big Bands, 68, 116, 131

The Observer's Book of Jazz, 56, 116, 131

"The Occupational Subculture of the Jazz Musician," 24

Of Minnie the Moocher and Me, 80, 90

Oh, Didn't He Ramble, 77, 91

The Okeh Record Catalog, circa 1920, 158

The Omni-Americans, 39

On the Road, 186

On the Trail of Negro Folklore, 11, 16

100 Facts on Swing Music, 66

144 Hot Jazz Bluebird and Victor Records, 162

Opening Bars, Beginning an Autobiography, 98

Organizing and Conducting the Student Dance Orchestra, 165, 173

Organizing the School Stage Band, 165, 175

The Origins and Development of Jazz, 51, 172

Owning Up, 83, 100

Panorama of American Popular Music, 4, 20

Paramount 12000/13000 Series, 160

Paris Blues, 181, 185

The Peculiar Institution: Slavery in the Antebellum South, 11

"The Pedagogy of Lennie Tristano," 175

"The Personality of the Contracted Studio Musician," 22

The Pete Johnson Story, 78, 98

Piano in the Band, 185

Piano Jazz, 125

Piano Man, the Story of Ralph Sutton, 105

Piano Method for Blues, 36, 120

Pictorial History of Jazz, 49, 53

A Pictorial History of the Negro in America, 10

The PL Yearbook of Jazz, 64, 111, 125

"The Place of the Dance Band in the High School Educational Program," 165, 168

"The Place of the Dance Band in the High School Program," 165, 175

"The Place of the Dance Band in the School Music Program," 164, 176

A Plain Man's Guide to Jazz, 54, 116, 127

"A Plan for Stimulating Interest and Motivation," 166, 177

Play That Music: A Guide to Playing Jazz, 130, 178

Playback, 25

The Pleasures of Jazz, 72, 85, 112, 120

Plus Blood in Their Veins, 188

The Poetry of the Blues, 30, 35

Pop Music and the Blues, 24, 34, 39

Pops Foster, 78, 95

The Popular Arts, 20

"Popular Dance Music in High School Instrumental Teaching," 164, 170

Popular Music, 21, 151

"Popular Music as a Medium of Instrumental Instruction in Secondary Schools," 164, 178

Popular Music of the Twenties, 21

Popular Music Periodicals Index, 1973, 151

Popular Music Record Reviews, 151

Portraits of New Orleans Jazz, 15, 58

Preservation Hall Portraits, 56, 84

"The Problems of the Black Jazz Musician," 22

"The Professional Dance Musician in Chicago," 21

The Promised End: Essays and Reviews 1942–1962, 10

"A Proposed Guitar Method for High School Dance Bands," 174

"Proposed Listening Course on Ten Styles of Jazz Using Call Charts for Use in the General Music Class," 175

"A Proposed Plan for the Integration of the Dance Orchestra into the High School Music Program," 178.

Queen New Orleans, 26, 58

Rags and Ragtime, 6, 19

Ragtime Rareties, 6, 19

The Ragtime Songbook, 6, 18

Raise Up Off Me, 81, 97

"Rapid Development of Stylistic Techniques in Secondary School Stage Band Drummers," 172

The Raw Pearl, 89

Reader's Guide to Books on Jazz, 146

Readings in Black American Music, 3, 17, 55

The Real Jazz, 108, 127

The Real Jazz, Old and New, 64, 125

Really the Blues, 78, 100

Record Collecting, 162

Record Dating Chart, 159

Recorded Information, 158

Recorded Jazz: A Critical Guide, 143, 156

Recorded Ragtime 1897–1958, 142, 156

Recording the Blues, 36

Records for the Millions, 160

Reflections on Afro American Music, 3, 22, 171

"Relationships between Experiential Factors and Percepts of Selected Professional Musicians," 24

The Reluctant Art: Five Studies in the Growth of Jazz, 79, 85, 113, 122

Remembering Bix, 75, 89

Reminiscing with Sissle and Blake, 86

Rev. Gary Davis—Blues Guitar, 37

"The Rhetorical Dimensions of Black Music Past and Present," 34, 116

Rhythm: An Annotated Bibliography, 1900–70, 145, 148

Rhythm and Blues Scrapbook, 39

Rhythm on Record, 136, 159

"Rhythms of Negro Music and Negro Poetry," 15

Right On: From Blues to Soul in Black America, 22, 33, 37

The Robbed Heart, 185

Robert Johnson, 30, 35, 98

Rock Folk: Portraits from the Rock 'n Roll Pantheon, 39, 99

The Rock Giants, 90

Rock Is Rhythm and Blues, 41

The Rockin' 50's, 61

"The Role of Black Music in the Los Angeles School District," 176

Roman Joy, 188

Rough Sketch, 188

Rum Bum and Concertina, 83, 100

"Sacred Music of the Negro in the U.S.A.," 13

Satchmo, Collector's Copy, 88

Satchmo: My Life in New Orleans, 72, 88

Savannah Synocopators, 27, 29, 40

Scott Joplin, 6, 19

Scott Joplin and the Ragtime Era, 5, 18

Scott Joplin and the Ragtime Years, 18

Screening the Blues, 29, 40

Second Chorus, 83, 100

Second Ending, 186

Second Movement, 83, 98

Secrets of Dance Band Success, 129, 164, 168

A Select Bibliography of Music in Africa, 146

Selections from the Gutter, 37, 85

A Selective Bibliography, 147

"A Selective Bibliography of Periodical Literature in Jazz Education," 147, 176

"A Self-Instructional Audio-Imitation Method Designed to Teach Trumpet Students Jazz Improvisation in the Major Mode," 167

Send Me Down, 188

Serious Music—and All That Jazz, 127

The Seven Lively Arts, 65

78 RPM Records and Prices, 159

Shadow and Act, 120

Shining Trumpets: A History of Jazz, 45–46, 50

A Short Survey of Modern Rhythm on Brunswick Records, 156

Sideman, 185

Sidewalks of America, 9, 56

Simon Says, 67

Sinatra, an Unauthorized Biography, 104

Sinatra and the Great Song Stylists, 104

The Sinatra File, 104

Sinatra: Twentieth-Century Romantic, 104

Sinful Tunes and Spirituals, 3–4, 12

Singers of the Blues, 42, 87

Six Black Blues Guitarists, 39, 86

Six Blues-Roots Pianists, 32–33, 38, 125

60 Years of Recorded Jazz, 153

Slave Songs of the United States, 3, 11

Slavery in America: Its Legal History, 10

Slavery: A Problem in American Institutional and Intellectual Life, 10

So It Doesn't Whistle, 188

So This Is Jazz, 44, 54

"The Sociological and Psychological Implications of the Texts of the Antebellum Negro Spirituals," 17

Sold, 188

Some Aspects of the Religious Music of the United States Negro, 16

Some of My Best Friends Are Blues, 104

Somebody's Angel Child, 82, 104

Sometimes I Wonder, 83, 91

Somewhere There's Music, 186

The Songs of Our Years, 13

The Soul Book, 33, 37

Soul Music—Black and White, 16

The Sound, 74, 181, 187

The Sound of Soul, 33, 36

The Sound of Surprise, 113, 117

The Sound of the City, 33, 37

The Sounds of Social Change, 22

Source Book of African and Afro-American Materials for Music Educators, 147–48, 177

The Spirituals and the Blues, 12, 31, 35

Sportin' House, 26

"The Stage Band as a Part of the High School Music Program," 178

"The Stage Band as a Teaching Tool for the Performance of Contemporary Band Literature," 176–77

"The Stage Band in the Secondary School," 166, 174

The Standard Stan Kenton Directory, 160

The Stardust Road, 83, 91

Stars of Swing, 62

"The Status and Administration of Student Dance Bands in Colleges and Universities in the United States," 165, 173

Stomping the Blues, 39

The Story of American Folk Song, 11

The Story of Bing Crosby, 82, 92

The Story of Dance Music, 19

The Story of Jazz (Berendt), 47, 50

The Story of Jazz (Harris), 52

The Story of Jazz (Niemoeller), 54

The Story of Jazz (Stearns), 46, 55

The Story of Music in America, 65

The Story of the Blues, 29, 40

The Story of the Original Dixieland Jazz Band, 43, 57

Storyville, New Orleans, 7, 26

Storyville Portraits, 26

Straight Ahead, the Story of Stan Kenton, 80, 99

Straight Life, 103

The Street That Never Slept, 49, 59

Strictly Ding-Dong and Other Swing Stories, 185

Strike the Father Dead, 188

Strike Up the Band, 85

"Structural Development in the Jazz Improvisational Technique of Clifford Brown," 129

Studies in African Music, 27

Studies in Jazz Discography, 116, 167

"Studio Musicians," 22

"A Study of Ability in Spontaneous and Prepared Jazz Improvisation," 169

"A Study of Certain Similarities between Classical Music (1700–1961) and Jazz (1900–1961)," 132

"A Study of Influences from Euro-American Art Music on Certain Types of Jazz," 117

A Study of Jazz, 55, 112, 130

A Study of Jazz (Jacobs), 173

"A Study of Popular Music and Reactions to Its Use in High Schools," 167

"A Study of the Effectiveness of Public School Music in the Opinions of Selected Dance Band Musicians," 172

"A Study of the School Jazz Ensemble in American Music Education," 171

"The Style of John Coltrane, 1955–67," 91, 118

"A Stylistic Analysis of Ten Selected Dance Band Stock Orchestrations," 128

"A Stylistic Study of the Blues as Recorded by Jazz Instrumentalists, 1917–1931," 41, 129

The Subterraneans, 186

Such Sweet Thunder, 113, 117, 189

"A Suggested Curriculum for Utilizing Jazz Music in the High School Programs," 178

Super-Drummer: A Profile of Buddy Rich, 103

"A Survey and Analysis of Teacher-Training and Experience," 175

"A Survey-Appraisal of Jazz-Oriented Curriculum in Higher Education in the State of Florida," 173

"A Survey of Published Jazz-Oriented Clarinet Study Materials," 176

"A Survey of Stage Band Curricula in the High Schools of Florida," 169

"A Survey of Texas High School Dance Bands," 165, 174

Sweet as the Showers of Rain, 29–30, 35

Sweet Man, 187

Swing It High Sweet Saxophones, 186

Swing Music, 66

The Swing Music Murder, 187

Swing Out: Great Negro Dance Bands, 66

Swing Photo Album, 162

Swing That Music, 72, 88

Swingtime in Tottemham, 49, 58

Synopating Saxophones, 63

Take It from the Top, 83, 100

Tambourines to Glory, 181, 186

Tangle Weed, 188

Teach Yourself Jazz, 125, 170, 174

Teacher's Guide to the High School Stage Band, 164–65, 172

"Teaching Musical Improvisation," 171

"The Teaching of Jazz in Junior High School General Music Classes," 174

"A Technical Analysis of the Development of Jazz," 55, 130

"The Technological and Sociological Influences on Jazz as an Art Form in America," 25, 69, 131

Tell Your Story, 151

Ten Modern Jazzmen, 71, 85–86

The Tenor Saxophone and Clarinet of Lester Young, 1936–1942, 154

The Tenor Saxophone of Ben Webster, 1931–1942, 154

The Tenor Saxophone of Coleman Hawkins, 1929–1942, 154

The Tenor Saxophone of Leon Chuberry, 154

The Tenor Saxophones of Cecil Scott, Elmer Williams and Dick Wilson, 154

The Tenor Saxophones of Henry Bridges, Robert Carroll, Hershchal Evans and Johnny Russell, 154

Tex Beneke and His Orchestra, 155

That Crazy American Music, 127

That Crazy Music, 127

That Jazz, 24

These Jazzmen of Our Time, 71, 85, 114, 124

They All Played Ragtime, 5, 18

"The Third Stream," 117

This for Remembrance, 91

This Is Jazz, 62, 131

This Is Our Music, 182, 187

This Is Ragtime, 6, 19

This Swing Business, 116

A Thousand Golden Horns, 48, 66

Three Brass, 86

3 Jazz Greats, 87

To Be or Not to Bop, 61, 122

To Be or Not to Bop (Gillespie), 95

Tommy and Jimmy: The Dorsey Years, 80, 93
Tommy Johnson, 31, 36, 98
Tony Pastor and His Orchestra, 155
Toward Jazz, 53, 110, 123
Trad Mad, 58, 125
Trad: An A–Z Who's Who of the British Traditional Jazz Scene, 152
A Treasury of the Blues, 30, 37
Treat It Gentle, 76, 89
Tremolo, 184
Tribute to Huddie Ledbetter, 31, 38
Tripticks, 128, 187
Trombone Jazz, 65
The Trouble with Cinderella, 79, 104
The Trumper in Jazz, 64, 125
The Trumpet of Henry Red Allen, 154
The Trumpet of Roy Eldridge, 155
Trumpet on the Wing, 100
"Trumpet Techniques in Selected Works of Four Contemporary American Composers," 130
Trumpeter's Tale: The Story of Young Louis Armstrong, 88
The Trumpets of Bill Coleman 1929–1945 and Frankie Newman, 154
21 Years of Swing Music on Brunswick Records, 156
The Two Worlds of Johnny Truro, 187

Understanding Jazz, 68, 110, 126, 175
"Unit Organization of the Topic Jazz in the Senior High School," 177–78
Units in the Study of Modern Jazz Music, 177
Uptown—The Story of Harlem's Apollo Theatre, 4, 11, 59
Urban Blues, 32, 38

Vamp Till Ready, 187
The Victor Master Book, 158
The Voice, 104
Voodooism in Music, 27

Wake Up Dead Man, 4, 13
Walking to New Orleans, 33, 34–35, 56–57
Ways of the Hand, 129
The "Wax Works" of Duke Ellington, 142, 152
We Called It Music, 57, 78–79, 92
The Weary Blues, 182, 186
What Jazz Is All About, 51, 115, 120
What's That Sound?, 20
Where's the Melody?, 115, 131
White and Negro Spirituals, 18
Who Walk in Darkness, 184
Who's Who in Jazz Collecting, 143, 161, 162
Who's Who of Jazz, 134, 148
The Wild Faun, 188
William C. Handy, Father of the Blues, 96
Willie Geary "Bunk" Johnson, 77, 99
Women in Jazz, 62
The Wonderful Era of the Great Dance Bands, 48, 67–68
World in a Jug, 180, 185
The World of Big Bands, 49, 66
The World of Duke Ellington, 73–74, 93
The World of Earl Hines, 77, 97
The World of Pop Music and Jazz, 24, 68, 126
The World of Soul, 16–17, 41
The World of Swing, 66
The Worlds of Jazz, 110, 124
"Written Jazz Rhythm Patterns," 176
Wunnerful, Wunnerful, 106

Yes I Can: The Story of Sammy Davis Jr., 93
You Don't Look like a Musician, 79, 95

Young Man with a Horn, 75, 89, 180, 184

Your Jazz Collection, 144, 161

The Zonophone Studio House Bands, 140, 158

Text design adapted from first edition by Ellen Pettengell
Cover design by Ellen Pettengell
Composed by A & A Typesetting Co. in VIP Caledonia
with Helvetica display type
Printed on Warren's 1854, a pH neutral stock,
and bound by Braun-Brumfield, Inc.